JAS PONTES, BRAZIL, 1962.

Before the eyes of his three sons a farmer walks toward a ball-like object stationed six feet above ground. He is enveloped in smoke; the craft disappears. No trace of the man has ever been found.

FORT MYERS, FLORIDA, 1965.

A man suffers medically unaccountable burns after he approaches a round, lighted object hovering low in the air. Examination of the site reveals a perfect circle of scorched treetops.

CANBERRA AIRPORT, AUSTRALIA, 1965.

Air traffic control officers spot an Unidentified Flying Object shortly before a nearby tracking station is scheduled to pick up Mariner signals. It zooms away when an Air Force plane is sent in search of it.

Despite official attempts to discredit saucer sightings, UFOs have been seen by thousands: including airmen, astronauts, police officers, respected professional men in varying fields, and, once, a whole dormitory of college̶̶̶̶̶̶̶̶̶̶̶̶̶̶̶̶̶̶̶̶ the most compe̶̶̶̶̶̶̶̶̶̶̶̶̶̶̶̶̶̶itten, world̶̶̶̶̶̶̶̶̶̶̶̶̶̶̶̶̶̶̶̶̶̶nzen warns ̶̶̶̶̶̶̶̶̶̶̶̶̶̶̶̶̶̶̶̶̶̶̶̶ reconnoitering earth's water reserves and military defenses, gathering flora fauna, and tracking our space missiles.

Other SIGNET and SIGNET SCIENCE Books
You Will Want to Read

WE ARE NOT ALONE   by Walter Sullivan

Winner of the 1965 International Non-Fiction Prize, this is a comprehensive account of the search for intelligent life on other worlds, by the Science Editor of *The New York Times*.   (#T2872—75¢)

FRONTIERS OF ASTRONOMY   by Fred Hoyle

An assessment of the remarkable increase in our knowledge of the universe.   (#T2309—75¢)

THE EXPLORATION OF THE UNIVERSE by H. C. King

The story of man's exploration of the cosmic universe from ancient times to the present.   (#T2601—75¢)

THIS IS OUTER SPACE   by Lloyd Motz

A concise explanation of modern scientists' most recent discoveries about the universe.   (#P2084—60¢)

FLYING SAUCERS

THE STARTLING EVIDENCE OF THE INVASION FROM OUTER SPACE

Original Title: THE GREAT FLYING SAUCER HOAX

The UFO Facts and Their Interpretation

Coral E. Lorenzen

A SIGNET BOOK

Published by The New American Library
of Canada Limited

IN MEMORY OF
MY LATE BELOVED MOTHER

GRACE WOOLDRIDGE LIGHTNER

Preface

When an idea as unacceptable as that embodied by the Unidentified Flying Object (UFO) presents itself, we tend to play a game of self-deception in order to avoid the necessity of facing up to anything resembling a final judgment—at least until time and repetition lower our threshold of acceptance. We go through the motions of appealing to Authorities for answers, but we make certain that we choose Authorities whose hands have been carefully tied by convention and precedent—thus the answers will be safe ones.

Recent national attention given to a number of cases in this country suggests to me that we may be tiring of the game. Various public information media seem to be awakening simultaneously to the ominous importance of the subject. In 1953 a scientific committee convened at United States Air Force (USAF) request and among other things recommended that the UFO be publicly debunked. Air Force public information policy has followed this guideline for thirteen years but it hasn't worked too well lately; this year they went back to committee.

I do not align myself with those who make their chief work the denigration of the USAF program. I feel that these groups are dealing with an unconsciously contrived substitute problem. Their efforts tend to elevate official public information statements to an importance which they do not merit, while contributing little or nothing to the advancement of the general body of knowledge of UFOs.

An underlying premise with me is that the UFO problem is planetary in scope—it knows no national boundaries. It is my feeling that the evidence should be allowed to provide the answers; therefore I present the evidence with as little prejudgment as possible and suggest such meanings and patterns as seem to be valid.

I hope that this, the result of fifteen years' work, is helpful in elucidating some final answers—and I hope it is not too late.

Coral E. Lorenzen

Introduction

It is a distinct pleasure to write an introduction to this book —not only because the author is a gentle woman and an interesting person, but because she offers here a unique contribution to the study of Unidentified Flying Objects. In any field of study, a careful investigator should consider three factors: the adequacy of his data; his competence in analyzing and interpreting the data; and his values or reasons for studying the data. Mrs. Coral Lorenzen unquestionably qualifies in all three areas. She has conducted a thorough investigation of UFO reports and of persons who submit these reports; has carefully analyzed and interpreted the patterns of UFO reports; and has probed deeply into her own personal values for investigating UFO reports.

The interested reader probably knows that there are increasing numbers of persons and organizations who contribute to the empirical study of UFO phenomena. Those of us who have sighted unidentified flying objects are aware of the dramatic change in orientation and attitude which such sightings can effect—in those who consider themselves "open-minded," as well as those who call themselves "skeptics." But after increasing numbers of viewers, it now should be less difficult for the average person to describe his observations of unusual aerial phenomena. However, Coral Lorenzen, with the able assistance of her husband, Jim Lorenzen, established the Aerial Phenomena Research Organization (APRO) during a time when intense interest in "flying saucers" brought ridicule and scorn. Starting with a limited budget and few personnel, APRO grew until it became a worldwide organization for collecting, analyzing, and disseminating UFO information.

Flying Saucers offers the reader the results of patient investigation of many UFO sightings; but it also offers a startling conclusion, based on careful interpretation of the patterns of UFO sightings. This interpretation has led to testable hypotheses about future UFO sightings—not only in regard to the periodic cycles of reports, but also in regard to the expected locations of sightings.

Systematic description of data and insightful analysis of patterns have been characteristic of Mr. and Mrs. Lorenzen and their colleagues. However, in my opinion, Mrs. Lorenzen has made a unique contribution in her discussions of her personal reasons for studying UFO phenomena. Recent scientific trends have tended to obscure or de-emphasize the view that every investigator is a valuing, biased, desiring, purposive participant. The image of a calm, objective, dispassionate observer characterizes the investigator *after* he has made decisions about *which* data, *which* techniques of analyzing the data, and *which* criteria for evaluating the data he should employ. But the choices of data, techniques, and criteria are in themselves indications of the investigator's personal view of the universe.

Coral Lorenzen has been willing to state publicly her personal values; to describe her fears about potential dangers of the UFO phenomena; to challenge sharply the statements of those military and political leaders who claim that citizens have not seen "flying saucers"; and to differ courageously from those who take a "head in the sand" approach. Furthermore, instead of expending energy in an unending battle with "The Establishment," she has continued with her own work. She realizes that censorship probably is controlled at the highest levels of governmental administration. She infers that political and military leaders believe they have important reasons for maintaining the censorship program, and that they are in need of continuous information about UFO reports. Thus, she believes that each citizen must look to his own conscience for answers to questions such as these:

Am I afraid to learn about UFO reports?

Should I blame "The Establishment" (or the Russians or the Devil) for these disturbing reports?

Am I afraid and angry because I believe that information about UFOs is being withheld from me?

If there is a special reason for governmental censorship, should I attempt to expose the reason, or should I become as informed as possible within the limitations of the censorship?

Should I assist recognized organizations and agencies to gain more information about the UFO mystery?

It may be that the earth is the object of a survey by spacecraft whose occupants intend no harm to the United States. However, regardless of the intent of UFO occupants, it behooves us to learn as much as possible about their persons, powers, and purposes. Mrs. Lorenzen realizes that her present conclusions may not all be verified, but she also is aware that it may be too late for mankind to react to a potential threat to world security. It is to her credit that she has avoided feelings of panic on one hand and feelings of hopelessness on the other. She has demonstrated a courageous approach: the continuation of the process of gathering, analyzing, and evaluating information, and the encouragement of the efforts of others to come to grips with the emotional and political aspects, as well as the technical and scientific aspects, of the UFO phenomena.

Our generation may discover the physical, biological, psychosocial, and spiritual implications of UFO sightings. The emergence of this knowledge—be it helpful or hurtful to our present view of ourselves—will be due in large measure to the persistent and courageous efforts of a new breed of space-age pioneers. Mrs. Coral Lorenzen, and others like her, have been willing to face the doubts and anxieties in others and in themselves, and to meet the challenge of finding modern answers to an ancient mystery: Unidentified Flying Objects.

R. Leo Sprinkle, Ph.D.
Counselor, and Assistant
Professor of Psychology
University of Wyoming

Contents

1
The Beginning

"IT had been silent as it approached, but now at close range the two sentries heard a distinct humming sound coming from the disc-shaped interloper. Then came the nightmare. . . . The sentry got the horrible feeling his clothes were on fire. A wave of heat suddenly enveloped him. He was filled with horror and he began to scream desperately, running and stumbling and crying, from side to side like a trapped animal. . . ."

A page from a science-fiction story? No. The quotation is taken directly from a carefully documented report of the attack of an unconventional aerial object on a military base in November, 1957. The reporter is a reputable Brazilian medical scientist whose objective and meticulous investigation of UFO reports is unassailable. I laid the report aside, settled down in my chair and began to formulate a letter of congratulation and thanks to the Aerial Phenomena Research Organization (APRO) special representative for Brazil, Dr. Olavo T. Fontes. His eighteen-month search for the facts concerning the Itaipu fort incident had paid off, and the pieces of a twelve-year-old puzzle began to fall into place.

The beginning of the mystery of UFOs was, for me at least, on a sunny summer day in Barron, Wisconsin, in 1934. The details of that sighting are still fresh in my mind, and, although I was only nine years old at the time, I was very much impressed by what I saw. Barron in 1934 was a small town of about 1500 populaton. Airliners were rarely if ever seen, it would be safe to say weather balloons were never seen and, indeed, even a small monoplane was an event in that area. The "thing" was in the west-southwest when I first noticed it. I called it to the attention of my two play-mates, and one said she thought it was a parachute. Its color was a glowing white. The object was about as large as a dime held at arm's length, there were no ropes or lines suspended from it—and, therefore, no parachutist. It could best be described as resembling an open umbrella without the ribs or spurs. It made no sound as it wobbled in a north-west direction across the clear, cloudless sky. It wasn't going fast—rather, it was poking along at a leisurely rate of speed and with a rather strange motion, that has been described in recent reports as "undulating."

We watched the object for perhaps twenty seconds. Then it appeared to go over the horizon, or perhaps it came to rest north of Barron in the vicinity of a body of water referred to locally as the "Upper Dam." I went home and told my father, who made inquiries, and the matter was dropped. No one had seen the object we three children had watched, and there was no news of a parachutist landing north of the dam.

The day had been usual for a summer day in Douglas, Arizona, on June 10, 1947. It had been very warm. After my daughter Lesli and I had our dinner at seven, we bathed and I put her to bed. By nine I was in my favorite spot on the back porch looking at the stars and watching for meteors. At about eleven o'clock my attention was arrested by a light to the south which began to glow at the foot of the range of hills south of the Arizona-Mexico border in Mexico. Just a light at first, it soon took the shape of a tiny but well-defined ball, then rose into the air very quickly and was lost to sight among the stars. From the time I first saw the light until it had disappeared into the sky, a period of from four to six seconds had elapsed.

I sat there a long time, puzzled about what I had seen. The "seeing" that night was perfect. If there was an inversion, it wasn't evident. The stars and planets had little or no twin-kle, and the atmosphere was very steady. It couldn't have been a meteor . . . meteors come down, they don't go up. It was no plane of any kind. I was familiar with jets, for I had seen several in 1945 at Love Field in Dallas, when my hus-band was stationed there with the Army Air Force. There are many other currently favored possible explanations which would not fit the sighting—even if it were seen today, with guided missiles, advanced aircraft and high-altitude research balloons common things in the sky. As a civilian employee

of the Air Force in the Range Scheduling Office at Holloman
Air Force Base in 1955 and 1956 I saw many missile and
balloon launchings. I emphatically deny the slightest possibility that the object I saw in 1947 even remotely resembled
any of these. It was traveling too fast.

The next day I wrote to Mr. Lorenzen, who was in
Phoenix. I described the sighting in detail and said that,
fantastic as it might seem, there was only one explanation
for the thing I had seen: there might be intelligent life on
other worlds, and their ships were the strange things people
had reported in the heavens from time to time through the
years.

In the coming weeks the heavens seemed to open up and
expel all manner of odd things. On June 24, 1947, the
famous Kenneth Arnold sighting was made near Mount
Rainier, Washington. Arnold, a competent private pilot, was
voluntarily participating in an air search for a missing transport plane. His attention was drawn to a flash off his wingtip
and he spotted nine disc-shaped objects flying along a chain
of mountains to his left. He said they flew together in a
single-file formation like "geese," in and out of the mountain
peaks. Arnold attempted to compute the speeds, using various
landmarks as points of reference and the time intervals which
elapsed during the travel of the objects between the two
points; he concluded that the disc-shaped things were flying
at a speed of not less than twelve hundred miles an hour. He
reported what he saw and before many hours the wire
services were carrying the story of the "flying objects"
spotted by Arnold. Because of his experience and good repu-
tation, Arnold's story was believed, and he is given credit
for bringing the mystery of the UFO to world attention.

Just three days after Arnold's sighting, and seventeen days
after my own observation in Douglas, southern Arizona
played host to many enigmatic flying objects, a few of
which will be listed here. It might be worth noting that at
the time of these visitations southern Arizona had no military installations of importance.

On June 27 John A. Petsche, an electrician working at the
Denn Shaft of the Phelps-Dodge Corporation copper mines
near Bisbee, spotted a disc-shaped, mirrorlike object which
moved "like a flash of light." Reporting his observation later,
Petsche said the thing wobbled as it moved, but made no
sound. Two men were within shouting distance of Petsche,
but he didn't call their attention to the object. Later in the

locker room the other two men said they had seen the object, and Petsche then announced he also had seen it and was certain it was no reflection or illusion, but a real, solid flying object. Three other men, John C. Rylance, an electrician at the Cole Shaft, I.W. Maxwell and Milton Luna were at Cole Hill, a mile and a half from Petsche at the time of the sighting. They observed the object as it came down out of the northwest at an angle of seventy-five degrees. As it came into view the object was clearly outlined against one of the hills overlooking an area called "Tintown." Rylance, Maxwell and Luna also said they were positive the object was a material thing and not a reflection or illusion. It did not look very large, they said, and seemed to be elongaged at the rear, or more oval-shaped than round. All these observers were of the opinion the object appeared to have landed at Tintown. Vernon C. McMinn, electrician gang boss for Phelps-Dodge Corporation, in an interview with reporters, said several other employees also saw the object and independently given descriptions tallied.

On that same date and at approximately the same time, 10:30 A.M., Major George B. Wilcox, U.S. Army, Ret., watched eight or nine light-colored, disc-shaped objects flying a west-to-east course at about a thousand feet above the mountains in the Lowell-Bisbee area. The objects were perfectly spaced in single-file formation, traveling at high speeds and dipping in a "rocking motion" as they flew.

Quite often observers hesitate to make public their experiences with UFOs, and the sighting of a huge object at sea in June, 1947, did not come into our hands until Edgar Jarrold, an Australian researcher, forwarded the text of a letter from Mrs. A.M. King of Nairobi, South Africa, in 1954. Subsequent accounts years later indicate that Mrs. King observed one of the huge "mother" or interplanetary ships, possibly the source of the many smaller atmospheric craft seen that summer. I quote:

I left Mombasa at the end of June, 1947, on the SS *Llandovery Castle* en route to Cape Town and, going through the Straits of Madagascar about the beginning of July, was on deck with another lady passenger at approximately 11 P.M. when we noticed a particularly bright star. It was traveling very fast and approached the ship. Suddenly a searchlight appeared which flashed a strong beam of light on the water within fifty yards of the ship. It descended, its beam shortening and becoming brighter as it neared the water, and the next instant there was no more light, but an object appeared, apparently made of steel and shaped like a cigar cut at the rear end. It remained in the air about twenty feet above the sea, parallel with the *Llandovery Castle,* and traveling in the same direction.

Gaining a little in speed, after a second or two the whole shape disappeared without a sound, from the rear issuing fierce flames which shot out to about half the length of the object. It appeared that there must be something like a huge furnace inside the thing, but still we could hear no noise from the flames. No windows could be seen, only a band of metal round the entire thing which, if it had been a complete cigar shape, would have been centrally situated.

The object was very large, about four times the length of the *Llandovery Castle* and at a rough guess about four times as high. We had a wonderful view, but in a few seconds it disappeared. No light was seen forward as it left; it just vanished soundlessly in the darkness. For a while we thought we were the only ones on deck at that late hour but, walking to the prow of the ship, we saw there one of the ship's officers with a few passengers; the entire party had seen the same thing. Whether or not it is recorded in the ship's log, I know not.

If Mrs. King's estimate of the object's size in comparison to that of the ship is fairly accurate, we must assume the object was at least sixteen hundred feet long and possibly larger (ocean-going vessels vary considerably in size).

To return to the United States, where in other parts of Arizona as well as in other western states the then so-called "flying saucers" were being reported very frequently. Douglas lies twenty-five miles east by southeast of Bisbee and is almost entirely ringed by mountains. In early July Douglas residents reported unconventional aerial objects in the skies, all of which, including the foregoing reports, were recorded in the Bisbee *Review* and the Douglas *Dispatch*. On July 8 Mrs. Ray Wilder and Mrs. Earl Moore reported watching a disc-shaped object flying across the sky from west to east, changing shape slowly and glinting in the sun. At 11:45 A.M. on July 10 Mrs. L.B. Ogle reported seeing a small, bright object which "quivered" and appeared to hover in the area immediately outside a downstairs window. Mrs. Ogle said the object seemed to be about seven inches in diameter. The window was located about five feet from the ground. On July 11 Mrs. W.P. Hopkins, also of Douglas, watched an object which appeared to be disc-shaped, reflecting floodlights at the Fifteenth Street Park. Several weeks later, about twenty-five residents of Douglas, including B.L. Fields, watched an object which appeared as a cluster of small lights as it circled the town ten times at great speed, finally disappearing with a burst of speed.

Elsewhere in Arizona the discs were putting in their appearances. At Yuma on July 9 Henry Vardela of the Arizona State Highway Department observed two discs flying single-file formation above the mountains. At Nogales, Guy Fuller, Western Union office manager, police sergeant Pete Mincheff, Sam Marcus and Arthur Doane observed objects there which they referred to as "flying tortillas." (A tortilla is a Mexican pancake of sorts, round and quite thin.) On July 8 William Holland, William Harman and Lewis Zesper, a former Air Force pilot, observed an oval metallic-gray object at an estimated four thousand feet above the mountains east of Tucson. The object appeared to be about twenty-five feet in diameter, and "wobbled" as it flew in a general north-to-south direction.

During this period discs were the favorite topic of conversation, especially in those areas where they had been sighted, and many who had seen unconventional objects in the past came forward to relate the details of their observations. One of these was Gene Holder, game warden in the Winslow-Tonto Rim area of Arizona. He told the Bisbee *Review* of his sighting of a bright object which appeared to be a "silver tin plate" soaring through the skies. The object appeared to be only a few hundred feet above his head, and watching it pained his eyes. Holder was riding horseback in the Tonto Rim area when the incident took place in 1913 or 1914.

An interesting fact about each of these sightings is very evident even without prolonged study—the objects were in the vicinity of, traveling along or among *mountains*. There are hundreds of other sightings which bear out this finding, many of them well-publicized "major" sightings of 1947. A government-employed civilian working at Holloman Air Force Base in New Mexico related to me two different UFO incidents he observed in 1947. One, involving a glowing, globe-shaped object, took place above the San Andreas Mountains to the west of Alamogordo and Holloman. The thing resembled the "bouncing musical ball" used in movie "community sings." The object followed the peaks as it flew at high speed from north to south. The second incident took place in the vicinity of the Sacramento Mountains, east of Alamogordo and Holloman. The object in this instance was a red, glowing ball-shaped object which flew along the mountain peaks from north to south. In many other flying saucer reports during 1947 the objects were flying along mountain ranges. Yuma, Nogales, Bisbee, Douglas and Tucson are in mountainous areas. Arnold's sighting took place in the Rocky Mountains, and the sightings last mentioned took place above mountains. What does this correlation mean? In my opinion it means only one thing: the objects were painstakingly mapping the geographical features of the country, as they were doing in 1954 and 1955 in South America when reports of unconventional objects were headlines in the newspapers there. One South American area in particular received a great deal of attention from the discs—the Avila Mountains, located near Caracas, the Venezuelan capital.

The pattern which later developed suggests that the UFOs mapped the United States in those early years, progressing from mountain ranges to rivers, coastlines and eventually lakes. In 1948 they began their disturbing visits to military installations. Doubtless, no major military base was overlooked. Those 1948-50 reconnaissance flights dealt primarily with military targets, including atomic installations. UFOs in comparatively unimportant areas, such as farmlands and forest regions, were apparently observed as they flew by. Those objects observed near military reservations were *hovering* or *maneuvering*, while those seen in sparsely populated areas were almost always in flight and seemingly in a hurry to get somewhere.

One evening in the summer of 1947 Ronald Larsen, a high-school student in Sturgeon Bay, Wisconsin, observed a kelly-green, teardrop-shaped object which appeared to follow the coastline along Sturgeon Bay and the canal that connects the bay and Lake Michigan. This object "trailed" an object which was an exact duplicate in size and shape, but much lighter in color. Larsen, who was familiar with the contours of the land in the area surrounding Sturgeon Bay, was certain the object was following or tracing the coastline. Both the Pacific and Atlantic coast areas have been hosts to objects which took either north-to-south or south-to-north routes, appearing to follow the coastlines. The most recent "coastal reconnaissance" flight in our files took place in 1955. The object was tracked from Portland, Oregon, to Pasadena, California, on the civil defense coastal radar network. The over-all distance was six hundred miles, and the speed of the object was sixteen hundred miles an hour. Observers along the coast and Mount Tamalpais radar estimated its altitude at nearly sixty thousand feet. Filter Center workers in Oakland were told that sent-up "scrambles" were unable to intercept the object.

Sixteen hundred miles an hour is a high speed even in these days of jets and guided missiles. It is unlikely that these high-speed objects are experimental planes using the air over populated areas for test flights, and it is doubtful whether we had operational planes capable of that speed in 1955.

During 1947-1950 newspapers throughout the world recorded many sightings of the unexplained objects reported by astronomers, pilots and trained weather and aircraft observers. The Mantell case, involving National Guard pilot Captain Thomas Mantell, took place on January 7, 1948, when Mantell and two other pilots attempted to overtake a "large, glowing object" in the skies near Godman Field, Kentucky. They were flying F-51s and were not equipped with oxygen for flight above fifteen thousand feet. Though unable to get close to the object, Mantell described it as tremendous in size and apparently metallic. First spotted at 1:45 P.M. by the assistant tower operator, the object was not sighted by Mantell until about 2:45 P.M. He had pulled out ahead of his wingmen, who apparently never did see the UFO. He announced to tower personnel that he was going to twenty thousand feet. At 3:50 the tower lost sight of the object and minutes later received a report that Mantell's plane had crashed and the pilot was dead.

Considering the many vague references to various aspects of the incident, it is not clear just what happened. It was widely believed that Mantell had chased the planet Venus, but the fallacy of that theory was evident—Venus was not at maximum magnitude at that specific time and, although Venus can be seen on clear days at peak brilliance if one knows just where to look, it would have been impossible for Mantell to chase something that would not have been visible on that partly cloudy day. Captain Edward Ruppelt, a one-time chief of the UFO investigation project at Wright Air

Development Center, says in his book, *The Report on Unidentified Flying Objects*, that he came to the conclusion the object being pursued by Mantell was actually a large skyhook balloon. I am not prepared to dispute this theory except to say that no balloon flight for that particular area has been discovered in military archives. Also, Ruppelt did his investigating of the case during his tenure as project chief, sometime between 1951 and 1953—at least three years after the incident; the trail had grown cold. As far as I'm concerned the Mantell case should be listed as "unknown" until the "object" can be positively identified.

This is one of the incidents heavily relied upon by some UFO enthusiasts to bolster their theory that UFOs are interplanetary space vehicles. More rumors surround it than any other sightings in UFO history. The latest to reach me was from a captain in the USAF Reserve who claims he took part in the investigation of that incident, including the location and inspection of the crashed F-51. He supports an old theory that the "spaceship" removed Mantell from his ship and then allowed it to crash. The captain says Mantell's body was never found.

Some other claims are equally interesting. One woman who claims to have seen the crash said the plane came down in a screaming dive, but nosed up just before striking the ground. The plane may have encountered a strong moving layer of air near the ground which lifted the nose just before the crash, or Mantell, who may have "blacked out" due to anoxia (oxygen starvation), could have regained consciousness just before the crash, and attempted to pull out of the dive.

In the September 1956 issue of the *APRO Bulletin* we published a letter originally sent to Ken Purdy, editor of *True* magazine, by Captian William B. Nash, Pan American Airlines pilot. Writing about the Mantell incident as described by Ruppelt in his *True* article, "What Our Air Force Found Out About Flying Saucers," Nash's letter was never printed by *True*:

As a pilot he [Ruppelt] *must* know that he wrote pure deception when he said of the Mantell case, "The propeller torque would pull it into a slow left turn, into a shallow dive, then an increasingly steeper descent under power. Somewhere during the screaming dive, the plane reached excessive speeds and began to break up in the air." Any Dilbert knows that as the speed of an airplane increases its lift increases, and the plane's nose would come up until the speed decreased again and the nose dipped once more to pick up speed and lift, thus creating an oscillation all the way to the ground—not a "screaming dive." The plane could spin or spiral instead of oscillate, but a spin is a stall maneuver, and planes do not come apart in a stall. This oscillation would be especially likely to occur if the airplane had been trimmed to climb, and at the beginning of the same paragraph containing the above-quoted hogwash, Ruppelt says, "The wreckage showed that the plane was *trimmed to climb.*"

Captain Nash is a World War II pilot, a respected, capable airman with a lot of flying hours to his credit. His interest in UFOs was aroused in 1952 when he and his copilot sighted UFOs near the East coast.

The next "big" one of 1948 took place on July 24 near Montgomery, Alabama, when an Eastern Airlines DC-3 piloted by Charles Chiles and John Whitted encountered a "B-29 fuselage"-shaped object with a "deep blue glowing underside" and "two rows of windows from which bright light glowed." The object sported a 50-foot trail of orange-red flame. The time was 2:45 A.M. and the night sky was dark. One other person observed the object; he said he saw only an eerie streak of light of great intensity, all he could observe because his eyes were not adjusted to the darkness. At about the same time a crew chief at Robbins Air Force Base in Macon, Georgia, reported observing a very bright light pass overhead at high speed. Later another report came in which seemingly corroborated the observation made by Chiles and Whitted. Flying near the North Carolina-Virginia state line, a pilot reported he had seen a "very bright shooting star" in the general direction of Montgomery.

According to Chiles and Whitted, Captain Chiles had first seen the object and called it to Whitted's attention. The thing was only a bright light at first and they thought it might be a jet, but as it approached they realized even a jet couldn't close in that fast. Chiles pulled the plane into a tight left turn, and the object flashed by at what was estimated as about seven hundred feet to their right. As it passed, the DC-3 hit extremely turbulent air and, looking back, Whitted saw the object pull up into a steep climb.

In his book Captain Ruppelt says shortly after this incident "the people at Air Technical Intelligence Command" decided the time had arrived to make an "estimate of the situation." The situation was the UFOs and whether they were interplanetary.

On October 1, 1948, another mysterious incident took place in Fargo, when a North Dakota National Guard pilot, twenty-five-year-old Second-Lieutenant George F. Gorman, chased a small light for some twenty minutes. This sighting has been thoroughly discussed in other books dealing with UFOs. According to Gorman, the light blinked on and off continuously until the object put on speed, at which time it increased in intensity and became steady. The light was six to eight inches in diameter, sharply outlined, and made sharp turns which Gorman could not duplicate with his F-51. Twice the light took a collision course with Gorman's plane, and twice Gorman dived to prevent a crash. Suddenly the light gathered speed and disappeared. Although three other people (the pilot of a cub plane, the cub's passenger and an oculist) observed the light, they didn't observe all the maneuvers.

Captain Ruppelt and Air Technical Intelligence Command personnel say the light was a balloon. But: (1) Ruppelt and the ATIC people didn't see the light or its maneuvers; Gorman did; (2) the "balloon" hung around the airfield, simulating dogfight maneuvers for twenty minutes, then some errant wind wafted it, at high speed, out of sight; (3) the light was clearly defined, blinking on and off, except when it appeared to put on speed, at which time it remained steady. A balloon?

Ruppelt lists three other cases of "meandering night lights," one of which was seen between the observer and the moon. In the Gorman incident the light was the only thing seen; nothing is mentioned about the diffuse plastic body of a balloon, which certainly would have been evident.

In November, 1947, we moved to Phoenix, and in 1949 we left for Los Angeles. UFO sightings were not receiving the publicity they had in the previous two years and, except for an occasional wire-service story, things were pretty quiet. In 1951 a Burbank acquaintance who was also very interested in UFOs suggested I attempt to organize a civilian research group. I was considering it when we moved to Sturgeon Bay, Wisconsin, in August 1951. In January 1952, after contacting other amateur astronomers who were interested in the subject of UFOs, the Aerial Phenomena Research Organization came into being. In July 1952 our first mimeographed bulletin was mailed to fifty-two members. In the fall of 1952 I started doing news correspondent work and feature writing for the *Green Bay Press-Gazette,* and consequently I met a lot of people who were of great assistance to me in tracking down early, unpublished sightings in Wisconsin.

One particularly interesting sighting was related to me by a minister who in the summer of 1910 observed a most peculiar sight. Because of the unusual nature of the sighting, he remembered the year. He had returned home from a church meeting, went into the back yard and started out to the barn for a last check on the animals before retiring. Suddenly the yard was flooded with light—white as though moonlight. He looked up and saw a single-line formation of round objects proceeding across the sky from west to east. He said he couldn't judge how high the objects were, but each object was round, clearly defined and a glowing white in color. The night was cloudless and clear, and the stars were bright, but there was no moon. His first impression was that he was observing one long, slender object, for the glow continued the whole length of the formation, although not quite as brilliant as the objects themselves. He then realized he was observing a number of objects in single-line formation, each traveling in the light or vapor trail of the object ahead of it. However, each object appeared to be a single object unconnected with the others in the line. The objects were proceeding at a high rate of speed and, not being familiar with astronomical phenomena, he automatically tabbed them as meteors, until he inquired about UFOs thirty years later when "flying saucers" came into the news.

In October 1951 another Wisconsin resident, John Schopf of Algoma, observed a globe-shaped object at about 8 P.M. The night was dark and Mr. Schopf, driving from Lincoln to Algoma, was coming down a hill which overlooked Lake Michigan when he spotted the object below the car visor (the object had to be quite low on the horizon to be seen). It was heading into the northeast very slowly and banked at a 30-degree angle. The color, Schopf said, was aluminum and it had the appearance of a light bulb painted a silver color with the light shining through. It finally disappeared in the distance over Lake Michigan.

2
No Other Answer

DESPITE many claims to the contrary, issued stentoriously and often by unnamed Air Force spokesmen, there have been many reports of the sighting of unconventional aerial objects by qualified observers which definitely indicate the extraterrestrial nature of the objects. Although APRO has in its files hundreds of sightings providing sufficient evidence in support of the interplanetary theory as an explanation of UFOs, for the sake of brevity I have selected only two to illustrate the point.

Our first report is of the cigar-shaped type of UFO, and is significant because it took place at Holloman Air Force Base, and was photographed. Holloman is an Air Force research and development center located in the Tularosa Basin, nine miles west of Alamogordo and approximately thirty miles north of the White Sands Proving Grounds. Military and civilian personnel stationed at the base have seen many strange objects in the skies over Holloman in the past nineteen years. The observer, an electronics engineer who submitted the report, had previously seen high groups of shiny objects and had accepted the idea that some kind of phenomena existed which had not been identified by scientific and technical people. On a hot summer day in July, 1950, he was having lunch in his office at a private contractor's building at Holloman. The range telephone rang and the engineer and an Askania operator were informed by one of the range stations that an unidentified aerial object had been sighted. They were requested to proceed to another range station, which was equipped with a manually operated Askania theodolite and located about three miles north of range control. The men rushed to the designated station and, using the azimuth and elevation readings of the object supplied to them, they focused the theodolite and found their subject.

(The description of the maneuvers of the object observed by the two men could be sensationalized to read far more excitingly than described here, but the basic facts are more important than the impression they create. I have maintained this attitude during the fifteen years I have edited the *APRO Bulletin* and still feel it is the best course.)

Through the finders on the theodolite the object presented a side view to the observers and appeared to be cigar-shaped and metallic, with a straw-colored irridescent radiance or luster. Fins one-third of the way back from the front of the fuselage with a row of at least three oblong ports extending from the fins to the rear of the object and located above the center line of the fuselage complete the physical description. The ports were dark, somewhat a "smoky" gray but not luminescent. The object hovered in an almost horizontal position, elevation 20-25 degrees, azimuth northeast. Shortly after the men had focussed their theodolite on the object, it began maneuvering. Turning toward the camera, the object moved in, and the men had a front view of the object—it was round, with the fins extending out from the sides. It then dropped abruptly, as though beginning to fall, but arrested the drop. Again, it moved toward the camera, turned sideways, then dropped as before, but this time it exposed the side view again.

At this point the operator left the azimuth controls, went to the range telephone and called Queen-1 to report their contact so other range facilities could be put into action. Because the Askania manually operated theodolite requires two operators, one for azimuth and one for elevation, while the operator was on the phone the engineer was unable to continue tracking the object. When the operator returned to the controls the men could not relocate the object—it was gone.

The men turned over their exposed film to the Data Reduction Division for development and analysis. They didn't hear anything for from seven to ten days; then they were called in and questioned by a young first lieutenant. They didn't recognize the officer, although he wore a Base identification badge. They were asked over and over again if they had taken pictures, and to describe over and over the object they had observed. Then the two men were asked if they could identify the film of the object they had photographed. One of the men became quite angry about the questioning, telling the officer he had seen what he had reported, had photographed the object and was convinced the object was some sort of a vehicle from outer space. He was shown a film of fourteen frames on a Recordak projector. The black-and-white presentation showed a blurred ellipsoid with a dark center, but no details. (Puzzled about the film he later talked to a mathematician-analyst employed by Land-Air, Inc.; she conjectured the object had been oscillating in the air, preventing good photography.[1]) The men were then told by their superiors to forget the whole incident.

There is a definite parallel between this case and the report of the following sighting, namely, after the sighting the interrogating officials who obtained all the available information instructed the principals to "forget" what had happened. Any individual who has observed an unidentified flying object for some time and noted all the unorthodox features, such as color, configuration and maneuverability as well as the maneuvers does not easily forget what he or she has seen. Obviously, as early as 1950, and possibly 1948, the Air Force was fully aware of the portent of the many sightings and reports they had received relevant to what they designated "unidentified flying objects."

Here is how I happened to find out about the following particular sighting. Mr. Lorenzen and I made a trip to Los Angeles in April, 1956, to have some bass viol work done by Robert Roberti, a master craftsman and one of many friends whom we visited while in the City of the Angels. While visiting one of our old friends one afternoon, our host, who shall remain anonymous for obvious reasons, told us a friend was in town and had expressed interest in APRO and would very much like to meet us. Always glad to meet anyone interested in UFOs, because new opinions and fresh ideas are vital to research, we said we'd like to see the fellow, and our host arranged for him to be at the house the next evening. Our friend mentioned that this man had served as a Navy airman during the Korean War and was one of six who had a sensational experience with two unconventional flying objects. On the way to our lodgings, Jim and I discussed whether this might be another false lead, a minor sighting

---

[1] APRO consultants do not support this opinion, considering it more likely the camera recorded the existence of an enveloping field—probably ionic—not visible to the naked eye.

with few if any details or another crackpot claim.
The next evening we heard the following story:

Very early one morning in September, 1950, three fighter-bombers took off from the flight-deck of a U.S. aircraft carrier riding off the coast of Korea. The sun hadn't risen and there was a bite in the air. Two men—a pilot and a radar gunner—occupied each of the three planes assigned to a routine mission, bombing and strafing a truck convoy that combat intelligence expected to be winding along the floor of a valley about a hundred miles from the Yalu River. The takeoff was routine, as was the flight to the target area. At about 7 A.M., just as the sun was breaking above the mountains in the east, the aircraft were proceeding north, ten thousand feet above the valley floor. Radar observers had their eyes peeled for the target. The target was never seen, but what did show up caused those six airmen considerable puzzlement. It is not difficult to understand their surprise or concern, for they probably observed the largest unconventional aerial objects at close range (considering the circumstances, time of day and perfect visibility) for a longer time than any human beings up to then.

Mr. Douglas (as we'll call him) sat quietly while he told his story, but it was evident, as he related his experience, that he was reliving every minute of it. "I was watching the ground below for the convoy," he began, "and I was startled to see the two large circular shadows coming along the ground from the northwest at a high rate of speed. We were flying north above a valley which was surrounded on the east and west by mountains, with a pass directly ahead of us to the north. When I saw the shadows I looked up and saw the objects which were causing them. They were huge. I knew that as soon as I looked at my radar screen. They were also going at a good clip—about 1000 or 1200 miles per hour. My radar display indicated one and a half miles between the objects and our planes when the objects suddenly seemed to halt, back up and begin a 'jittering,' or 'fibrillating motion.' My first reaction, of course, was to shoot. I readied my guns, which automatically readied the gun cameras. When I readied the guns, however, the radar went haywire. The screen 'bloomed' and became very bright. I tried to reduce the brightness by turning down the sensitivity, but this had no effect. I realized my radar had been jammed and was useless. I then called the carrier, using the code name. I said the code name twice, and my receiver was out—blocked by a strange buzzing noise. I tried two other frequencies, but couldn't get through. Each time I switched frequencies the band was clear for a moment, then the buzzing began.

"While this was going on the objects were still jittering out there ahead of us, maintaining our speed. About the time I gave up trying to radio the carrier the things began maneuevering around our planes, circling above and below. I got a good look at them. I had never seen anything like them before, and I learned after we reached our carrier that the other men in that flight were of the same opinion. They were huge—I said that before. Before my radar set was put out of commission, I used the indicated range plus points of reference on the canopy to determine their size. They were at least 600 or possibly 700 feet in diameter.

"The objects had a 'silvered mirror' appearance, with a reddish glow surrounding them. They were shaped somewhat like a coolie's hat, with oblong ports from which emanated a copper-green colored light which gradually shifted to pale pastel-colored lights and back to the copper-green again. Above the ports was a shimmering red ring which encircled the top portion.

"When the things maneuvered above us, we saw the bottoms of them. In the middle of the underside was a circular area, coal black and nonreflective. It was simply inky black, and it is important to note that although the whole object 'jittered' while maneuvering, the black circular portion on the bottom was steady and showed no indication of movement."

Mr. Douglas completed his narrative and Jim and I began shooting questions. Mr. Lorenzen has had a good deal of experience with radar and radio. He asked if Mr. Douglas had noted any other peculiarities. Douglas said that he and all the men in that flight had noticed a feeling of warmth in the airplane, and also what he described as a high-frequency vibration.

When the objects seemingly finished their inspection of the Navy planes, they took off in the same direction from which they had come, and disappeared at a high rate of speed. The three planes then proceeded back to the carrier, where reports were made. The six men were questioned individually and then in a group by combat intelligence. They were thoroughly tested for radiation, as was their aircraft. The men never knew the results of the Geiger-counter tests, but they did learn that the instrument dials on their ships had become extremely luminous and all the gun camera film had been fogged or exposed, although none of the crews had used either guns or cameras.

The usual explanations offered by many "experts" do not fit this report. Meteors, balloons, hallucinations, reflections, revolutionary new aircraft—are all insufficient. As Mr. Douglas said, "Mrs. Lorenzen, those things were real—intelligently controlled machines." I asked, "Where do you think they could have come from?"

"I would be presuming a lot if I were to try to definitely give their origin, but I do know this—those things were the product of intelligences far beyond ours—a science far in advance of ours. They must be from outer space. There's no other answer," he affirmed.

3
The Sturgeon Bay "Flying Saucer"

I TURNED the corner at Third and Michigan and walked toward the drugstore. Suddenly someone called, "There's the 'flying-saucer woman'—ask her what it is!" Third Avenue, the main street in Sturgeon Bay, Wisconsin, was literally full of people watching the sky to the northeast. I looked up and saw it too—a silver, ellipsoid object.

This incident took place at about 7 P.M. on May 21, 1952. I had been writing features and doing news correspondent work for the *Green Bay Press-Gazette* in 1951 and 1952, and on that particular evening had gone downtown to interview a local dancing teacher. She was late for our appointment, so I walked a couple of blocks to Kellner's Drugstore for my second after-dinner cup of coffee.

One of the reporters for the *Door County Advocate*, located next to the drugstore on Third Avenue, and the editor's son were among the crowd on the street. It was the reporter who pointed out my presence. "What is it?"—"Is it a flying saucer?" the crowd wanted to know. I told them I didn't know, and immediately wondered if it would be possible to reach someone reliable in the northern part of the county to attempt a triangulation. (Door County is the upper portion of the "thumb" that juts out into Lake Michigan.)

I entered the drugstore and called Jim Cordier at the police station. Jim was the radio operator for the local and county police. I asked him if there was a radio car "up north," and he said that City Policeman Harry Londo and County Patrolman Daniel O'Herne were near Fish Creek. I told him what we were watching in the sky and asked him to call O'Herne and Londo and find out if the object was visible from their location. I hung up, dashed into the street again and asked the onlookers if anyone had a pair of field glasses. Mr. Eames, proprietor of Eames Restaurant across the street, said he had a pair of low-power glasses in his apartment, and ran across the street to get them. I looked back at the object just in time to see the bottom of it begin to glow with a reddish tint.

Eames hadn't returned with the field glasses, so I went back to the drugstore and called home. My husband had never observed a UFO, and I wanted him to see the object. There was no answer. When I had left home, he was doing some yard work, and I later learned he hadn't heard the phone. I called Jim Cordier at the police station again. He had talked to O'Herne and Londo by radio, and he described what they were watching. In Sturgeon Bay the object was at a 45-degree elevation in the northeast. At Fish Creek the object appeared not as an ellipsoid but as an almost perfect circle, with a brilliant round red light about one-third the diameter of the object in the center. The elevation at Fish Creek was 60 degrees. All descriptions, at Fish Creek and in Sturgeon Bay, agreed that the object was moving very slowly in a north-easterly direction.

I went back outside. The field glasses had arrived. With the aid of the low-powered glasses we saw the thing as a clearly defined, apparently metallic object. The glow on the bottom was a deep red through the glasses.

For a triangulation of the sighting I stood against the drugstore building and lined up the object with a television antenna mast on a building across the street. The mast did not quite obscure the object. At 7:40 P.M. the object was no longer visible at Sturgeon Bay. It was visible in the northern part of the county for five more minutes and then was lost to sight because of trees in the vicinity. Altogether, I had observed the object intermittently for about thirty minutes. I later learned that the object had been spotted at 6:50 P.M. by observers in the northern part of the county, when it was almost overhead. All those to whom I talked had the impression the object had been traveling in a general northeast direction, following the Lake Michigan shoreline. When there was no more to see, the people in the streets continued about their business, and I went home to discuss with Mr. Lorenzen what I had observed. The next day Jim went down to the exact spot where I had stood, computed the distance between my point of observation and the television mast and took the measurement of the mast. A straight-line measurement of the distance between Fish Creek and Sturgeon Bay gave us eighteen miles. This gave us the base line of the triangle, and we were on our way to calculating the object's approximate distance from the ground and its diameter.

The Sturgeon Bay saucer was about 780 feet in diameter, traveling slowly at an *approximate* altitude of forty miles. In releasing the story we realized that people wouldn't believe or accept the 780-feet diameter, so we stated that it was at least 400 feet wide. We ourselves found the actual measurements difficult to believe, despite the fact that we had worked out all the contributing figures very carefully.

The "explanations" which were forthcoming within the next few days were of interest. The Air Force didn't investigate this sighting, which had all the earmarks of a "major" sighting, but General Mills Co. of Minneapolis, then engaged in the manufacture and launching of huge "skyhook"-type balloons for upper-air research, stated to the press that we "probably" had seen one of their balloons which had been launched that morning and "could" have been over Door County at the time of the sighting. Not explained was the bright light on the bottom of the object; it wasn't even mentioned in the press release. The reliability of the observers wasn't mentioned either. I had had a good deal of experience with estimating degrees of arc in the sky, and both policemen who had observed the object in Fish Creek were World War II veterans and capable observers. The General Mills statement did not attempt to discredit Mr. Lorenzen's triangulation, nor did it mention the facts that the big balloons were considerably less than four hundred feet in diameter and were not equipped with huge riding lights.

Since that sighting I have given a lot of thought to the nature of that huge (about two hundred and ninety feet in diameter) red light which suddenly appeared on the bottom of the object. Was it possibly some type of special light used in high-altitude photographic techniques? The sun had not gone down, so it wasn't needed for illumination; besides, a light that far from a subject wouldn't light it up to any appreciable extent.

The day after the Sturgeon Bay saucer was observed I talked with O'Herne and Londo. Both had been "saucer skeptics" before observing the object, but admitted that they *had seen something* and that *something* couldn't be explained. O'Herne said, "I don't know what that thing was, but I can tell you it was no balloon or reflection or hallucination, or any of the other explanations." This was the attitude of some twenty different individuals which whom I talked after the incident.

One year later I talked about the saucer mystery with the famous astrophysicist, Dr. J. Allen Hynek. Giving him all the details, including our estimated size of the object, I asked him if he thought the object could have been a balloon, and he answered, "No." "Well, Doctor, what do you think it could have been?" I asked. "I don't know," he said.

Air Force officials might say there was "insufficient data" to provide an explanation, because of their inability to explain the object by conventional means. This would be an entirely false premise. We had a sufficient number of observers at a number of different locations, enabling us to get a good description of the configuration of the object—it was definitely round and flat. If it had not been for the huge, brilliant light on the bottom of the object one might stretch a point and assume the object was a high-altitude research balloon of extraordinary size which had "pancaked" between two layers of dense air at an extremely high altitude. One might attempt to explain the light as a reflection of the sun, etc. That light, however, cannot thus be explained away. It was observed by about a hundred people who described it as a brilliant glow at the bottom of the UFO. At a point eighteen miles to the north observers described it as a perfectly symmetrical light of such brilliance that one could not comfortably observe it through binoculars, and that it was located precisely in the middle of the object. If it had been a mere reflection, even of the sun, this would not have been true. And so we must rule out that possibility; the Sturgeon Bay saucer was no balloon and the light it sported was no reflection.

4
1952–The First Landing

AFTER the initial interest in the flying discs had been aroused during 1947-1950 several interested people began documenting available data and speculating about the possible origin and motives of the strange crafts. Among these were Major Donald E. Keyhoe, a retired Marine officer who wrote *The Flying Saucers Are Real,* and Frank Scully, a professional writer and author of *Behind the Flying Saucers.* Both books were big sellers and further increased interest in UFOs. Scully concentrated on several stories which had been passed on to him regarding crashed discs and their occupants in the New Mexican desert at the beginning of the UFO saga. Keyhoe, however, dealt factually with sighting accounts gleaned from pilots and weather observers, and personally investigated and documented many of them.

APRO was founded in January, 1952, with a handful of members. By the time the "flap" (Air Force slang for the period during which many reports of UFO are made) of that year had come upon the world we had garnered a few more members, but nevertheless were short-handed. The Washington, D.C., "blip" incident, which involved radar returns and placed unidentified flying objects over the Capitol on several nights, seemed to be the height of an influx of mystery flying craft. With limited member activity we could not gather the reports we should have had for proper evaluation. Despite this, before the year was out a general scrutiny of our 1952 files yielded undeniable evidence that the elusive sky objects had visited the whole earth. The most disturbing fact was that the machines were observed in most cases over vital defense areas in the United States and Canada. Inasmuch as those early years have been so well documented by other writers I will confine my accounts to those incidents which have not been fully covered and which, I feel, need further clarification.

As early as April the Albuquerque, New Mexico, area was visited by a really strange appearing object—a black sheep among the usual discs, "cigars" and globes. Sighted by Carl Hawk, the object resembled a long rectangular flying wing with a clear v design on it. The object was black, but the v was a bright yellow. It made no sound as it streaked through the sky. Hawk, a Sandia Corporation engineer, said that he and his friend Marvin Harvey were at the base when they looked up to see a jet fighter zooming across the sky. They then spotted the object as it came streaking out of the Tijeras Canyon area on an east-to-west trajectory, disappearing into a cloud which appeared to be approximately over downtown Albuquerque. The observation period was ten seconds, as timed by Hawk. An amateur artist, he immediately sketched what he had seen and jotted down his impressions as to size, distance and speed. Although he admitted he could make no reliable estimate of the object's size or speed, he judged its altitude was about two thousand feet and its speed between 200 and 400 miles per hour. Later, after making a report to the Air Force, he received a letter from Air Force officials commending him for his objective and unbiased report and referring to him as a well-qualified observer. In a personal conversation with me in 1958 he said that as far as he knows the Air Force still considers his sighting unexplainable.

Things were quiet during the first months of 1952, but the summer saucer season was opened with a bang when Pan American Airlines pilots William B. Nash and W.H. Fortenberry sighted six glowing red discs while in flight near Newport News, Virginia, on the night of July 14. The objects, a mile below them, appeared to be about a hundred feet in diameter, flying in a stepped-up echelon formation. They executed a 150-degree turn when below and just in front of the airliner, heading in another direction to be joined by two more discs which came from behind and underneath the Pan-American plane. As they sped into the night the discs' lights blinked out, one by one.

Fifteen days later, on July 29, photographic supplies salesman Sid Eubanks of Wichita, Kansas, was almost swept off U.S. Highway 81 between Bison and Waukomis, Oklahoma, by a low-flying yellow-green, then yellow-brown, streak of light which appeared to the frightened Eubanks to be about four hundred feet long. He was still trembling with fright when he told his story to police at Enid. He could supply no more details than that the object was ball-shaped when it was above him. The press wire story reported the basic facts.

Since the big flap of 1952 the history of the flying saucers has been well recorded in books and periodicals edited by dedicated UFO-mystery fans. Every periodical in the world chronicled the events of the summer of 1952. Out of the amassed pile of sightings came a thread of continuity—the aerial and terrestrial defenses of the United States and Canada had been thoroughly reconnoitered by unidentified flying objects. In addition to the mass visitations in these two countries the discs visited the rest of the world, but on a lesser scale. Infant Israel was saluted over Haifa in August by a bright green elliptical object with a broad, rapidly revolving belt around its middle. An oval-shaped object of great brilliance, emitting tail smoke and flying at great speed, was reported over Bogota, the Colombian capital. An object flashed out of the stratosphere and stopped for about twenty seconds over Rome before it disappeared. One of the more sensational reports was from East Germany where a man and his daughter claimed they had seen a flying disc on the ground and two men in silvery suits near it. Three high-flying, speedy saucer-shaped objects scouted Madrid at night, leaving vapor trails. In the Baltic Sea the crew of a Danish destroyer, participating in "Operation Mainbrace," spotted a "flying body" traveling at great speed over the southern rim of the sea, fifty miles from a Russian guided-missile base. The wire services recorded stories of flying saucers over the battle lines in Korea and also over Japan. In some of the Japanese sightings the objects were tracked by radar and chased by jets.

On March 29, 1952, Lieutenant David C. Brigham was flying a prop-driven reconnaissance plane at six thousand feet over Northern Japan. An F-4 Thunderjet drew alongside and Brigham saw a very shiny disc-shaped object, about eight inches in diameter, to the right and just behind the jet. It appeared to be going 30 to 40 miles an hour faster than the jet, and closed in rapidly. Just before it would have flown into his fuselage, the object almost instantaneously accelerated to the jet's airspeed, flipping on edge in approximately a 90-degree bank. It appeared to flutter about twenty feet from the fuselage for perhaps two or three seconds before it pulled away and around the right wing, appearing to flip once as it hit the slipstream behind the jet's wingtip fuel tank. Brigham said it then passed the jet, pulled in front of it and then up abruptly, appearing to accelerate, and finally shot out of sight in what appeared to be a steep, almost vertical climb. Brigham said that its flight characteristic was a slow, fluttering motion, rocking back and forth in approximately 40-degree banks at possibly one-second intervals and pulling away much more sharply than a plane could have done. He said the maneuvering seemed purposeful and precise. Because of the proximity of the jet, Brigham was able to fairly accurately judge the distance—about 30 to 50 feet away. Although the sighting lasted only about ten seconds, Brigham got a good look at the object, and Air Force Intelligence apparently was sufficiently impressed with the report to release it to the wire services without qualifying remarks or denials.

The object may very well be related to, or the same as, the small, vari-colored lights of amazing maneuverability quite often seen at night. However, the size of night lights cannot be estimated, for they could be merely lights on craft larger than their own apparent diameter.

An AP report from Seoul noted the July 10 sighting of two objects by a Canadian destroyer, and radar confirmation. The Navy report placed the objects two miles high and seven miles away. A second Navy report dismissed the objects as Jupiter, whereupon one officer commented that Jupiter doesn't come in pairs and Jupiter was several million miles out of range of the ship's radar.

Except for the Canadian and Baltic sightings, those in countries other than the United States and Canada were made after August 5. The Canadian and American flap had ended. Random observations of sightings during August and September appeared to be only of afterthoughts to the main purpose of the visitations, perhaps the preliminary reconnaissance of other areas. The sightings in Europe, Africa and South America after the major 1952 flap apparently were merely orientation flights, for these continents received a good deal of attention two years later.

The climax of the 1952 influx of saucers was, of course, the visitations over Washington, D.C. Keyhoe, among others, reported that in one visit an object was over the White House and another over the Capitol itself. The Washington area is surrounded by air fields, and Fort Monmouth, then the location of the Army's secret defense laboratories, was in nearby New Jersey. It would seem that Washington, D.C., itself was not the primary target for those after-dark visits. Inas-

much as visits were mainly confined to military installations
it is possible the occupants of the discs may have mistaken
the Capitol and the White House, as well as other imres-
sive landmarks, for military objectives. In 1957 Mr. Lorenzen and I visited friends in Nogales, Arizona; while in the
area we stopped at Fort Huachuca, which was the new location of Monmouth activities. We were not surprised to learn
that shortly after the reactivation of the base there had been
a flurry of UFO sightings in the fort area. The saucers
were keeping well-posted on all new developments!

On July 16, 1952, at 9:35 A.M. what researchers considered
a "good" UFO picture was snapped through a dirty window
at the Coast Guard Air Station photo lab in Salem, Massachusetts. The picture made history and was flashed around
the world on the news wires. It showed four glowing objects resembling two soup bowls clamped together. The photographer, Shell Alpert, said he watched them for five or six
seconds before he tried to photograph them; by the time he
had clicked the shutter they had dimmed their light considerably. The Coast Guard's statement was that it had no
opinion as to the cause or source of the "objects" and was releasing the photo only because of the widespread public interest in aerial phenomena. Later, of course, it was theorized
in official statements that Alpert had merely photographed
lights reflected against the photo lab window. It was never
learned whether there were other witnesses, but similar objects have since been seen and photographed, for example,
the remarkable "Saturn-shaped" UFO pictures taken by an
IGY photographer near Trindade Island in January, 1958.
(see *Plates 5 A-D*.)

In 1952 a landing of sorts took place near West Palm
Beach, Florida. This account has been debunked, distorted,
embellished and generally messed up. After years of digging
it is apparent that something did land and that a man did get
close enough to see the object.

On August 19 at about 9 P.M. Scoutmaster D. S. "Sonny"
Desvergers and three boy scouts in his troop were driving
along Military Trail about five miles west and twelve miles
south of West Palm Beach. Suddenly Desvergers spotted
what appeared to be something burning a few hundred yards
from the road. There were no houses in the surrounding area
of a thicket of scrubby palmettos. Desvergers, thinking a
plane had crashed, stopped the car and turned it around for
a better view. He told the boys to stay in the car, and if

he wasn't back within ten minutes they should go for help. He then made his way to the edge of the thicket and started toward the light with his machete and a flashlight. As he approached the lighted area he realized something was wrong; there were no cries for help, no sounds of burning— just an eerie red glow. Then he looked up—something circular with a phosphorescent glow was hovering just above his head. Instinctively, he ducked and backed up, simultaneously striking out at the object with the machete. A misty round flare blossomed from the underside of the object and floated straight toward his face. He flung an arm in front of his face and fell to the ground, almost unconscious. The smell of the thing that hit him in the face registered in his mind. "It was a sickening, a nauseating stench—worse than rotten eggs and more like burning flesh," he said later.

The three scouts in the car by the side of the road became alarmed when ten minutes passed and then stretched to twenty. They had seen strange-looking lights flare up where their scoutmaster had disappeared. The boys, David Rowan, Bobby Ruffing and Charles Stevens, got out of the car and ran north on the highway until they came to the house of J. D. Brynteson. There they told their story, their fright obvious to Mr. Brynteson, who telephoned Deputy Sheriff Mott N. Partin at Boynton Beach, five or six miles away. He raced to the highway and found the car with its lights still burning. He heard stumbling footsteps in the water-filled ditch alongside the road. He focused his flashlight and saw Desvergers approaching. He was lurching, almost drunkenly, his face pale, and, according to Partin, he appeared as if suffering from shock. He jerkily related his experience. He said he had tried to scream and run, but couldn't and didn't remember getting to the edge of the road. According to estimates, Desvergers had been gone an hour and a half. The hair on his forearms was burned off, as it would have been if he had used his arms to protect his face from heat or fire. The sheriff found nothing in the thicket except Desverger's flashlight imbedded in the ground with only the lens exposed. Back at the car Partin examined Desverger's cap and found three small holes which appeared to have been burned into it.

These are the bare essentials of the story. Later, however, more facts and near-facts came to light. In his book, *The Report on Unidentified Flying Objects,* Edward Ruppelt, one-time chief of the saucer investigative branch at Wright Air Development Center, on page 239 admits that the Air Force investigators tried to prove that the Desvergers incident was a hoax. Relying on an investigation of Desverger's background, the Air Force team decided to stick around and check the story carefully. Grass samples taken from the scene of the incident were tested. Although the grass had not been affected the roots were charred. Except for the charred extreme tips of the longest blades the grass showed nothing; the lab report reasoned that these long tips had been bent over, touched the ground and had been charred. The lab duplicated the charring by placing live grass clumps in a pan of dirt and sand and heating it over a gas burner to about 300° F. Neither Ruppelt nor the lab had any idea how it could have been done outside a laboratory.

But there were other facts which interest me far more. In 1957 Captain William B. Nash, an APRO member and one of the principals of the Nash-Fortenberry sighting near Newport News in June 1952, sent me a photo of the area in which the incident took place. The "thicket" was stubby palmetto and the area where the photo was taken was easily visible from the road. Yet, Ruppelt on page 241 says that he and his cohorts had gone to the area at night and, under approximately the same lighting conditons as existed at the time of Desverger's adventure, had attempted to duplicate the scene. Even by standing on top of their car, he says, they couldn't see the spot where Desvergers purportedly fell. I would like to know how he produced the *same lighting conditions,* how he could determine what they were, how they could approximate something Desvergers couldn't adequately describe or understand. Did he know from experience, for instance, just how much light that certain type of UFO was capable of producing?

The boys' stories were not discredited and the charred roots supported Desvergers's story. Yet Ruppelt states that the Air Force wrote off the whole story as a hoax. This admission suggests to so many civilian researchers that the Air Force is not conducting a scientific investigation of UFOs. Something had hovered over that clearing, burned holes in Desvergers's cap, shot fireballs into the air and charred the roots of the grass—evidence of the existence of aircraft so superior to our best that the earth's finest looked like so many kiddie cars in comparison.

The front-page banner story for the Tuesday, July 29, issue of the Milwaukee *Sentinel* was fairly representative of the news being featured throughout the United States. JETS ON

24-Hour Alert to Hunt Saucers, it read, with subtitles: Discs Over D.C. Latest of One Thousand "Seen" in the U.S. and Air Force Report Tries to Quiet Public.

The INS story began by saying that on Monday, the day before, the Air Force had issued an order to its "hottest" jets to maintain a twenty-four-hour alert for "flying saucers." Then the story played down the excitement by saying that an official statesmen "sought to quiet public excitement" over the recent rash of saucer reports. The day-and-night alert was issued by Colonel Jack C. West, commanding the 142d Fighter-Intercepter Squadron in New Castle, Delaware, following the weekend of saucer sightings over the Washington, D.C., area. The article said that preliminary Air Force investigation, including pursuit of the objects, indicated that the *"latest"* [italics mine] saucer fleet did not constitute a threat to the United States. Then followed the usual birds, "misinterpretation of conventional objects," mild hysteria, meteorological phenomena or hoax malarky. The Air Force report also pointed out that the unexplained sightings appeared in haphazard fashion and showed no pattern which would indicate the objects were being controlled by a "reasoning body."

It is obvious that someone stubbed his toe early in the game. Ruppelt's book tells of a group of sightings on the Eastern seaboard which started with a sighting in Boston and then one at Fort Monmouth. He states that without injecting any imagination or wild assumptions—a UFO had come across Boston, thence across Long Island, stopped for a time at the Army's Fort Monmouth lab, then continued southwest, heading toward Washington, D.C. Sure enough, the report came in later: a UFO was spotted in Washington, D.C. And even later, after Ruppelt's book was published, civilian UFO researchers pinned the sightings on a map, applied their thread or rulers and found a straight-line course. Indeed, a UFO had come down over Boston, across Long Island, stopped at Fort Monmouth, then later hovered north-north-west of Washington, D.C.

But let's go back to that July 19 statement. Speaking of the possible threat to the United States, the Air Force statement said: "the latest saucer fleet does not constitute a 'threat' to the United States." Why specify the *recent* saucer fleet? What about the "fleets" which had been seen in the past and which might come in the future? The earliest ones involved reconnaissance of our atomic laboratories, and the authorities knew it. By July 29, 1952, the Air Force and other agencies of the government were aware that the saucers had visited every major military installation in the United States. And if Ruppelt had discovered a straight-line pattern of sightings by the first of July, surely the UFO investigation center at WADC was aware of that fact, and so were top Air Force brass who made the July 29 official statement. It would almost seem that they were making the statement to reassure themselves.

5
1954—Europe and South America

ALTHOUGH a fair number of sightings were made elsewhere in the world during the 1954 Mars opposition, by far the largest number was in Europe and South America. Researchers found no meaningful pattern among the hundreds of sightings of unidentified flying objects during the year, though it was quite obvious that the discs were concentrating on two general areas. Efforts by APRO to find orthotenic lines for South America during the 1954 flap yielded nothing. Not until later was the "straight-line" pattern discovered by Aime Michel. As Michel so ably points out, it is necessary to obtain correct dates to carry on such an analysis. Unfortunately, even by 1954 we did not have sufficient coverage or sufficiently interested workers to gather the data we needed. But it was definitely established that a close-up survey of South American countries and Europe was in progress.

It was also the year the Mars Committee, after viewing hundreds of feet of film taken by the special committee during the Mars opposition, announced that life of a sort did exist on that planet. The contention had been purely conjecture until then. E. C. Slipher returned from his stint as a Mars observer at the Bloemfontein, South Africa, observatory in October and gave his startling conclusion to the world in a press release from Washington, D.C. He said that Mars had to be alive, for if things did not grow there, changing with the seasons, dust from its red deserts would have settled long ago over its entire face, making the planet all one color. This was good news to many amateur astronomers and UFO researchers, tired of the ridiculous theories accounting for the many mysteries of the Mars disc. (One of these, for instance, considered the green stuff on Mars to be only volcanic ash which seasonally blew across the surface of the planet. The theory, however, did not explain what kind of wind would also seasonally blow the stuff back into conveniently located crevices so that, except at the poles, during the winter season the planet would again appear to be covered by the red desert.) This news was important, too, for it appeared evident as early as 1952 that the flying discs had some connection with the planet Mars. The largest number of sightings were made during the proximity of that planet and earth. For years popular magazine and newspaper articles had pointed out that saucers were seen usually during the summer months; they were but reflections of ground lights on inversion layers in the upper atmosphere which occurred during hot weather. Some even went so far as to insinuate that those who sighted UFOs were victims of the heat. Since these "experts" were bent on explaining away the problem rather than solving it the coincidence between saucer influxes and Mars proximities of 1952 and 1954 and the fact that no rash of sightings was recorded for the summer of 1953 were conveniently overlooked.

Opinion among researchers concerning the actual relationship of Mars proximities and UFO "flaps" is divided. Some feel that Mars cannot support intelligent life and that the discs, if they are indeed extraterrestrial, must hail from a planet in another star system than that of the sun and its planet family of nine. Others, including myself, feel that we do not know enough about Mars to make an informed statement on her ability to support intelligent life. It is not generally realized that many accepted "facts" about our neighbors in space are not facts at all, but only none-too-well supported theories in most instances. Recently it has come to the attention of astronomers that Jupiter could very well be a warm rather than the cold world it has long been supposed to be. Astronomy has not yet solved the many mysteries of our own natural satellite, the moon, and it is doubtful that much more will be learned until we are finally able to land a manned space ship on its surface.

After reading Michel's book, *The Flying Saucers and the Straight-Line Mystery,* I decided against a comparison study, superimposing his straight-line plots over a map of France's defense centers; I assumed that he had already conducted such a study. Later I was to regret this decision, for Dr. Fontes suggested that the straight-line patterns of UFO close observations and landings in France in 1954 coincided with the French terrestrial and air-defense installations. Possibly M. Michel realized this but didn't consider it sufficient evidence to indicate military reconnaissance. On the other hand, it may be that Michel knew the significance of those correlations but hesitated to make it public. Considering the meticulous method he employed in his study and his strict adherence to fact, in my opinion the latter explanation is the correct one.

Joseph Rolas and Horacio Gonzales were APRO's foremost contributors of information on the 1954 "flap" in South America, but being Venezuelans the bulk of the information they forwarded to APRO's headquarters dealt with Venezuelan sightings, and information from the other South American countries was sketchy. However, when APRO's South American membership began to enlarge in 1956 and 1957, after the 1954 flap brought the subject into focus, sightings from the 1954 period, which had been gleaned and saved by the new members, were forwarded to us. The overall close observation in South America was quite evident in disclosing another kind of pattern. Michel's book dealing with the straight-line pattern indicated the beginning of the European reconnaissance with many carefully documented sightings. Comparing the French "flap" to the performance of an orchestra, Michel commenced his documentation with the incidents of late August and early September, 1954 ("The Orchestra Tunes Up"), went into the fully developed flap of September 17 through September 30 ("Crescendo") covered October 1 to October 11 ("Full Orchestra") and noted the slackening of reports after October 12 ("Diminuendo"). Even a casual examination of APRO's file of periodicals and case reports for that fall immediately indicates that another pattern had begun elsewhere as sightings diminished over Europe. During October 17 through November 1 scattered reports came from Italy, Spain and Portugal. Some told of small men in glowing craft, stopping only momentarily here and there, then zooming off into the sky as silently and swiftly as they had come. But there were not many of these sightings. It seemed that most of the objects which had swooped down on Europe, and especially France, during September and October had retired for a time. This, in my opinion, leads to the possibility of a satellite where maps, reports, specimens and other findings could be examined before another foray was planned. It certainly seems to be a logical explanation for the October hiatus—the objects, or most of them, made a return trip to their home planet or permanent base.

But this would belie their apparent respect for time and distance, in coming en masse at two-year intervals, with only a small number on hand during the intervening months to keep an eye on things.

If we use the reverse-identity procedure in attempting an analysis of the actions of the discs and their occupants, we gain a much clearer idea of the whole operation: If and when earth men perfect means of space travel and begin to explore space, the result will be exploration and—because of man's talent for overpropagation—eventually space colonization. When man begins his exploration of a planet which is populated but technologically inferior to earth, he will do a geographical survey and then a military reconnaissance of the most highly developed and industrialized areas—*after* utilizing any available natural satellite and orbiting an artificial one closer to the surface of the planet. He will look for a remote area on which to establish a permanent base of operations. To space travelers no mass in space will be uninhabitable. If they can make a space ship livable for long periods of time it will be no insuperable task to convert a lifeless body such as the moon into a tolerable abode. Occupants of temporary bases will be relieved of duty by fresh crews from the home planet. During briefings of new crews men and vehicles will be available for manning the temporary base or bases, as well as for sweeping surveys of points of interest on the planet under surveillance. A constant spot-watch will be kept by the occupants of the artificial satellite, and any new defense operations or weapons testing of sufficient size to be noticeable will be investigated. Large-scale operations will take place during the interchange of crews and space vehicles when the home planet is in position for "short hops." After a complete military reconnaissance of specific land areas has been completed the search for a satisfactory base location on the planet will be in order. The most desirable location will be an undeveloped and therefore unpopulated area. Accessibility will be of little importance if observational craft were sufficiently maneuverable. A mountainous area will be the most likely selection.

If we apply this pattern to the activities of the discs during the past decade we find they are almost identical. Their future operations, however, are what concerns us now.

In November, 1954, Joseph Rolas's Venezuela reports of UFOs were bulging with clippings and translations. Few were of the type that could be discarded as obvious atmospheric or astronomic phenomena, and most of them very evidently were observations of unusual aircraft. In 1954 South America became aware that the United States had no monopoly on the strange sky objects, and the idea that they might by Yankee secret weapons became more and more ridiculous. The November 1954 *APRO Bulletin* recorded the first wave of sightings in South America in early November. The 1954 "flap" in South America mainly concerned two countries, Brazil and Venezuela. The findings of Keyhoe, Michel and others concerning the relation of the speed of the saucers to the color and intensity of their glow were confirmed by many observations. On October 23 a disc-shaped object was seen by workers and policemen as it maneuvered over Buenos Aires, Argentina, stopping and changing course many times. The object gave off luminous rays which changed colors alternately. On October 24 air-base personnel in Porto Alegre, Brazil, observed objects which they could not definitely identify as conventional phenomena—they were circular, silvery in color and maneuvered at great speed with occasional abrupt changes in course. In the Chicama Valley of Peru an engineer observed a brilliant elliptical object on October 27. It pulsated brilliant flashes of light and for several minutes it moved slowly, at other times with great speed and at one time it fell diagonally. The engineer reported that the object hovered at a height of three hundred meters and recovered its luminosity which had paled during the diagonal fall. The orchestra was tuning up.

And then on November 10 a Porto Alegre agronomist out for a ride with his family saw a disc from which emerged two apparently normal-shaped men with long hair and over-all-like clothing. They approached the car with their arms above their heads, but the driver, urged on by his wife and daughter, accelerated and left the strange men behind.

The motorists saw the men enter their disc-shaped craft and mount the sky at a dizzying speed. In Curitiba, Brazil, a railroad worker told authorities that at 3:30 A.M. on November 14 he saw three beings in tight-fitting, luminous clothing examine the ground around the railway tracks with a lantern. When the strange creatures saw the man they entered an oval-shaped craft which elevated rapidly. On that same day a bright oval object giving off a yellowish glare was seen by many in Buenos Aires as it traversed the sky. Also on the 14th, three hundred members of an anti-aircraft division in Berna, Argentina, watched a silvery, disc-shaped object give off a reddish trail. Observers using binoculars said it appeared to be at nine thousand feet when it was first spotted hovering in the air; suddenly it began to fly south at great speed, disappearing into the clouds. Reports elsewhere at this time were scattered and few. The lull in the middle of October was followed by a spurt of sightings about the middle part of November; then another lull from the 20th to December 1, when "all hell broke loose." The "little men" made their appearance in various sections. Full orchestra.

Some detailed and well-substantiated South American-"little men" stories will be dealt with in another chapter, but it is necessary now to elucidate the extent of the travels and actions of these creatures during the crucial December, 1954, period. In the early part of December (unfortunately there is no exact date for this incident) a respected and well-liked teacher and director of an educational institution in Barquisimeto, Venezuela, related how he was pursued by a glowing, disc-shaped object while driving along the highway to Guanare. The object when first seen resembled the moon, and he gave it no further thought. Then he noticed that the object was moving toward him and was huge in size. Seized with panic, the professor fired a small revolver he carried in his car at the pursuing object as it maneuvered above his car. The bullets didn't seem to bother the object and, thoroughly frightened, the man pushed the accelerator to the floor. He managed to stop another car occupied by a lawyer, a sheriff and a policeman, bound in the opposite direction. They accompanied the professor back to where he had last seen the object, and they were just in time to see the object heading into the southern sky leaving a bluish trail behind.

On the evening of December 10 a well-known Caracas doctor witnessed a strange sight while driving with his father in the vicinity of Floresta. He was later interviewed by the press, though his identity was withheld since, like most observers, he did not care to be ridiculed for what he saw. At 6:30 P.M., between La Carlota Airdrome and Francisco de Miranda Avenue, his father suddenly pointed. The doctor stopped the car. Together they watched two little men running from the brush. Shortly after they disappeared in the thickets a luminous, disc-shaped object emerged from behind the brush and, with a sharp "sizzling" sound, darted off into the sky at a high rate of speed.

On that same day an American engineer employed by a petroleum company in El Tigre took snapshots of a covey of five saucers as they flew in formation from south to north. They resembled "turtles," with a beam of light at the front and another at the rear of the formation. The photos were shown to the police and the press and were discussed in various newspaper articles; though they were not published. The description of these objects tallies with the objects photographed by a Salem, Massachusetts, coastguardsman in 1952 and the famous Trindade photo of January, 1958.

A group of prominent professional and scientific men in Venezuela realized by now that something was definitely afoot and they set about attempting to find an answer. Horacio Gonzales was one of them. Another, Astronomer Dr. Aniceto Lugo who publicly professed his interest in UFO, had more than a passing interest in them, for in September, while Europe was under close scrutiny of hovering disc-shaped objects and little men, he had observed flashes of light inside Crater Kepler on the moon. A similar observation of unidentified light flashes of one to two minutes' duration in Crater Copernicus was made by Mr. Venegas, secretary to the Minister of Communications.

The peak of the sightings, whether of objects or little men, appears to have been reached during December 10-14. Brazil also was being initiated, the Brazilian Air Force making public an appeal for the united efforts of all governments toward the solution of the UFO problem. Caracas, Venezuela, newspapers devoted whole pages to a briefing of Brazilian Air Force officials by Colonel Joao Adil Oliveiera who, incidentally, gave good coverage to many "classics" in UFO history. The Brazilians had good reason to be excited.

On November 4 Jose Alves of Pontal was fishing in the Pardo River near Pontal. The area was deserted, the night quiet with only a slight breeze blowing from the east. Suddenly Alves spotted a strange craft in the sky, apparently heading toward him. He watched, transfixed, as it closed in with a wobbling motion and landed. It was so near he could have touched it, he said. The object appearing as two wash-bowls placed together, looked to be about ten to fifteen feet in diameter. He was too frightened to run. Three little men, clad in white clothing with close-fitting skull caps, emerged from a windowlike opening in the side of the small craft. Their skin appeared to be quite dark. Alves stood terror-stricken, watching the small creatures collect samples of grass, herbs and leaves of trees; one of them filled a shiny metal tube with river water. Then, as suddenly as they had come, they jumped back into their machine, which took off vertically as swiftly and as silently as it had come. Residents of Pontal, who heard Alves's story when he came back to town, told the press that he was a quiet man who lived only for his work and his family. He had never heard of flying saucers and he was sure the little men were some kind of devils.

The Air Force base at Santa Maria, Rio Grande do Sul, was the scene of a strange incident on November 22. At 9:45 P.M. radio operator Arquidmedes Fernandez left the meteor-ological station and walked toward a small building a hun-dred feet away which he had built to store the thermometers and other instruments. Gathering readings for the next weather bulletin, he took a customary look at the sky and noticed a thin dark cloud hovering above small eucalyptus trees be-hind the building. He observed it very closely. It was not a cloud—it was a black object, enormous in size, shaped like a washbowl hanging upside down, and seemed to be about 160 feet long, suspended just above the trees. Not motionless as a cloud would appear to be, it had a slow, oscillatory mo-tion. Fernandez became alarmed and ran back to the sta-tion, watching the object all the time. It slowly lowered itself into the trees and then began climbing again, rather swiftly. He then noticed a small light on top of it. It dived again between the trees, almost to the same place he had seen it originally. The object moved again, now glowing faintly in the darkness. Fernandez radioed Porto Alegre and reported what he was seeing; the object was still there. At 1:15 A.M. his substitute arrived. Fernandez had watched the object for almost three and a half hours. Fernandez's startling report was corroborated by the testimony of others who also saw the strange object. At midnight another radio operator, Ruben Machado, had seen it from the window of his room in the Canobi Hotel, some distance from the base. To him it appeared to be hovering over the base—a luminous object, larger than the full moon. He pointed it out to others who saw it clearly before it disappeared into the north. There was further substantiation when Varig radio operator Jurandir Ferreira reported he had spotted the UFO over the base. He saw it as it was gaining altitude; after some maneuvers it headed into the north and was gone.

On the evening of December 9 a farmer, Olmiro da Costa e Rosa, was cultivating his French bean and maize field in Linha Bela Vista, two and a half miles from Venancio Aires, Rio Grande do Sul, when he heard something with the sound of a sewing machine. The animals in the pasture next to the field scattered and ran. Costa e Rosa looked up and saw a strange-appearing man. Beyond him was an unusual object hovering just above the ground. It had the shape of an explorer's hat, cream-colored and surrounded by a smoky haze. There were two other men, one in the craft, his head and shoulders sticking out, the other examining a barbed-wire fence. Costa e Rosa dropped his hoe and the stranger nearest to him raised his hand, smiled and picked up the hoe, which he turned in his hands, examining it carefully. Then the man placed the hoe in Costa e Rosa's hands, bent down, and uprooted a few plants and started toward the craft. Costa e Rosa had stood as though paralyzed. Then, assuring himself that they meant him no harm, he advanced toward the craft. The man who had taken the hoe and the one in the craft made no move to stop him, but the one at the fence made a gesture which seemed to mean that he should stop. Costa e Rosa stopped. Some of the farmer's animals approached and the strangers looked at them with great interest. With words and gestures the farmer tried to tell them he would be happy to make a gift of one of the animals. The strangers didn't seem enthused about the offer. The departure of the strangers was as unexpected as their appearance. Suddenly they trooped into the ship which rose about thirty feet, accelerated abruptly and flashed away into the western sky at high speed.

Costa e Rosa's description of the men was detailed—he had had time to observe them at fairly close range. They appeared to be of medium height, broad-shouldered, with long blond hair which blew in the wind. With their extremely pale skin and slanted eyes they were not normal looking by

earth standards. Their clothing consisted of light brown cov-
erall-like garments fastened to their shoes. Afterward Costa
e Rosa said the shoes seemed especially strange because they
had no heels. After the men had left he searched the ground
over which the objects had hovered but found nothing. However, he did notice the smell of burning coal which remained
in the air for some time after the craft's departure. Costa
e Rosa was questioned for several hours by authorities
from Porto Alegre. It was determined that he didn't read
science fiction; indeed, he read with difficulty and had never
heard of "flying saucers." He seemed to believe that these
men were visitors from another country. This incident was
reported in the magazine *O Cruzeiro* by one of Brazil's outstanding reporter-writers, Joao Martins, who is also a crack
UFO investigator.

Two days later at 5 p.m. Pedro Morais, who lived less than
a mile from Costa e Rosa's home, was preparing to go to a
warehouse for supplies. He heard the frightened squawks of a
chicken, and he went out to investigate. The day was hot, with
no wind. He still heard the chicken but couldn't find it (and
never did), for what he saw hovering in the air took his mind
off the chicken and the sparrow hawks he had thought were
molesting it. The object had the sound of a sewing machine;
it oscillated as it hovered and appeared on the topside to be
shaped similar to the hood of a jeep. The bottom resembled
an enormous polished brass kettle. Morais's attention turned
to the cultivated fields nearby where he saw two human-shaped
figures. Indignant at this trespass, he started toward the craft.
One of the men started running toward him, while the other
raised his arm in a gesture which appeared to be a warning not
to come any closer. Morais, still angry, did not obey, and continued toward the machine. He noted that as one ran toward
him the other kneeled down and quickly picked a tobacco
plant out of the ground. Then both got into the craft which
disappeared from view in the sky within a few seconds. Morais said the little men were human in shape, but didn't have
any faces. He got the impression that they were enveloped in
a kind of yellow-colored sack from head to toe. After their
departure he looked for footprints, but found none. But the
hole from which the plant had been uprooted was still there.
Morais, too, turned out to be a rather simple, uneducated
man; he did not know even the alphabet. But, unlike Costa e
Rosa, he thought the men were saints or ghosts. When he was
told that the government was anxious to have one of these

"men" dead or alive he vowed to shoot one if he ever had another opportunity.

And so the picture of the 1954 saucer invasion of South America is fairly clear—first, a scattered observation, then the landings; the pattern is very similar to that of the European visits in September and October. The incidents reported here are only a sampling of the hundreds brought to public attention by the press in Brazil and Venezuela as well as in other South American countries. The seeming lulls may be due to our inadequate coverage of other areas on the continent; however, the many reports which did come to our attention were startling in that most of the sightings were in the vicinity of defense installations. The possibility that these objects, which had kept their distance in years past, were merely American or Russian secret weapons became invalidated. No reasonable, intelligent individual with any command of the facts would any longer fall for that one.

Humberto Garcia Galindez of Venezuela wrote a letter to *Time* regarding the South American incidents, but the letter was never published. APRO's Venezuelan representative, Horacio Gonzales, forwarded a copy of that letter to us. I quote from it:

> It was great relief that I read (*Time,* November 7, 1955) that the United States Air Force has explained, in non-sensational ways, almost all the "saucer sightings" to date. I was also more relieved when you quoted Secretary Donald A. Quarles as saying that the projected Air Force saucer-shaped craft "if manned, will be manned by normal terrestrial airmen." If, then, we here happen to see *again* any small, strange, humanoid, hairy bipeds emerging from grounded saucers to frighten the citizenry, examine railway lines, pull boulders and dirt off the highways and load it aboard their strange craft, we will know that they are only United States Air Force pilots sent by Quarles to collect samples of Venezuelan dirt and rocks, and in the event of any complications arising we will know where to direct complaints.

What the little men did in South America is most important. They took samples of rocks, soil and plants. It does not require a vivid imagination to explain their actions. Idle curiosity? Hardly! Why would they traverse space, spend years on military reconnaissance, pull boulders out of the ground, uproot plants and take soil samples? I envision a huge laboratory somewhere in space in which experiments involving the adaptability of other types of plant life to earth soil are being carried out. What are their plants? They may intend to establish a base on earth, and if the visitors intend to bring along their own agriculture they plan to stay a long while.

6
Shadows of the Unknown

ON December 16, 1954, President Dwight Eisenhower, in a press conference said in essence that flying saucers are not from outer space and exist only in the imagination of the viewers. On that same night a young man, Jesus Paz, in San Carlos, Venezuela, was set upon by small hairy manlike creatures, and spent the rest of the night in a hospital for treatment of shock. What had happened to him was not imagined; he had the physical marks to prove it, and he has not forgotten the experience. His is one of the first believable accounts of contact with occupants of UFOs.

Paz and two friends had dined in a San Carlos restaurant. On the way home by car the party neared the Ministry of Agriculture's Exposition Park, and Paz asked the driver to stop while he went into the bushes to relieve himself. His friends in the car suddenly heard a piercing scream. They rushed to where Paz had entered the brush and came upon their friend lying unconscious on the ground. A short distance away a hairy-appearing little man was running toward a flat, shiny object which hovered a few feet above the ground. One of the men, Luis Mejia, member of the National Guard, reached for his gun, but remembered it was back in the barracks. He picked up a stone and futilely threw it at the craft which, with the dwarflike creature now inside, was rising into the air with a deafening buzzing sound. Paz was rushed to the city hospital. Authorities who interviewed the men said that all three were obviously frightened and that Paz was in a state of shock. Paz had several long, deep scratches on his right side and along his spine, as if he had been clawed by a wild animal. It was apparent that when Paz entered the brush he surprised the little man, who turned on him. Paz, who had only tried to get away and hadn't attempted to fight, fainted from fright.

At about the same time as the Paz incident an encounter with dwarfish men was being related by two boys who, on December 10, had been rabbit hunting near the Trans-Andian Highway between Chico and Cerro de Las Tres Torres. The boys, Lorenzo Flores and Jesus Gomez, saw a bright object off the highway and thought it was a car. Approaching the object, they saw what appeared to be two huge washbowls placed one atop the other, hovering about two or three feet off the ground. They estimated the size as about nine feet in diameter, and said it ejected fire from the bottom.

"Then we saw four little men coming out of it," Lorenzo said. "They were approximately three feet tall. When they realized we were there the four of them got Jesus and tried to drag him toward the thing. I could do nothing but take my shotgun, which was unloaded, and strike at one of them." "The gun seemed to have struck rock or something harder, as it broke into two pieces," Flores said. Reporters asked the boys if they had noticed the facial features of the the little men. Flores said: "No, we could see no details, as it was dark, but what we did notice was the abundant hair on their bodies and their great strength." Gomez could remember little of the incident. The boys said they hadn't seen the object leave, for when Gomez regained consciousness they ran as fast as they could toward the highway. Exhibiting scratches and bruises, their shirts torn to shreds, the boys were rushed to the nearest police station.

Investigation by authorities revealed signs of the struggle where the boys said the incident had taken place. Both were questioned intensively by the police and psychiatrists and were found to be sane, responsible young men. One doctor said that both boys had been badly frightened by something very unusual, for they both were almost hysterical when he talked to them. Horacio Gonzales, APRO representative in Caracas, in a letter shortly after the incident wrote that the boys were obviously telling the truth, that no young man of the working class would deliberately destroy a cherished possession as expensive as a gun just to perpetrate a hoax.

Early in the morning three days after Jesus Paz encountered his little man, Jose Parra, an eighteen-year-old jockey from Valencia, rushed into the National Security office. He was winded, flushed and apparently very frightened as he tried to relate his experience near a local cement factory. Parra said he was out running on the highway that night to lose some excess weight. He did his running at night, he said, because it was cooler then and he'd be less conspicuous. He had stopped near the factory when he spotted six little men pulling boulders from the side of the highway and loading them aboard a disc-shaped craft which was hovering less than nine feet from the ground. Parra started to run away, but one of the little creatures pointed a small device at him; it gave off a violet-colored light and prevented Parra from moving. He stood there helplessly while the little creatures leaped aboard their ship, disappearing rapidly into the sky. Only then was Parra able to move, and he hurried to the National Security office to report what he had seen.

One hour later, a brightly lighted, disc-shaped object was seen hovering a few feet off the ground near the Barbula Sanitorium for Tuberculars at Valenica. Two hospital employees saw the object at different times, first at midnight and then at 3:15 A.M. The man who witnessed the object at midnight didn't notify anyone for fear of disturbing the patients. The one who saw the object later, approached it for a better look, but the thing moved away and then ascended and disappeared from sight. While Parra was being questioned, detectives who were sent to the area he had described found tracks which they were unable to identify as either those of a human or an animal.

On the morning of November 28 two men in Caracas also underwent an experience with small, hairy men—this time wearing loin cloths—and reported the incident to the police. Gustavo Gonzales and his helper Jose Ponce had set out in a panel truck for Petare, a twenty-minute ride from Caracas, at 2 A.M. to purchase foodstuffs. The two men had not gone far when they were startled to see a luminous sphere, some eight to ten feet in diameter, blocking the street. It appeared to be suspended about six feet off the ground. Gonzales and Ponce got out of the truck to investigate, and a dwarfish-looking man came toward them. Gonzales grabbed the little man. (Gonzales later said he intended to take the little fellow to the police.) He was immediately impressed by the light weight of the creature who, he estimated, weighed about thirty-five pounds. The little man, whose body seemed to be very hard and covered with stiff, bristly hair, gave Gonzales a push with one hand which threw him about fifteen feet. Ponce watched the scuffle, became frightened and ran to the police station about a block and a half away, but not before he saw two other little men emerge from the bushes with what looked like chunks of dirt or rock in their arms. With apparent ease they leaped into the sphere through an opening in the side.

Gonzales, meanwhile, was having his troubles. The little creature which had knocked him down appeared to leap into the air and come toward him with eyes glowing. Scared almost out of his wits, Gonzales pulled out his knife and, as the creature approached him with claws extended, he made a stab at its shoulder. To his amazement, the knife seemed to glance off as though it had struck steel. Then another of the hairy little men emerged from the sphere, holding a small tube; he beamed a light at Gonzales and blinded him momentarily. The little men then climbed into the sphere which took off swiftly and was lost to sight within seconds. Overcome with exhaustion and fright, Gonzales stumbled toward the police station, arriving there shortly after Ponce. The men were suspected of being drunk, but examination showed they had had nothing to drink. They were both given sedatives, and Gonzales was put under observation for a long, red scratch on his side.

Several days later one of the doctors who had examined Flores and Gomez after their experience admitted that he had witnessed the fracas at Petare. He had been out on a night call and had driven into the street where Gonzales and Ponce had stopped their truck. He stayed only long enough to see what was going on, and then left, apprehensive that he might be involved in undesirable publicity if he stayed. In his statement to the authorities he stipulated that his name should not be connected with the incident. A member of the Caracas press informed our representative there that, following his statement, the doctor was invited to Washington, D.C., to talk with American authorities regarding the "little men" incident.

On May 7, 1955, the Caracas daily, *El Universal,* carried a weird sequel to the events of the preceding fall—an aeronautical engineer's 1950 encounter with a saucer and its dead occupants. (The engineer, Dr. B., at first preferred to remain anonymous, although he has since been identified. He never attempted to exploit the incident, but rather has done everything to find out more about the discs and their mission on earth.) He was driving along the highway in isolated Bahia Blanca in Argentina when he saw a metallic-appearing, disc-shaped object resting on the ground just off the road to his left. He stopped the car and watched the object for a few moments. Except for a flashing light on the top of the thing, nothing transpired, and he decided to approach it. There was an opening or door in the side, and he looked in. A red light was pulsating in the dome at one-second intervals, but the craft seemed to be empty, and he crawled through the small opening.

Inside, he began looking around, and immediately saw that the thing was not deserted—there were three small men in the circular enclosure. One sat at what appeared to be a control chair in the center, and two were lying on lounges along the curved wall of the ship. Another curved couch was empty. All three were dressed in brown tight-fitting overalls that exposed only the hands and the face, and their feet were encased in some kind of boots. Dr. B. estimated that they were about four feet tall, their skin a tobacco-brown, their eyes light colored. He could not distinguish colors too well, for the light was not good. In front of the little man in the center chair varied-colored rays were playing across what looked like a television screen, on top of which was a rotating globe of glass or other transparent material.

Dr. B. touched one of the creatures, and it felt rigid. It was then, he said, that he got the feeling he was in the presence of some kind of alien life; he rushed out of the object, got to his car and sped off. He didn't stop until he reached his hotel, where he related the incident to friends. They decided to photograph the thing, but as night had fallen they waited until the next morning before they set out. They had a difficult time finding the exact spot, for the disc was gone. However, they did find a pile of gray ashes which were warm to the touch and which turned their hands green on contact. The men siphoned some gas out of their car and washed the stuff off their hands.

Looking for additional clues, they searched the sky above and noticed a cigar-shaped object with two small disc-shaped objects near it. Dr. B. photographed one of the closer dics. In all, he took five pictures, only two of which showed the object with any degree of clarity. A few seconds later, the two discs approached the larger object and appeared to merge with it, whereupon the large object turned a blood-red color and ascended swiftly out of sight.

Horacio Gonzales, our Caracas representative, interviewed Dr. B., who said that although the saucer looked like metal it had a curious resiliency like rubber and there were holes or vents in the floor of the cabin. For weeks afterward Dr. B. suffered from a strange skin irritation, fever and blisters. They could not be diagnosed, though the greenish spots first visible on his skin were washed away with an application of an antiseptic. He had been wearing green-tinted glasses when he entered the saucer, and the areas around his eyes and where his clothes covered his body were not affected. Dr. B. stated that he had noted two odors in the saucer—ozone and garlic. In his APRO report Gonzales noted that Dr. B., a respected member of his profession and the community, was an ex-war pilot, about forty-five, of Italian extraction and spoke English as well as Spanish and Italian.

More than four years later, the Swedish papers, the Halsingborg *Dagblad* the *Svenska Dagbladet,* the Stockhom *Tidningen* and the *Dagen Nybeters,* and the magazine *Se* played up what was, to my knowledge, the first Swedish "contact" case. APRO representative in Sweden, K. Gosta Rehn, forwarded clippings, translations and some well-founded interpretations and opinions regarding the incident, the first in which hypnoanalysis was used to get the facts.

Twenty-five-year-old truck-driver Hans Gustavsson boarded with his friend, Stig Rydberg, a thirty-year-old student, and Rydberg's mother in Halsingborg. Photos showed both to be clean-cut young men. Returning home from a dance in Hoganas on December 20, 1958, at 2:55 A.M., and nearing Domsten, they saw a peculiar light through an opening in the pine woods. Their curiosity aroused, they left their car and walked some thirty-five feet toward the light. Its source was a disc-shaped object resting on three legs, its diameter about sixteen feet, its height about three feet, three inches. It appeared to be self-illuminating, but was not blinding or warm. In the center of the light they thought they could distinguish a darker core.

"All of a sudden we were attacked by four lead-gray creatures, about four feet tall and about fourteen inches in breadth," said Rydberg. "They seemed to lack extremities, looking sort of like scones or skittles, but when they attacked us they clutched us firmly and attempted to drag us toward the craft. It was difficult to defend oneself because we could get no real hold on the jellylike creatures. My right arm sank as far as the elbow into one of them when I tried to box myself loose. They smelled like stale marsh."

"At one time all four were on me," Gustavsson said. "It is difficult now to explain, but I got the impression the things could read my thoughts. The second before I had time to get a hold on them they parried the hold I was planning. Their raw strength was not great, but they were very technical. Luckily, there was a camping sign near where I was standing and I clasped my arms about the pole. It was my rescue."

Rydberg, taking up the narrative again, said, "We have estimated that the struggle lasted between four and seven minutes. The creatures concentrated their efforts on Hans, and suddenly I found myself free. They just ignored me. I took the opportunity to run to the car, and began to blow the horn. I watched through the windshield and saw Hans clutch the pole, and the creatures tore at him to get him loose. He was holding the pole, and they had him spread out horizontally from it. As soon as the horn sounded they released him, and he fell to the ground with a thump. I rushed to him, and the saucer rose into the air. The light from it became more intense and we were aware of a smell that reminded us of ether and burned sausages. But most remarkable of all was the sound the object made—a thin, high, intense sound you felt rather than heard. When the object left we were shaken by powerful, extremely rapid vibrations that quite paralyzed us."

Gustavsson thought the craft arced out over the nearby water, but Rydberg thought it rose straight up. The men then dazedly staggered back to their car. They later admitted they were both near hysteria, with tears streaming down their faces as they realized the full portent of what had happened to them. After about fifteen minutes trying to regain their composure they drove into Halsingborg. Not until they were well inside the city were they able to speak, and they vowed they would not tell anyone of their experience because they knew they would be ridiculed. But because of their strained manner and appearance their friends asked them what was wrong. It was then they decided to tell their story to the Defense Department and to the newspapers.

The word was out. On January 8, 1959, both men were examined by Dr. Ingeborg Kjellin, who signed a sanity testimonial for them. Excitement about the incident rose and on January 10 the newspapers reported a new examination of the men by Drs. Lars Erick Essen and Kilhelm Hellsten, both of Halsingborg, who applied the technique known as hypno-analysis. This is, essentially, the same as questioning the subject while he is under the influence of sodium amytal or sodium pentothal, except that the subject is put into a state of hypnosis. According to the physicians it permits a cross-examination that is as incisive as any conducted by the military or the police. Dr. Essen tested them particularly for possible hallucinations, but the tests disclosed that their experience came directly *from the outside* and that they could clearly coordinate experiences other than those in issue. Their description of the occurrence was correct; the only wrong impression they might have gotten concerned the shapes of the "little men," and that was understandable, the doctors said. Though the analysis revealed no clues as to "contact" with the creatures, the doctors felt that Rydberg and Gustavsson had actually encountered a field force of enormous strength. The account of the experience through hypnoanalysis was substantially the same as the publicized account, deviating only in a few minor details. (APRO representative Rehn felt that this fact strengthened the view that the experiences related during the test were more complete and credible.) Dr. Essen told the press: "It may be added that the men's attitude was of a very sober kind. They do not want to put any frills on any feature of the incident, exaggerate or embellish it, or even attempt to interpret their experiences. They want only to communicate them." He also said: "They were both very receptive to this form of analysis and I hold, as a matter of result, that it was one of the most successful analyses I ever made."

In his communique Mr. Rehn wrote: "By this time the Swedish defense organization had rallied. It arranged a police and military examination of the young men. On January 18 the newspaper *Svenska Dagbladet* revealed that the military psychologist, Dr. Michael Wachter, conducted most of the hearing which lasted twelve hours." Here is a summary of the findings reported in the *Svenska Dagbladet*:

It developed that Rydberg was excused from military service in 1948 because of agoraphobia (morbid fear of being in an open space). Both men have no real training for any trade. Rydberg appeared to be the leader. He is more talkative than Gustavsson. Rydberg gives an impression of nervousness. He shifts his position according to what he deems to be most favorable to support his trustworthiness. He seems somewhat afraid and tries to guard himself. When he is pressed his constant resort is to refer to his experience and state that he cannot help that he has experienced it.

That the scuffle or fight was kept secret for some time the investigators find peculiar. His statements lack stringency, they are diffuse, sometimes directly unreasonable or also proven incorrect. He exploits his situation to a certain extent, emphasizing the fact that he has voluntarily put himself at the disposal of the cross-examiners with regard to the interest of the press and other circles in the matter.

Gustavsson is not so talkative, says Dr. Wachter. He often replies as if he rattles off a lesson. He refers to what he has said earlier and does not intend to say anything else. Somebody might have told Gustavsson to stick to his story and not to deviate from it one bit. Gustavsson is a fit victim for suggestive influence. As to Rydberg, it is not unreasonable to hold that the spiritistic interests of his mother might have given him considerable impulses toward his world of conceptions.

Summing up: The credibility of both men ought to be strongly put in question. They are to be deemed as possessing a lesser reliability. Both seem to be convinced of the truth of their experiences. The possibility that the issue here is of a direct invention cannot be excluded. Most probable is that Rydberg is a victim of autosuggestion and that he in his turn has influenced Gustavsson. Irrespective of their subjective conviction, there are weighty reasons present to seriously question the trustworthiness of both men as witnesses in this matter.

In view of the negative attitude and conclusions of the military hearing it is necessary to air the opinions of Rydberg and Gustavsson. In later questioning by Mr. Rehn, they stated that (1) the representatives of the military were very skeptical and the investigation was conducted in a humdrum, routine and nonchalant manner; (2) the psychologist was German-born and they could only partially understand him; (3) no earth specimens were taken for examination although defense-staff men roamed the area with tape measures for a couple of hours. The only other equipment they brought with them was a tape recorder, which was out of order.

In light of the statements by Dr. Essen and Dr. Hellsten, based on their hypno-analysis investigation (a dependable method of getting at facts without having to sort out the embellishments of the conscious mind), the "summation" of the military hearing is somewhat mystifying. It is a well-known fact that any subject under cross-examination may be influenced by fatigue, boredom and the constant pounding of questions. It is also a fact that if one searches back far enough one may find some personality information which another personality might interpret as discrediting. It would seem that the two doctors in the first examination were conducting an impersonal, objective investigation, whereas the military team was biased, fault-finding and determined to discredit the men. Why? Because of the obvious attempts in 1954 to keep the evidence of the South American "contacts" from becoming pulbic knowledge throughout the world, I am inclined to believe that the system of ridicule, as demonstrated in the military summation of the Rydberg-Gustavsson case, was calculated to discredit the subjects in the case, and to serve still another purpose: to discourage other possible future disclosures by people who might have similar experiences. This denigration method is probably what discouraged Rydberg and Gustavsson from disclosing their experience in the beginning. The fact that the military made a point of drawing attention to Rydberg's agoraphobia, to the lack of training in both men, to the fact that one was more talkative than the other, etc., leads one to believe that they were deliberately using any personality trait they could detect which might be construed by the layman to be undesirable and therefore discrediting. In fact, Rydberg's statement that he had put himself at the disposal of the examiners could have been his fair reminder of their mutual relationship when the questioning became too repetitious and tiring, when the examiners' accusations and possible attempts to make him refute his story became too obvious.

One of the two most fantastic tales of strange airships and their even stranger crews to come into my hands, had its beginning on the night of October 5, 1957. The principal, Antonio Villas-Boas, twenty-three, was a farmer by profession living with his parents and family near the town of Francisco de Salles, state of Minas Gerais, Brazil. On the night in question there had been a party at the man's home and the family had retired at 11 P.M., which was rather late for them. Because of the heat, Antonio opened the window in the bedroom which he shared with his brother Joao, and as he did so, he saw that the corral area was lighted as if by a giant searchlight. He saw nothing in the sky, but tried to wake his brother so that he could see the strange sight. Joao woke just enough to tell Antonio to go to bed, so Antonio got up again and looked out. The light was still there. In closing the shutters he woke his brother, who got up and also saw the light. Finally it disappeared.

The second episode took place on the night of the 14th between 9:30 and 10:00 P.M. when Antonio was plowing in the field with his tractor. His brother was with him. They suddenly saw a bright red light which hurt their eyes at the northern end of the field. It had the appearance of a cartwheel and seemed to be located about 400 feet above the ground. Antonio suggested to his brother that they approach the light to see what it was, but his brother declined so he began walking toward it. As he did so the light moved to the southern end of the field, maintaining its altitude all the while. Villas-Boas attempted to follow but it moved quickly and this sequence of events was repeated some twenty times. Antonio got tired of the chase and went back to his brother and the two watched it as it shot out rays of light in all directions, after which it disappeared as though it were only a light which had been turned off.

On the next morning at 1 A.M. Antonio was plowing with the tractor in the same location. In this area of Brazil field work is often done at night because of extreme daytime heat, and this particular evening was clear, cool and exhibited a starry sky. Antonio's attention was arrested by an unusually bright star which began to increase in size as if approaching. Within a few minutes the "star" gave the appearance of a very bright egg-shaped object approaching at high speed. The movement was so swift that it was hovering overhead at about 175 feet altitude before the witness realized what was happening. The object hovered, lighting up the ground as brightly as daylight, with a bright red light.

Panicked, Villas-Boas considered his chances of getting away but realized he wouldn't have a chance on foot in the soft plowed ground, so he sat rooted to his tractor seat. As he sat there the object moved again and stopped about ten to fifteen yards away, slowly settling to the ground. He got a good look at it. The object looked like an elongated egg, with small purplish lights all over it. On the leading end was a huge, red light which apparently was the light which had lit up the ground and prevented him from seeing its shape and size while in the air. Three metal bars, sharp at the ends, protruded from the rear end of the thing. On top of the object was "something" which rotated at high speed and gave off a sharp fluorescent reddish light which began to turn green the moment the object slowed in preparation for landing. As it slowed, the top became more visible and appeared as a round plate or "squashed cupola." These details were not taken note of consciously at the time because of his extreme fright, but were recalled later. When three metal legs or props began to emerge from the belly of the thing, Antonio lost what control he had left and attempted to move the tractor away. At this point the tractor engine quit and its light went out. He tried desperately to start the engine but was unsuccessful. He then opened the door of the tractor, jumped out and started running.

Villas-Boas was caught up short by something grasping his arm. He turned to shake off his pursuer and came face-to-face with a small "man" wearing strange clothes, who came only to his shoulder. By then in a state of panic, he gave the creature a push which sent him reeling to the ground about eight feet away and started running again. Within seconds he was attacked by three small men of slightly larger size than the first, from the side and the back. They lifted him off the ground and dragged him toward the ship. He called for help, cursed his tormentors, demanding to be freed. Each time he resorted to yelling and cursing they would stop and watch him curiously, but they did not loosen their grip on him. When they finally got to the machine, a door was open in the middle of the thing, and a ladder of sorts extended to the ground. He was lifted and shoved up this ladder, which was a difficult maneuver for the ladder was flexible and not large enough to hold more than one person at a time. Villas-Boas caught onto a round railing the size of a broomstick which extended down both sides of the ladder, in an attempt to keep from being hauled bodily into the craft.

The inside of the ship was made of bright metal and lit by fluorescentlike light which came from tiny holes in the joining of the ceiling and walls. When the outside door was closed he couldn't see where it had been except for the location of the ladder, which was rolled up and fastened to it. The area in which Antonio found himself was small. When one of the "men" beckoned him toward an open door he decided to cooperate since the outside door was closed and he had no opportunity to escape. He went into the designated room which was oval in shape with the same lighting and silvery polished metallic walls as the first. There was a metal bar running from floor to ceiling in the middle of it and the bar was thicker at the ends with a narrower part in the middle. The only furniture was an oddly shaped table that stood at one side of the room surrounded by several backless swivel chairs, similar to bar stools. They were of the same material as the walls, floor and ceiling, with one "leg," which narrowed toward the floor where it was linked to a movable ring held fast by three hinges which jutted out on each side and were riveted to the floor.

The men held Villas-Boas in their grips for some time while they looked him over and talked among themselves. The "talk" reminded Antonio of the noises dogs make, like howls, varying in pitch and intensity. He felt as though he was among animals and could not simulate the noises they made, he later told questioners. After this "conversation" the five men present seemingly had made a decision for they began to forcibly undress their victim. Antonio fought, cursing and screaming at them, but they kept on with their task, only occasionally stopping to stare. Although they persisted in their task, at no time did they hurt their subject, and a tear later discovered in the shirt was possibly caused by Antonio sometime prior to his adventure. He was not sure. After Antonio had been reduced to nakedness, one man approached him with a wet spongelike object which he began to rub all over his body. The liquid being used was colorless like water but much thicker. When he had been rubbed all over with the liquid, one of the men, howling and gesticulating at Antonio, led him to a door at the opposite end of the room from which they had entered, put his hand against the middle of it, which caused it to open into another room. Villas-Boas compared this door to the "swinging doors" of a bar room. The door, apparently of the same metal as the rest of the ship, had inscriptions in bright red lettering which appeared to protrude about two inches out from the surface. Antonio said he had never seen any writing which resembled these marks. He later drew them for our investigation team but apologized for his inability to remember their exact form.

The room in which Villas-Boas now found himself was squarish, small and lit like the others. The door closed and he could not see where it had been. The two men were with him. A moment or two later the wall "opened" again and two men entered carrying with them two very thick rubber pipes in their hands—each of which was about forty inches long. One end of one of the pipes led into a chalice-shaped apparently glass container and the other had a spout like a "cupping glass" which was put to the skin on his chin and Villas-Boas watched some of his blood filling the chalice-shaped glass. He felt no pain or prick while this was being done but later the area where the tube was applied began to itch and burn. He later discovered that his skin at that point was raw and lacerated. The same procedure was carried out with the second tube which was applied to the other side of his chin. After this operation was finished, Villas-Boas was left alone for quite some time, perhaps a half hour. Feeling tired, he took advantage of a bedlike furnishing which looked like a bed but had no legs and was humped up in the middle. It was soft like foam rubber and covered with a soft kind of thick gray material. While sitting on the "bed" he began to feel sick and was aware of a strange smell, like painted cloth burning. He lay down on the bed and it was then that he noticed a series of tiny metal tubes jutting from the wall at about the height of his head, which were pouring the gray thick smoky vapor into the room. His nausea increased and shortly he hurried to a corner of the room where he vomited. The difficulty he had felt in breathing before ceased, and he felt better.

Villas-Boas had no idea of the facial features of the "men," at this point, for all five of those he had encountered were dressed in tight-fitting suits made of soft, thick, unevenly striped gray material. The garment reached up to their necks where it was joined to a kind of helmet of gray material that looked stiffer than the suit and appeared to be strengthened, front and back, by thin metal plates, one of which was three-cornered, at nose level. The helmet hid everything except their eyes, which were protected by two round glasses. Through them he could see the eyes, which seemed to be quite small although Antonio admitted that might have been a result of the distortion of the lenses. Their eyes appeared to be light blue but he couldn't be sure. The "skull" area of the helmet was so high above the eyes as to give the impression of a head twice the size of a normal adult human head. From the middle of the top of the helmet there erupted three silvery round tubes a bit smaller than a common garden hose, smooth and bent backwards and downwards toward the back of the men's suits. One was fixed to the suit at about the center of the back (shoulder blade level) and the other two were fixed to the side, below the shoulders, about four inches below the armpits. The sleeves of these garments were narrow and tight-fitting to the wrists and ended in five-fingered gloves of what seemed to be thick material. Villas-Boas deduced that the garments were uniforms of a type for at the center of the chest he saw a red "badge" about the size of a pineapple slice which reflected light. From this "badge" there came a strip of silver material which joined into a broad, tight-fitting claspless belt, the color of which he could not recall. He saw no pockets or buttons anywhere, and the trousers fitted over the buttocks and thighs so that there was not a wrinkle or crease to be seen. The general appearance of the shoes was like that of a tennis shoe although there were no laces or buckles, and the soles appeared to be 2 to 3 inches thick, and the toes turned up like "harem" slippers. All but one of the men appeared to be as tall as Villas-Boas, except for the tall helmet and thick-soled shoes. With these removed they would have been considerably smaller. The remaining one was noticeably smaller than the others—the one who first grasped Villas-Boas in the field, and he only reached to his chin—helmet, shoes and all.

After what seemed like an eternity to Villas-Boas, the door opened again and in walked a small but well built and completely nude woman. She walked slowly and seemed amused at Villas-Boas's open-mouthed amazement at seeing her. Her blonde, nearly white hair, big blue, slanted eyes and even features contributed to an unusual beauty. The hair was smooth, not very thick, less than shoulder length and was parted in the center and turned up slightly at the ends. She wore no makeup, her nose was straight and small and her face fine-boned. The contour of her face, which showed very prominent cheekbones and a severely pointed chin, as well as slit-thin lips, were the only outstandingly unusual features. Villas-Boas noted that the prominent cheekbones made her face appear to be very wide, even wider than that of an Indio native (Brazilian). The woman's body was well built with high, separated breasts, small waist, flat belly, well-developed hips and large thighs. Her feet were small, her hands long and narrow. Villas-Boas estimated her height to be about 4 feet 6 inches, he being about 5 feet 5½ inches. He later deduced that she was probably the smallest of the five "men" in suits who had been the first to grapple with him in the field.

The woman's purpose was immediately evident. She held herself close to Villas-Boas, rubbing her head against his face. She did not attempt to communicate in any way except with occasional grunts and howling noises, like the "men" had uttered. A very normal sexual act took place and after more pettings she responded again. For a while after each one she breathed with difficulty. After the second act the woman began to shy away from the man and he became a little annoyed at this. The howling noises she made during the togetherness had nearly spoiled the whole act for they reminded him of an animal. At no time would she allow him to kiss her and his overtures in this respect were met by a gentle bite on the chin. Some of the physical features noted by Villas-Boas were the woman's very light skin, freckled arms, and the deep red pubic and underarm hair which contrasted vividly with the almost white hair of her head.

As soon as the woman had repelled Antonio, the door opened and one of the men came and called out to the woman, who turned to Villas-Boas, pointed to her belly and, smiling a little, pointed to what he thought was south, and then left. He thought this meant that she would return to take him with her and gave him much food for agonizing fear for some time.

A man then came in bringing Villas-Boas' clothing and everything was intact except for his lighter which he thought might have been lost during the struggle in the field. He was taken to the room where the swivel chairs were located and three of the crew were conversing in their peculiar manner. The man who took him to that room joined the others and left Villas-Boas near a table in the middle of the room. Trying to pass the time, Villas-Boas made a point of observing everything in sight and eventually riveted his attention on a square box with a glass top which had markings at the 3, 6 and 9 o'clock positions of a regular clock. Where ordinarily the 12 o'clock mark would be, however, he noted only four vertical parallel black marks. One of the men would occasionally look at the box, but the "hand," which was at

"6," did not move in the estimated 15 minutes that Villas-Boas watched it. Wanting something by which to prove his experience, Antonio attempted to take it but it was immediately and angrily taken from him and put back on the table. He then backed against the wall and held still, trying to scratch the metal surface to get some under his nails but his fingertips slid off as though it were glass. Four of the men were in this room with him and Villas-Boas deduced that the fifth, or the woman, was in another room which must have had its door partially open and from which he occasionally heard noises as if someone were moving about.

At last one of the men stood up, motioned to Antonio and took him out of the main door to a narrow platform which entirely circled the ship. They walked around the ship back to the main door and the man pointed to the ladder, indicating that Villas-Boas should descend, which he did. The man stayed at the "threshold" of the door, pointed to the ground, then to the sky, motioned Antonio to step back, then went inside and the door closed. At this, the saucer-shaped thing on top began to spin at great speed, the lights got brighter and the machine lifted straight up. The legs and the tripod to which they were attached lifted up and into the ship and it was airborne with no visible evidence that the legs or tripod had ever been there. It kept going until it was about 100 feet off the ground, stopped still for a few seconds, then grew brighter. The disc on top made a buzzing noise as it rotated, going faster and faster, the main light changing color, finally settling to bright red. As this happened, the machine abruptly changed direction by turning quickly and unexpectedly and making an even louder noise and the ship darted off like a bullet toward the south. It was out of sight in a matter of seconds.

Villas-Boas ran back to his tractor. It was about 5:30 A.M. when he left the strange ship, so that in all, he had spent over four hours in the craft. When he tried to start his tractor it would not work, so he examined the engine and found that the wire ends of the battery had been unscrewed and were out of place. Obviously, he said later, this had been done after he had been abducted for it was all right when he had left the house that night.

The above is condensed from a 23-page report which was submitted to APRO by Dr. Olavo Fontes, Professor of Medicine at the Brazilian National School of Medicine. It in-

cludes a verbatim report given to him by Villas-Boas and
recorded by journalist Joao Martins and translated by Mrs.
Irene Granchi of the languages department of the University of Brazil. I have presented this case in detail because of
its controversial nature, and have a few comments to make
concerning Dr. Fontes' observations, findings and comments
concerning his physical examination of Villas-Boas on February 22, 1958, in Dr. Fontes' private consulting room.

Villas-Boas was found to be a very healthy physical specimen, psychologically stable. His medical history after the
incident indicated that he had suffered from some sleepless-
ness, nervousness, irritation of the eyes with attendant water-
ing and a profusion of strange-appearing sores which erupted on his body. The two marks made by the "tubes" on
Villas-Boas' chin were still very much in evidence when he
was examined by Fontes. Mr. Villas-Boas originally contacted Martins after reading one of his articles which made a
plea for citizens to come forth with information about UFO
sightings. He wrote to Martins, whereupon Martins contacted
Fontes and the two men made arrangements for Villas-Boas
to visit Rio de Janeiro for the interview and physical examination.

At this point, some of Dr. Fontes' comments are illuminat-
ing:

"For about four hours we listened to his story and submitted him to close questioning, trying to clear up certain
details, trying to make him contradict himself, to call his
attention to certain inexplicable facts in his deposition, or to
see whether he would get mixed up or fall back upon his
imagination. From the beginning it was obvious that he was
not a psychopath. He was poised, spoke fluently, didn't re-
veal any signs of emotional instability and all reactions to
queries seemed to be perfectly normal. His uncertainties
seemed to be those natural to a person faced with a strange
situation which offered no natural explanation.

"Villas-Boas would not put into writing certain details referring to the "woman" and the "sexual contacts"—and this
is normal. These details were never given spontaneously
nor was any description of such given freely. During questioning about these details, Villas-Boas revealed embarrass-
ment and shame and it was only after much insistence that
we were able to obtain the details from him." Unquote.

When Dr. Fontes visited Mr. Lorenzen and me during
one of his trips to the United States, I asked him point-

blank, "Do you believe Villas-Boas' story, Olavo?" His reply: "It is too bizarre to believe." This is the usual reaction of most people when they are first exposed to such sensational tales and yet Dr. Fontes has been examining reports of strange UFO occupants for years. My own first reaction was almost one of scoffing until I began to add up some important factors:

If an alien race bent on contact and possible colonization were to reconnoiter this planet, one of their prime tasks would be to learn if the two races could breed. To do this they would need a human subject. Either sex would be all right, but it would be much more efficient to pick a male by some means. If a human female subject were used, the chances of no conception, or conception followed by miscarriage, would be great due to the considerable nervous strain of removing that female subject from her familiar surroundings to a completely foreign location and alien companions, and then literally subjecting her to forcible rape. It should be quite well known, especially to an advanced culture, that the psychological makeup of women, especially where sex is concerned, is considerably more delicate than that of her male counterpart. The ideal situation, then, would be for the experimenters to pick their own female subject whose ovulation period would be known beforehand, and proceed exactly as the strange UFO occupants apparently did with Villas-Boas.

Unfortunately, due to the great distance involved in transporting Villas-Boas, as well as not only his preoccupation, but Dr. Fontes and Mr. Martins, with their own daily pursuits, it was not feasible at that time to have Villas-Boas examined by psychiatrists. Since then, Villas-Boas has married and does not care to dwell on his experience because of his wife's feelings in the matter. Preliminary examination by Dr. Fontes, however, seems to assure us that Villas-Boas is stable, not a liar, and certainly not knowledgeable about certain information which he would have to have in order to concoct such a *logical* tale.

Villas-Boas has hypothesized that the liquid which was rubbed on his body was some kind of aphrodisiac to arouse him sexually. Dr. Fontes felt he might have been trying to justify his ability to perform sexually under such conditions, and thought that the liquid was more probably some kind of antiseptic. Antonio also thought that the smoke which emanated from the jets in the walls may have been something to adjust the atmosphere for the woman and of course this is quite possible. However, considering the circumstances, it is just as possible that the "smoke" was an antiseptic agent contrived to cleanse Villas-Boas' respiratory system of any active germs which could infect the female subject, who would naturally be in very close contact with him.

It is unnerving to me that, along with the thousands of sightings of flying, landed and occupied unconventional aerial objects, an incident such as the above could take place and not be objectively, scientifically and logically analyzed because of *emotional predisposition*! Our next case is also unacceptable to the squeamish:

On September 4, 1963, three men from the Sacramento area in California were bow-hunting in the mountains near Cisco Grove, not far from Truckee. At about dusk they separated and planned to meet at their camp at the foot of the ridge at which they were located. Two ascended on either side, and the third man, whom this narrative concerns, went along the ridge straight ahead. When he reached the edge he found a sheer drop and had to retrace his path in order to gain camp. By then it was dark and shortly he realized that he was lost. At this point he was in a canyon where there was sparse vegetation, some tall trees and a granite outcropping. He heard what he thought was a bear in the brush and climbed a 25-foot tree. Becoming apprehensive, he descended from the tree after he assured himself that the bear was gone and built three small signal fires, hoping to attract the attention of rangers. He was not aware at the time that they had left the area.

Shortly thereafter, he saw a bright light somewhat like a meteor, but on a glide path, come down out of the sky. It settled just above the rim of the canyon and not long thereafter he heard movements in the area and he went back up into the tree. What transpired later certainly justified his actions. Two "men" in white or light gray suits, their heads apparently encased in some kind of helmet which extended from shoulder to shoulder, came over to the base of the tree. Shortly, a strange-appearing "entity" which reminded Mr. X (he has asked that his name not be used) of a "robot" approached with a gliding motion as opposed to a walking motion, and stood at the base of the tree also. From then on through the night, several upsetting incidents were repeated:

The "men" would attempt to climb the tree by boosting

each other, but didn't seem to know anything about climbing trees. The "robot's" mouth (an aperture made when the "chin" dropped) would open, a puff of smoke would come out and shortly thereafter Mr. X would lose consciousness. After each of the latter incidents, X would wake up very nauseated and vomit and/or retch violently.

In an effort to drive off his tormentors X set fire to his cap, which had the residue of hair dressing on it and flared up brightly. He threw it down at the congregation below and it set a little grass fire. The two "men" moved away and stayed there until the fire died out and then came back. The fire did not daunt the "robot," however. At various times during the night X set fire to pieces of his jacket and his camouflage suit (somewhat like a jungle fighter's suit) which he had torn up, and the paper money and other papers in his wallet, with the exception of his driver's license. He hurled these burning items to the ground. Each time the "men" would desist in their attempts to climb the tree and they would retreat. The "robots" were dark in color and because it was night and there was only the light of a full moon, X was not able to see them in their entirety. At one time when a small grass fire was burning as a result of his arsonistic activities, he saw the robot approach the fire and saw a hand brush through the embers. X could not discern whether or not there were fingers or how many if there were. The details of the "face," which was dark and square, were visible only because of the light from the "eyes" which appeared orange and seemed to "flicker." During the course of the night X fired a total of three arrows at the "robot," two of which struck it, knocking it off balance. He managed to retrieve two of these steel-tipped arrows later, both of which were grooved as if by a file. One clearly showed traces of metal adhering to it. When the arrows struck the robot, they caused bright blue sparks. The arrow which had the foreign material stuck to it was handed over to the Air Force investigator who subsequently questioned Mr. X.

X said that he had climbed nearly to the top of the tree after the entities came upon the scene, straddled a branch and using his belt strapped himself to the tree, the trunk of which was only about four inches in diameter at the top. He broke off branches as he climbed upwards and used them as torches to toss at his antagonists, feeling that this would help deter them in their climbing efforts, which it did.

He said he felt that the "robots" were guided by some

kind of intelligence for at times they would get "upwind" of him to belch their sleep-inducing "smoke."

The final act in this weird tableau was played in the early morning hours when another robot "floated" down toward the tree, stood opposite the other, and a series of flashes like arc-welding flashes appeared between the two which were separated by only a few inches. At that, a huge cloud of the vaporous substance mentioned before issued from their general vicinity. Seconds later X blacked out and came to at dawn, sick, cold and miserable on his precarious perch. The object at the rim of the canyon was gone, as were his besiegers. After waiting some time, X got down and, using the spot where the sun had last been as a guide, headed for camp. The temperature in the area had reached an uncomfortable 38 degrees the night before and besides being sick and frightened he was nearly frozen. He dragged himself toward camp, finally collapsing on the ground from exhaustion. Hearing whistling and calling shortly, he roused and answered the calls and his friends found him. He told them his story and they believed him, for they had seen the descent of the strangely slow "meteor" the night before.

This story could be made much more interesting and spine-chilling if each episode of fire-setting were described in detail as it happened, along with the words of our principal. But for lack of space, which is the problem with trying to set down such a wealth of evidence between the pages of a single book, we have included only the barest of details for purposes of correlation, and to put them into the record.

X said little about his experience except to a relative who was a college professor. It was because of this confidence that we learned of the episode and began our investigation.

X had also reported the incident to the Air Force, and in his interview with APRO's investigator, Dr. James Harder of the University of California at Berkeley, he confided that the Air Force investigator had suggested that some "teen-agers" had played a joke on him. Needless to say, this didn't satisfy X. The preparation and staging of such a hoax would have been completely beyond the capabilities of trained actors, and hardly a playful pastime for even our most inventive youngsters. There was also the little detail concerning how the youngsters could have known that a man would be in that area at that time. Besides, an arrow shot at a target as close as the robot apparently was, would have caused no little damage, but X reported that the "robot" was unaffected except for being temporarily knocked off balance.

At this writing, this particular case is not closed. Professor Harder, after an initial taped interview, arranged to have X interviewed by a qualified practicing psychiatrist and at this writing only the initial interviews preceding and preparing the subject for deep trance hypnosis or sodium amytol questioning, have been conducted. X, at that time, did not show any predisposition to hallucinations or unusual exaggerations. The tape of his interview by Dr. Harder indicated that X could not be influenced to say things that were not true, nor to concoct evidence which did not exist. His hesitations indicated an effort to recall rather than to exaggerate or fabricate. He readily admitted his inability to describe certain features of the "entities" because of the darkness.

The suits worn by the "men," vaguely resembled those of the "men" in the Villas-Boas affair, and the "robots" resemble the strange-looking creatures seen by Mrs. Mary Starr from her bedroom window at Old Saybrook, Connecticut, between 2 and 3 A.M. on the morning of December 16, 1957. According to her account, she was wakened by bright lights outside her window and when she rose and looked out she saw a saucer-shaped object hovering outside. Through the lighted portholes she observed the upper portions of two creatures with square or rectangular heads of a reddish-orange color with what appeared to be a red bulb located in the center of the head. They appeared to be in profile, walking back and forth with one arm upraised, reminding her of waiters holding trays. When a third "man" came into view through one of the portholes, Mrs. Starr leaned forward to get a better view, whereupon the portholes faded, the whole shell began to glow and the object took off.

The suits of the men in the Villas-Boas narrative also resemble generally those apparently worn by the "men" in the Boinai, New Guinea incident, described later in this book. The glowing eyes of the "robot" also remind us of the strange creature, if indeed that is what it was, seen by Mrs. Kathleen Hill, Gene Lemon and several youngsters who climbed a hill near Flatwoods, West Virginia, on the night of September 12, 1952, to investigate a "meteor" which they had seen coming down in that vicinity. They saw a red, glowing hemisphere on the other side of the hill, then spotted the "monster" as it was later dubbed, which appeared at first as only two glowing eyes at the level of tree branches. It started toward them, and before they turned and fled in terror they all saw its "blood-red face" and greenish-orange glowing eyes.

The lower part of the "thing" was in shadow but Mrs. May thought she saw folds of clothing. This may have been the trunk or trunks of trees or imagination, for no one else noted the extremities. The important thing here is that the "creature" could have been smaller and floating above the ground at a higher elevation (they were heading uphill), therefore giving the impression of great height. Later, the whole crowd suffered from irritation of their respiratory tracts and complained of the acrid smell they had noticed. On the next day this odor still lingered in an area where the grass was flattened and where skid marks plainly showed on the ground.

These specific incidents are but a few of many incidents which indicate the presence, at least from time to time, of entities similar to humans but decidedly different in many ways. But it is difficult to convince orthodox science that these happenings need to be exposed to scientific inquiry; thus the "amateurs," with the help of a few dedicated scientists, have fallen heir to the thankless task.

Considered in their entirety, the "occupant" cases yield some correlations. It would be virtually impossible for any one of these observers to base his claims on past information about occupants, because for the most part, most of the cases have not been published and therefore have not been available to the public.

On rare occasions I have examined reports of UFO activity which are almost "too bizarre" to believe, and besides the Villas-Boas and "Mr. X" case, the case of Mr. and Mrs. Barney Hill is one of these. But because no stone should remain unturned, I must present this information also.

According to their own testimony, the young couple was driving home from a vacation in Canada on the night of September, 19–20, 1961, on U.S. Route 3 in the White Mountains of New Hampshire, when they encountered a UFO. At first only a very bright light about three times the apparent size of Jupiter, it slowly reconnoitered their car. They later realized that it was disc-shaped and huge. What had at first seemed to be only a lighted band around its circumference turned out to be a row of windows through which a cold blue light was shining. Hill stopped the car, left the headlights and engine running, took out his binoculars and got out on the highway to get a better look at the object.

Fascinated, he watched as the object slowly descended in his direction. Through the binoculars he could clearly see from eight to eleven figures which appeared to be watching him and his wife from the windows. Suddenly all but one of the figures turned their backs and began to hurry about, seemingly pulling levers on the wall. One figure remained at the window looking down at them, as two red lights began moving away from the object. Hill saw that the lights were on the tips of two finlike projections which were sliding outward from the object's sides. Mrs. Hill heard her husband repeat over and over, "I don't believe it, I don't believe it."

Hill said the figures were dressed in shiny black uniforms and he was reminded of "the cold precision of German officers." He felt that the man in the window was the leader and that he had some plan in mind for them. At this point, the object was estimated to be from fifty to eighty feet up and between fifty and a hundred feet away.

At this point Hill became hysterical, jumped into the car, repeating over and over, "They're going to capture us." He took off down the highway at high speed. Neither looked back immediately and when Mrs. Hill did finally look back she saw nothing. They had traveled only a short distance when they heard a series of beeping sounds, like code, on the trunk of the car. Each sound made the car vibrate. The sounds kept up for approximately thirty-five miles until they reached Ashland when the noises ceased as suddenly as they had commenced.

In a letter to Mr. C. W. Fitch, who investigated the incident, Mrs. Hill commented that "we have been quite upset by our experience. It seems to me unbelievable, so puzzling, with so many questions unanswered. We have discussed the situation with a psychiatrist who assured us that it is an impossibility for two people to have the same hallucination at the same time." It might be interesting to note here that the Hills are two highly respected individuals. Social workers both, Mr. Hill has received attention and reward for his community work from both New Hampshire's governor and Sargent Shriver. During the happenings in New Hampshire in 1965, the story of their encounter with the UFO became public and along with it the additional information that both had suffered a lapse of memory involving two hours during that eventful night. They had separately been examined by a well-known neuropsychiatrist and during these visits the details of those two hours were bared. The information is not yet available to the public, but considering what is already known as a result of studying the cases of "kidnapped" humans, we can make an educated guess.

Before closing this dissertation on "contacts" with UFO occupants, I feel it only fitting and probably very germane, to briefly report on an account still under investigation. It involves a man from Brazilia, Brazil, who claims he was captured in early 1965 by the crew of a disc and taken off the face of the earth to another planet. It has been established that the man was unaccountably gone from his home and his work for two weeks. While on the planet, the principal said he was put through a series of rigorous physical-strength tests. He said he saw thousands of what we call "UFOs" which his captors told him were being readied for a "peaceful invasion" of earth "next year," which would be 1966. The shocking thing about this man's claims is that he said that although he didn't know what planet he was on, he knew it was not the moon. The personnel stationed there lived in specially outfitted quarters, for the air was thin and would not support life. The planet, he said, was cold, extremely dry, and had craters on its surface.

In late 1965, American scientists revealed that Mariner's cameras had shown the existence of *craters on the surface of Mars.*

Once having established the authenticity of these accounts, we can make other observations. We note that there are different types of occupants described in this chapter. This indicates that the UFOs have widely varying types of entities for crews. What this means we cannot possibly know at this juncture but immediate speculation based on the evidence would seem to indicate several races involved in the observation of life on earth. It doesn't seem likely that they would originate on the same planet and therefore we are led to the speculation that there exists an interplanetary liaison of some type. If this should happen to be true, the human race is considerably more retarded than we are inclined to think we are.

These are some of the reports of "contacts" with the occupants of the discs. They have been accepted as authentic by many people who have investigated them and by many more who have read and studied the case reports. Other reports of similar incidents which took place in Europe earlier in the fall of 1954 are so thoroughly covered by Aime Michel in his excellent book, *The Flying Saucers and the Straight-Line Mystery*, that it is not necessary to expand on them here. They were investigated by American press representatives at the time they were reported, but for some reason their reports never reached the American public. It may be conjectured that those involved in these incidents were all perpetrators of hoaxes, and that none of the incidents ever took place. But it was apparent then, as it is now, that strange creatures were on a mission of some kind in that particular area and were either discouraged by the constant interference of those who came upon them or they had finished their business and simply didn't come back. Otherwise there would have been far more reported "hoaxes."

It is tempting when confronted with such cases to discount them entirely. Their bizarre nature offends human judgment. But he who discards all data that displeases him, keeping only that which he approves, certainly cannot be said to be conducting an impartial investigation. After considerable deliberation, including a careful examination of motivation, I came to the conclusion that the individuals involved in "contact" with beings obviously not entirely human did actually have these unusual experiences, and that any honest analysis of the general UFO mystery should include these incidents.

7
Flying Saucers and Censorship

ANYONE interested in the UFO mystery is familiar with the accusation that various government agencies have actually censored flying saucer news and reports. I am certain that those making the accusation believe they have sufficient basis for their stand. At any rate, the Air Force has been the prime villain. I do not propose to convince anyone that a military agency is directly censoring UFO information, but I present here two incidents which may have a bearing on this situation.

In the first incident, Miss Dorothy Madle, a reporter for the Milwaukee *Sentinel*, had written to me that she wanted to do a feature article on APRO and me. I arranged to be in Milwaukee on the weekend of June 12, 1953, for pictures and the interview, and I wrote to Edward Halbach of the Milwaukee Astronomical Society, stating that I would like to chat with him while I was in Milwaukee. Mr. Halbach informed me that Ohio State University astrophysicist J. Allen Hynek, a consulting astronomer to the Air Force at Dayton, and an Air Technical Intelligence Command representative were planning to be in Milwaukee on the preceding Wednesday and would like to talk to me. I replied that I would very much like to meet them but couldn't make the trip to Milwaukee from Sturgeon Bay until Friday, as planned. Halbach arranged for the two men to be in town on Friday, and that night we all met in my hotel and had dinner. The conversation was confined to UFO.

Throughout the evening I was well aware that the astronomer and the intelligence representative, Lieutenant Robert Olssen, were interested primarily in finding out where I stood on the UFO situation and what my opinions were. I was asked not to give Hynek and Olssen's names to the newspapers the next day. (I was somewhat amused the next day when the Milwaukee *Journal* called my room and asked for a picture and interview. It was quite apparent that the *Journal* knew about the meeting the night before. Not wanting to be uncooperative, I consented.) It was evident at the beginning of the conversation with Hynek and Olssen that they were prompting me to do most of the talking. They encouraged me to finish the book I had started, which would attempt to separate UFO fact from fiction. When I queried Olssen on several sightings, he made a few remarks that gave the impression the Air Force didn't consider the interplanetary theory a good answer to the UFO mystery. Olssen also stated that Air Force intelligence was in favor of groups such as APRO which attempt to get to the facts. He brought up the possible psychological ramifications involved in sighting flaps. He said the Air Technical Intelligence Command was of the opinion that a sighting in one location set off a chain reaction, bringing the subject to the attention of others through the subsequent publicity, and that the power of suggestion played an important role.

Then the lieutenant dropped the bombshell: "We're going to try keep such reports out of the papers." I was stunned. How could such a thing be accomplished in a free country with a free press? It would have to involve the cooperative efforts of the news wire services, and although this situation later existed I realize now that it must have been very subtly accomplished. During the flaps in the summer of 1954 and 1956 sightings were made throughout the United States in great numbers, but the wire services did not carry the reports. A man who observed an object in Texas, for example, would have no way of knowing that similar objects were being reported elsewhere in the country. The general public was not aware that a flap was on.

The young lieutenant may very well have been putting into words a general feeling about what should be done about UFO reports instead of referring to a specific policy. I don't know, and I would be assuming too much if I said I did. But I do have a few ideas.

In my experience I have noted that whenever UFO activity gains the attention of the press, there arises the inevitable surge of emotion among people which results in a considerable number of reports which turn out to be actual misconceptions of natural phenomena and ordinary objects such as planes. A few hoaxes invariably result also. It may have been to this that the 1953 scientific advisory panel alluded when the famous (or infamous, take your choice) recommendation was made, to wit: "Remove the aura of mystery."

In the early days of the UFO mystery, and to some extent since, every time a major sighting won the attention of the press, some pseudo religious leader who claimed fraternal relations with various spacemen from various places, would scoot to the nearest newspaper office and grant an interview. I cannot entirely account for the willingness of the press to print the sensational claims of these visionaries, but realize that they do make for humorous reading and are considered "colorful" copy. After all, that is what a news writer exists for—to inform and amuse his readers. It is revealing, however, to note that most of the contact-claimants named Venus as the origin of their "space-brothers." Venus is snynonymous with beauty, love and peace. If a serious researcher tried to inform the press about an objective observation or opinion concerning the UFOs, he usually got a quizzical look and a fast departure. But, despite the fact that the "contact claimants," as they are called, constituted a confusing factor as far as serious research was concerned, an attempt to block their efforts to get attention would be censorship—no matter who brought it about.

It was a strange coincidence that those who hated being ridiculed for their belief that the UFOs were real and interplanetary did not mind heaping ridicule on the heads of the visionaries when they had the opportunity.

In view of the foregoing, then, it is not impossible that some or many official investigators began to cast a jaundiced eye at practically all reports. The two men who have held forth at Wright-Patterson Air Base's Project Bluebook for the past few years are not, in my opinion, dedicated to a policy of secrecy or censorship. I believe their attitudes reflect their personal convictions rather than official policy. Mr. Lorenzen has talked with Major Quintanilla at length and we have both met and talked with Sergeant Moody. Neither of us got the impression that they were "holding back"; rather we noted that both held the strong conviction that if more information could be obtained on even the most detailed and authenticated case, it could be explained in terms of natural phenomena.

It seems to me that the largest problem in UFO research has been the emotionalism of the people involved. What has often been mistaken for censorship would not be so defined if the individuals making the judgments were not predisposed or conditioned by others to think in terms of "censorship."

When the subject of UFOs first came to public attention, much was said and written about them. Several popular books were written which immediately became best sellers. The authors felt that within a short time the "great truth" would be told, and when that did not happen within what they considered to be a reasonable length of time, charges of "censorship" were made. That charge has been nurtured and perpetuated through the years, often by twisting of the facts. But let's look at the position of the people responsible for investigating the UFOs and making pronouncements concerning their nature. What if the things had gone away, never to come back again? Then the responsible agency would have been left with red faces and no evidence to back up their momentous announcement about "interplanetary UFOs." An unenviable position.

If, however, sufficient data was available to warrant some

concern, it would be natural for those in charge to reserve opinions until more information on which to base a judgment became available. It might be judicious, then, to deny the existence of evidence indicating alien spaceships and continue to collect data. This seems to be what may have been done.

What has often been mistaken for censorship by overzealous UFO fans has really come about in the following manner. From time to time when a scientist made some pronouncement which seemed relatively "pro-UFO" and then shortly seemed to back off, the "censorship" crowd would scream "hush-up." In actuality, in many instances, the individual in question became aware of the notoriety he had received, the ensuing mail, the pleas from UFO fans for endorsement of their opinions, and he instituted his own brand of "censorship" by modifying his original statement and thereafter keeping his mouth shut on the subject. I know of several cases of this sort which I may be able to talk about some day.

If a sighting of a UFO is made within the confines of a military establishment, the people in charge have every right to keep that information from the public. Besides the involvement of statistics conerning classified craft and instruments (ours), it would not be good public relations for any military agency to admit that strange flying objects can violate their air (and land) space and get away with it.

It is not commonly known that within the American (civilian) UFO research field itself, there exists a type of censorship. It was instituted as early as 1954 when accounts of "little men" and landings began to come out of France and South America. Certain elements in the research field either did not accept the information because it came from "foreigners," or because the reports were too bizarre to believe. Although they operated under the guise of "scientific objectivity," they were incapable of the same objectivity where "unacceptable" reports were concerned. They seemingly overlooked the logical assumption that intelligently controlled interplanetary ships, which they endorsed, would have occupants of some kind and that they would be expected to land from time to time. These self-censoring elements have gradually departed from their narrow views but not until some rather well-authenticated accounts of landings and "little men" took place in the United States. The Zamora affair in Socorro, New Mexico, in 1964 was the incident which brought about the great change in thinking for the "keep them flying" crowd.

Censorship has become a dirty word in the American vocabulary for several reasons, some of which are political in nature. No thinking individual can reasonably say that censorship is *never* justified and I think that some censorship may have been justified in relation to the UFO subject.

The "anti-censorship" element has stated over and over again that the government has no right to censor UFO information, that "the public can take it," that they should be told the truth, and other such arguments. They seem to forget, for the most part, their own emotional inability to accept certain UFO evidence and the fact that they themselves had to be exposed to certain evidence for a *period of eight years* before they would even consider it. Because they have some inkling of the nature of the UFOs they want everyone else to believe as they believe and to recognize them as certain latter-day prophets. I see no great concern for the "public" in all of this. Instead, it smacks of just another religious movement.

The press is a most accurate barometer of the opinions and convictions of the public. Since the Zamora case in 1964 the press has become vitally interested in these elusive sky objects and UFO activity receives increasingly more space in newspapers and exposure on radio and television as time progresses.

But the overall picture concerning the availability of information about UFOs is a clouded and jumbled one. This particular facet of the UFO subject has been crying for a rational elucidation for some time. In and attempt to clarify the position of the press, a newsman friend of mine wrote to me in early 1957:

There is, as you note, the attitude of the press in general. That's the whole point: there it is, however contemptible one may feel it is.

Condemning it, however, is no more an excuse for refusing to understand it than is the attitude of the press toward unidentified aerial phenomena a justification for itself. I believe that the attitude of the press can be understood, although I must confess I haven't caught a single fellow newsman in the act of analyzing why we do what we do in this respect. I don't seek to excuse myself, but I have done some thinking about it and can offer an answer which, if somewhat oversimplified, is reasonably satisfactory to me.

One approach is to concede that the attitude of the press toward UFOs cannot be evaluated except within the context of our times. For the purposes of this discussion let us begin with the Arnold sightings of 1947. We had just fought our most distracting war. While seeking to get back to normalcy we were subconsciously seeking to avoid the burdens of the world leadership and responsibility which we knew were clamoring to be taken up.

In one single day in 1947 we were confronted with news which clearly implied to some of us the possible if not probable existence of intelligent beings from outside our own planet, fully capable of getting at us and implicitly superior to us in development. A corollary was the relative inferiority of our own scientific and technical stage. I feel strongly this must underlie the unwillingness of most scientists, who are supposed to be open-minded, to admit that Arnold and his successors actually saw something. There also was the implication that we were doing a certain amount of floundering and muddling in our laboratories.

But this was just the beginning. One suspects the saucers meant, to those religionists who are more concerned with their institutions than their faiths, the quite possible derangement of their whole systems of thought and the exposure of those aspects of our religious practices which probably have more to do with tribal custom and even superstition than they do with the spirit of man.

And in government—particularly among the armed forces and in the minds of all responsible for national defense—it meant: (a) a long step toward fusion with reality of a long-suppressed nightmare—that the population of the world might awaken to the meaninglessness of nationalism and national and racial distinctions; and (b) the equally possible realization that defense of the world could be futile. Ergo, why armies, navies, air forces, national governments, anyway?

In view of all these things presumably going on in the minds of government officials, priests and preachers, teachers and scientists, the rather silly performance of our press may not seem quite as churlish and stupid as

it has to most of us. We newsmen are of two kinds:
the reporters and editors who do the actual writing, and
the publishers who are, generally speaking, answerable,
to the pressures of business, as well as to journalism.
The publishers have the last word, of course, because
they are the bosses. They pay our salaries. Their
job is to run newspapers which will sell—and by sell I
mean not only circulation but, more important, space
to advertisers.

When the saucers hit us most reporters and editors
realized immediately, if dimly in a good many cases,
some of the implications of the Arnold sighting and
what followed. You will recall the incredible amount
of space devoted to saucers those first few days. This
was because reporters and editors were writing their
heads off about the hottest subject of the day—*and* because nobody had told them to hold down. Things got
pretty much out of hand, especially after the hoax boys
moved in with their garbage-can lids soldered together
and after several cases that sounded like mass hallucinations got a big ride.

When that happened publishers—and newsmen too—
began to get cautious, and for good reason. You don't
build circulation and hold advertisers by printing irresponsible rumors and wild yarns, and much of the
saucer copy was coming under that category. So staffs
got the word to go easy on saucer copy, especially since
the scientists and defense people by now were putting
out some pretty solid pooh-pooh stuff. And word got
around to the news agencies that saucer copy was going
increasingly into the wastebaskets of the newspapers
we serve; so we began to hold down too. There never
was any flat order except to exercise due caution, but
it became apparent that to get a saucer story printed
you had to have very solid evidence and attribution.
Later on it got so that you wouldn't even get a saucer
story on the wire.

One reason is that newsmen—both kinds—are like
anyone else: human. They don't like to put themselves
in the position of spreading unprovable reports, especially since it's their specific business to spread only the
kind of report that *can* be proved. With every government official and most of the reputable scientists in the
country either clamming up or denying that saucers
existed, the newsmen readily fell victim to the impulse
to shut up, too. You could write your head off, but

you knew it wouldn't be published and that you could be regarded as a bedfellow of George Adamski.

We thus arrived at our present stage: newsmen, still fully conscious of the vast but largely ignored interest in UFOs, resort to a tongue-in-cheek style or outright ridicule in order to get anything printed at all. I do not say this is in the least admirable or excusable. I do say it can be understood and, having been understood, can be related to the attitude of the other three estates involved. In this light—to me at least—the performance of the press looks no better and no worse than that of anyone else who refuses to face probabilities if not facts. For newsmen, as for anyone, it boils down to a choice between mustering credibility for the unknown (which could wreck our whole scheme of things) and sticking to what is known. If the press has given in to fear of the unknown (and I believe it has and that it has no real excuse for it) one can say in its defense only that it is not alone.

People seem to cherish fear, somewhat as a bored housewife is supposed to return daily to the miseries of the soap opera. We would rather, I suspect, fear the unknown than convert it to the known. What we may fear more deeply than the unknown itself is the prospect of actually knowing it.

Happily for all of us there are people like yourself who refuse to be bound by such mass refusal of reality, who are not afraid to seek and learn. But for most people this is an age of fear, and it is in their fear of fear, their reaction to it, their cherishing of this most vicious of all drugs, that we have to look for the key to the world we live in today.

Many who have avidly followed the UFO mystery for years may condemn me for my somewhat conservative attitude on this question of censorship, but I feel my position is justified. Too much has been written and said about censorship with no apparent beforehand investigation. The blame should be laid at the proper doorstep, yes, but irresponsible accusations which have no basis in fact are to be abhorred and avoided.

Perhaps the many misconceptions about UFOs have been engendered by the Air Force's secretive attitude. Some get the impression that sensational and shocking incidents and reports are being withheld because the authorities feel the danger of hysteria if they are revealed. This may or may

not be so. There is, certainly, sufficient available evidence to
indicate that unidentified, unconventional aerial objects, which
appear to be intelligently controlled flying machines are operating in the earth's atmosphere day after day, week after
week and year after year. Because they are unknown they
should be identified. The most logical conclusion as to their
identity is that they are from somewhere in outer space.

The following incident, involving insidious "suggestive"
censorship, concerns a letter written by Senator Richard B.
Russell (D., Ga.), chairman of the Senate Armed Services
Committee, in response to a request for information about the
sightings the Senator reportedly witnessed in Europe in late
1955. The letter, to Tom Towers, was printed in the latter's
January 20, 1956, "Aviation News" column for the Los
Angeles *Examiner*. Towers had originally contacted Senator
Russell's office by letter with the request that he be given
permission to "break" the story. That letter was not answered.
Senator Russell's letter, dated January 17, 1956, read: "Permit me to acknowledge your letters relative to reports that
have come to you regarding aerial objects seen in Europe last
year. I received your letter but I have discussed this matter
with the affected agencies of the government and they are of
the opinion that it is not wise to publicize this matter at this
time. I regret very much that I am unable to be of assistance
to you."

From Senator Russell's letter, I gathered that the Senator
did see something unusual, and also that "affected agencies of
the government" were most anxious that the incident remain
unpublicized.

The spring of 1966 saw editorials in all major United States
papers and in most small dailies clamoring for some kind of
recognition of the subject and explanation of the phenomena
known as UFOs. It seems that the public indoctrination which
is so badly needed is on its way at the request of the public
itself.

We have one judgment to make and that is whether the
"censorship" has been justified. Has it been instituted by
governments because of fear of panic, or to conceal attempts
to learn the propulsion secrets of the UFOs? Or has it been,
for a large part, unconsciously born and nurtured out of fear?

8
Test or Attack?

MR. LORENZEN and I had just finished our after-dinner coffee on that historic evening in October, 1957, when the Russians launched their first satellite. The doorbell rang repeatedly with what seemed to be special urgency.

The man at the door was one of my husband's co-workers; he pushed his way in excitedly and came into the kitchen where Jim was pouring another cup of coffee. "The cotton-picking Russians have launched an artificial satellite," he said. Jim almost dropped his cup. I said, "You're kidding!" The man replied, "The hell I am—don't you listen to the radio? It's on all the stations, and on television. I tell you, the Russians have launched their satellite!"

Despite my own often-voiced opinion that the United States might be lagging in rocket research, I was shocked and disappointed. Our friend went on to give us the details—maximum and minimum altitudes, approximate weight, purpose—everything he had heard on the broadcasts. Something told me this was not only the beginning of countless Congressional hearings, accusations and buck-passing by military and civilian committees, but also the beginning of increased UFO activity. I went to my desk at once and began to clear it of current work. Three days later the reports began to come in.

In the early part of 1957 UFOs had been operating in the Orient, as they had in the latter half of 1956. Filed reports indicated that the bulk of world-logged sightings had occurred there. Beginning in April, 1957, however, South America, and Venezuela in particular, had a definite increase in sightings, and these continued through October with only sporadic activity elsewhere. The sightings which came to my desk after Sputnik I showed a slight increase in the United States. By October, Brazil had joined Venezuela as co-hostess of the discs. Correspondence with Dr. Olavo Fontes of Brazil indicated that the increase of sightings in the United States did not signify a decrease in Brazilian sightings. It seemed that the increased sightings followed an increased number of UFOs being present.

Carrying a live cargo, the dog Laika, Sputnik II was hurled aloft on November 2 by the tremendous rocket engines developed by the Russians. That night the small town of Levelland, Texas, was visited by an egg-shaped glowing object which squatted on the roads and stalled car and truck engines. The object stayed well within a four-mile radius, according to observers who included law enforcement officers, truck drivers and motorists leaving or approaching Levelland. There is hardly an American able to read who does not remember that history-making week when tales of flying saucers were headline news; and the tales became more sensational as the days went by. Even with our large membership in the United States, APRO did not receive accounts of all the sightings; nonetheless the extent of the flap was magnified, in my opinion, by the amount of press coverage it received. The actual number of sightings reported by the press services and small-town papers were not many—indication that only a few vehicles were operating. To my knowledge there were no cases of two sightings involving distances which could not have been spanned by one fairly swift object. Diverse descriptions, however, indicated that there were several vehicles. Descriptions did vary, but the most popular and often-reported one was of the glowing, egg-shaped type seen in various parts of the United States. The Levelland sighting was the most interesting because of the number of observers. It seems likely that only a single object was seen at various times by the many witnesses. No two sightings were made at the same time.

The flap, as it developed, is much more important than the individual sightings, for it presents a fairly clear picture: After a few days of UFO comparative inactivity on a worldwide scale, Sputnik II was launched and the saucer put in an appearance at Levelland. It was generally conceded by UFO researchers that the Levelland sighting was a case of not being able to interpret the facts. The weather-phenomenon explanation offered later by the Air Force was discarded as ridiculous on the face of things.

At about 3 A.M. on Sunday, November 3, two military police, Corporal Glenn H. Toy and Private James Wilbanks, on routine patrol of the north part of the White Sands missile range, spotted a very bright object high in the sky. They watched it descend until it appeared to be about fifty yards above the A-bomb bunkers, when its light was extinguished. A few minutes later the object flared up "bright as the sun," fell at an angle to the ground and again lost its luminosity. The men later described it as being about seventy-five to a hundred yards in diameter and shaped like an egg. Its landing appeared to take place about three miles from them. Their report to the authorities was all but ignored until another similar observation was made seventeen hours later in the same vicinity by another two-man patrol. At about 8 P.M. Specialist Forest R. Oakes and SP/3 Barlow, driving in the same general area, saw a bright light which appeared to be hanging about fifty feet above the old A-bomb bunker. Oakes said the light suddenly took off at a 45-degree angle, went up into the sky, started blinking on and off and then disappeared.

Several points regarding these two sightings are outstanding: The sighting made at 3 A.M. followed the last recorded Levelland sighting by scarcely one and a half hours; the descriptions by witnesses at Levelland and the first patrol at White Sands were almost identical; there was no chance that the Army jeep patrol could have known about the Levelland sighting or the description of it; and it is a matter of record that the second patrol which saw the same object seventeen hours after the first patrol had had no opportunity to learn of the earlier sighting.

Ordinarily the following incident would not be considered for inclusion here because the names of those involved cannot be used. However, in view of the description of the object and the data and time involved, I believe it is germane to the sequence of events. A test pilot left Big Spring, Texas, at 1:56 Sunday afternoon, November 3, on his way across country to the Coast. His checkpoints were Wichita Falls, Oklahoma City, Amarillo, Texas, and Roswell, New Mexico. At 4:16 he landed at Holloman Air Force Base to visit an old friend from the Korean War days, an Air Force major. Checking in at Base Operations, he related his sighting of an unconventional aerial object en route. Traveling at five hundred miles an hour in an east-to-west direction, he had been startled to see a large, oblong glowing object pass over his aircraft. He didn't know whether the trail the thing had left was cast off by the light or was actually a vapor trail, but it did leave a trail. Within four hours, military police at the White Sands Proving Ground made a second sighting of a glowing object over the range.

I did not expect that the flap I had predicted would take place practically on my own doorstep. But James Stokes phoned on Monday evening, November 4, to tell me his car had been stopped by an object of huge proportions which made a couple of passes across the road as he drove south on Highway 54 near Orogrande, New Mexico. Stokes arrived later, quite excited. I invited him to sit down and give Mr. Lorenzen and me the facts in chronological order. He had been on his way to El Paso, eighty-three miles from Alamogordo. The highway to El Paso in 1957 was a comparatively narrow two-lane blacktop, its desert expanse broken only by two small towns, Orogrande and Newman in New Mexico. At 1:10 P.M., approximately ten miles south of Orogrande and nineteen miles northeast of Newman, Stokes experienced car trouble—the radio in his late-model Mercury suddenly faded out; then his engine began to falter and quit entirely. Up ahead he spotted several cars pulled off the road, the occupants standing on the highway and pointing toward the Sacramento Mountains to the northeast. Stokes looked up and spotted an oval-shaped object barreling in the direction of the highway and the cars. It turned and headed into the northwest after buzzing the highway. Traveling at a high rate of speed, the object made another pass at the cars and then disappeared into the northwest.

Stokes kept rubbing his wrists, his cheek and neck as he narrated his experience. I asked him what was wrong. He said he had an itching sensation in those areas. His skin was noticeably reddish. For half an hour I questioned Stokes closely on several points. He said he felt heat as the object passed over. It had no visible portholes or other external features. I asked him about its altitude, and he estimated that it was flying at about fifteen hundred to three thousand feet, but he had no points of reference except the clouds. It had rained that morning and scattered low-hanging clouds still filled the sky. He said he thought the object was traveling at a speed of at least Mach[1] 1. He produced a small notebook, turned to a page and handed it to me. I almost smiled—the "notes" he

[1] In aerodynamics, a number representing the ratio of the air speed of an object to the speed of sound in the same region of the atmosphere.

had made were illegible; he had been so busy and excited watching the object that he wasn't able to do more than scribble.

I asked him if he would like to tape an interview at the radio station. I knew the news director there would want a record of the incident. Stokes said he had called his military superior at Holloman Air Force Base (Stokes was an electronics engineer in the high-altitude research branch) who told him it was all right to talk about it. During the ride to Station KALG further questioning revealed something most ininteresting: the object had been flying among scattered, low-level clouds which dissipated in its path. Stokes had obtained the names of two other men at the scene, a Mr. Duncan from Las Cruces, who took pictures with a 35 mm. camera, and Allan Baker, who said he was from the White Sands Proving Ground.

The tape was made and KALG news director Terry Clarke released the incident to the press wires that night. I called local APRO members and it was decided that we should have a round-table discussion the next evening. On Tuesday morning Alamogordo and Holloman Air Force Base were the telephone targets for every newsman in the world assigned to the "flying saucer flap." The Lorenzen telephone also was busy as I tried to keep pace with the events of the day. From Alamogordo newsmen I learned that long-distance inquiries about the Stokes sightings and requests for personal interviews with Stokes were coming in at Holloman at such a rate that the switchboards were literally swamped. Stokes was called in from his post on the range for a press conference, and pictures of him with Holloman military personnel were published in the local newspaper. He was interviewed in the company of press representatives and the military men, and then was closeted with Air Force questioners for some time. One newspaperman said Stokes was obviously agitated as he entered another room for the military questioning.

On Tuesday evening local APRO technical advisers met at my home. Stokes was present. I noted that his "sunburn" was gone. Stokes told us he was scheduled for a physical examination at the Holloman hospital on Wednesday morning—and then began to cautiously advance the theory that what he had actually seen was "some kind of atmospheric phenomenon." We all exchanged glances, but we did not press him on that point. It was generally agreed later that Stokes had changed his story somewhat after his interview with the military authorities. As far as we were concerned we could go no further with the investigation; the case was closed.

The first hint of skulduggery was a Washington news release on November 5 in which the Air Force was quoted as saying that the Levelland sighting and "somewhat similar reports" from the Alamogordo area were nothing but exaggerations or misunderstood natural phenomena. This, however, was only a whisper of what was to come. The official release from the Office of Information Services, Holloman Air Force Missile Development Center, was dated November 5, one day after the sighting, and was issued shortly after Stokes was interviewed by the Air Force at Holloman. It contained the initial information about the sighting, qualified Stokes's position at Holloman and recorded the fact that he had been employed at AFMDC for eighteen months and was a retired Navy veteran (CPO) with twenty-four years of service. The headline story in the Alamogordo *Daily News* for November 5 covered Stokes's sighting and quoted Holloman spokesmen to the effect that his background and experience rendered him competent to observe and report on sky objects. The paper also stated that the Air Force was accepting Stokes's story as bona fide.

On November 6 the pattern began to show, with a release out of Washington stating that of 5700 saucer sightings none had been confirmed; that there was no physical or material evidence, not even a minute fragment, that a so-called "flying saucer" had ever been found; that there was no evidence these unknown objects were interplanetary spaceships. This blurb was printed and reprinted by countless papers throughout the world—soothing syrup for the fear-stricken. On November 7 a UP release out of Dayton, Ohio, stated that no physical evidence—not a single landing impression or footprint or "crew member"—had ever been found by the Air Force; it wound up pointing out that although three percent of the sightings the Air Force gathered were still unknown, it would have identified those, too, if complete reports on them could be secured, and that the sightings of unknown objects in Texas, New Mexico and elsewhere would almost certanly be explainable. Air Force anti-saucer propagandists were operating in high gear, but somehow they got their data mixed up—on November 15 the Stokes sighting was included in a group of three sightings which were labeled as "exaggerations or misunderstanding of natural phenomena"; on November 17 another wire service listed the Stokes sighting as a hoax, "presumably suggested by the Levelland reports." By November 20 few sightings were being reported—partly, I suspect, because of the "misconception" and "hoax" tag hung on the principal sightings of the preceding nineteen days, and partly because the objects simply were not making many further appearances.

Several things about the Stokes sighting make the "conclusions" of officialdom appear rather suspect: (1) the Alamogordo area in which Stokes lived had been having its fall period of scattered clouds and frequent rainfall. Despite the mild weather, there had been no opportunity for a sunburn. But the sunburn was there—I saw it. When I saw Stokes twenty-four hours later it was gone. (2) The location of the Stokes sighting is significant. It occurred very close to a White Sands Proving Ground access road which joins Highway 54. Highway 54 carries a lot of traffic between Alamogordo and El Paso on weekends, beginning Friday night and ending Sunday night, but during the week the traffic consists mainly of housewives on shopping trips to El Paso, salesmen, truckers and occasional business men. The only towns originating traffic between El Paso and Alamogordo are the two tiny desert stops, Orogrande and Newman. However, the White Sands Proving Ground is the home of thousands of civilian and military personnel. The sighting occurred on Monday. I believe the corroborating witnesses to whom Stokes spoke (he admitted he did not speak to all the people at the side of the highway) deliberately gave fictitious names because they did not want to be involved in the incident.

On New Year's Eve, almost two months after the incident, Mr. Lorenzen and I quite by accident met Mr. Stokes at a local supper club. We invited him to dinner with us there, and we discussed the sighting again. He was quite upset about the "hoax" label and said that if he ever saw anything out of the ordinary again he wouldn't tell anyone. I can't say that I blame him. Shortly after this, an officer at Holloman told one of APRO's contacts there that the Air Force had a lead on a corroborating witness to the Stokes sighting. We were never able to check this out, however.

But nine months later I got my first solid lead on a real corroborating witness. Our son had had a bad fall and we took him to the local hospital for emergency treatment. The doctor decided to hold him overnight for observation, because a head injury was involved, so we took turns staying up with Larry. Later in the evening a nurse came into the room and, seeing a copy of *Air Force Special Report No. 14* which I was reading, commented on flying saucers and asked if I believed they existed. I said, "Yes." The nurse then exploded a bombshell: "I know a couple who were on the highway near Orogrande when that engineer saw that saucer last November," she said. I immediately began to question her for details. She said she couldn't give me their names because they didn't want the unfavorable publicity and ridicule which might result if they corroborated the sighting. Her friends had almost come forward two days after the incident, but a press release labeling the sighting as a natural phenomenon stopped them. I asked the nurse if they thought it was a natural phenomenon and she said they didn't, that the thing appeared to be a machine of some kind, a real flying object. I could not convince her to give the names to me, but I did gather sufficient information to deduce who the people were—and then I realized why they couldn't talk—the man was a civil service employee.

The Stokes case was still front-page news on Tuesday, November 5, when Don Clarke, an electronics technician employed by a civilian contractor at Holloman, observed an orange-red cigar-shaped object at abut 15-degrees elevation in the western sky at 4:24 A.M. From his vantage point in the eastern part of Alamogordo, which rests on the slopes of the foothills of the Sacramento Mountains, Clarke had a good view of the object which appeared to be in the vicinity of Holloman. He ran into his house to get his camera, but when he returned the object was gone. Five minutes after the Clarke sighting Lyman Brown, Jr., of Alamogordo saw a weird phenomenon to the north of Alamogordo. It was a yellowish-orange light which, when he first spotted it, was at a 45-degree elevation in the northern sky. It was proceeding across the sky, arcing toward the east, and "went out" at about 15- or 20-degree elevation in the southeastern sky above Dog Canyon in the Sacramento Mountains. Then he observed another phenomenon—what resembled a searchlight beam did a "looping" maneuver just above where the light disappeared. The whole episode lasted about seven seconds. Conversation with Brown later revealed that he was acquainted with astrononomical phenomena. On the same day, a Bekin Van Lines driver, Delbert Boyd of Kellyville, Oklahoma, said he saw a mysterious light about five miles southwest of Albuquerque at 7:45 P.M. The light alternated from bright to dim and appeared to land southwest of the city. Also that day at Durango, Colorado, a silvery object was sighted by Richard Schaeffer of the Thompson Park area. Mrs. Harold McCabe, who also saw the object, said it looked like a moon, except that it was traveling rapidly.

Wednesday was quiet in the Alamogordo area, but elsewhere in New Mexico there were sightings of unidentified aerial objects and the reports continued to flow into APRO headquarters. On November 4 Mrs. Dale Van Fleet, an Albuquerque housewife, reported at 7 P.M. she had watched an object hover for five minutes at about 45-degrees elevation in the west. It appeared to be larger than the full moon and was gold in color. She went into the house and when she came out moments later the object was gone.

On Thursday an unidentified tourist informed policeman Erwin de Oliviera at Tucumcari, New Mexico, that at 6:15 he had seen a huge red object just outside of Vaughn on U.S. Highway 54. Vaughn is a small town northeast of Carrizozo and about eighty miles northeast of Alamogordo. No further details were obtained. Santa Fe residents Joe Martinez and Albert Gallegos, driving home at 12:15 that morning, saw an object in the sky with "red and green and yellow lights" and which gave out "a great glow all over." They would not give any further details, but their friends told the press the men had said the object came down over their car at least once. Gallegos and Martinez both said publicly that they didn't intend to say any more because they didn't want to be called "crazy." Two other Santa Fe residents, one of them named Frank Mares, told police they had seen a huge ball of fire which seemed to be traveling southeast as they drove in the southwestern section of Santa Fe. No exact time was given, but the press quoted Police Chief A.B. Martinez as saying the incident had taken place "early in the day.

Orogrande recorded another sighting of an uncoventional aerial object on November 7, confirming the description of the object Stokes saw. About twenty miles from where Stokes's car was stalled Mr. and Mrs. Trent Lindsey and their twenty-two-year-old-son Byron were driving south on Highway 54 at 9:20 A.M. Byron noticed that the speedometer on their 1954 Mercury was weaving wildly back and forth between the 60-miles-per-hour-speed at which they were traveling and the 110 mark. The three of them discussed the possible cause for this and then forgot it until they spotted a strange object in the sky to the south-southwest. Byron, whom I interviewed, said the object had sharply defined edges, no apparent glow, no trail or visible means of propulsion, and seemed to be highly polished metal. It appeared to be taking an arcing course into the southwest at high altitude. Byron compared its apparent length to the diameter of a dime held at arm's length, with a thickness considerably less than that. The Lindseys watched the object at high altitude for about three minutes, after which it disappeared over the Organ Mountains. When they looked at the speedometer again it was functioning perfectly, and has ever since. I spoke to Trent Lindsey, a respected businessman in Alamogordo, two days after their observation and he commented that he had never had trouble with his speedometer before.

The Lindsey sighting was the second in the White Sands Proving Ground area within four days. Albuquerque, which is within miles of Kirkland Air Force Base and the Sandia Base, was visited at least twice by UFOs. A red cigar-shaped object was seen in the vicinity of Holloman. This suggests a pattern of reconnaissance of military installations. Over the White Sands-Holloman Air Force Base range between 1:45 and 1:55 A.M., a little over six hours prior to the Lindsey sighting, airmen Bradford Rickets, James Cole, Dennis Murphy, Wayne Hurlburt and Harry Uhlrich sighted an unidentified aerial object while on duty near a salvage yard at the north side of the base between Alamogordo and Tularosa, twelve miles north-by-northwest of Alamogordo. They said the object made a whistling noise and turned from white to orange to red.

On the following Tuesday an item in the official section (mandatory reading for all Base personnel, military and civilian of the Holloman AFMDC *Daily Bulletin* reads:

Unidentified Flying Objects: On November 7 six airmen claimed they sighted an unidentified flying object and did not report this to proper Base authorities. They did, however, give this information to the local press. Request that each member of the military and civilian, employed at this center, refrain from any public statement on political, diplomatic, legislative or scientific matters or any controversial subjects, such as UFOs, without first contacting the Center Information Services Officer. This request is in accordance with AFR 190-6. Disciplinary action may be taken against offender.

Signed: LT. COL. McCURDY, HDN

(AFR 190-6 was probably used to quiet Stokes.)

A local APRO member employed at Holloman called the Information Services Office and asked a Lieutenant Martin there whether this order pertained to contractor personnel (employed by contractors at Holloman). The question was not answered specifically. The Base, he said, was in a difficult position when reporters called for further information and the office had no information on the incident. This is no doubt true, but the fact remains that the existing regulation restricts individuals at Air Force installations in relating the details of UFO sightings. I also believe that this regulation is a violation of the constitutional rights of civilians, and should be challenged.

It is interesting to note that while the Stokes story was labeled a hoax and the Levelland and many other sightings were explained away as atmospheric phenomena, Don Clarke's sighting of the red "cigar" over Holloman and the Lindsey sighting of the silvery object near Orogrande were not included in debunking press releases. The reason I believe, is that the latter were civilians, out of the reach of the military regulations (also, neither of these sightings received widespread press attention, and were not considered important in the context of the November flap).

The unidentified flying object sighted by the crew of the Coast Guard cutter *Sebago* two hundred miles south of the Mississippi delta on November 5 was first "identified" as Venus and later as a combination of two types of planes—a gas-engine light plane and a jet. The latter explanation was necessary to account for the widely varying speeds of the object. Official explanation did not, however, account for the fact that the object flitted off and on the radar screen several times during the 27-minute observation. This sighting by military personnel was debunked in the same press release which attempted to discredit Stokes and explain away the Levelland sightings.

The last sighting of the flap in the Alamogordo area took place at 7:20 P.M. on November 9 when a Tularosa housewife and several others, including a teen-age college student, observed a large, brilliant rapidly moving light which approached their car and apparently caused their vehicle's lighting system to fail. The incident took place near the junction of the White Oaks Road and U.S. Highway 54, about seventy miles north by northeast of Alamogordo and about twelve miles northeast of Carrizozo. First seen in the south, the object followed a south-north trajectory, approached the car, then changed course and finally disappeared into the southwest at a high rate of speed while the occupants got out of the car for a better look. At about 7:15 on the same evening Mr. Lorenzen and I were traveling east on Highway 380, about ten miles from Carrizozo, when we spotted a bright light silhouetted against the mountains to the east and which moved erratically until it appeared to move south. We could not obtain a clear, constant view of the object because of the frequent dips in the roads, but we believe we may have observed the same object the White Oaks group had sighted.

Mysterious happenings during Nobember, 1957, may have had some bearing on the appearance of UFOs throughout the world. On November 6, while strange objects were hopscotching around the world, an equally strange radio signal was baffling shortwave listeners and government officials in the United States. An AP release from New York stated that the signal was being heard "near the new Russian satellite's frequency," but it was of a different tone. The Federal Communications Commission first said that information about the signal was classified, but an FCC spokesman later said it wasn't classified, but simply that "we just don't know what it is." The signal, the AP said, was a long note of low pitch followed after a few seconds by two short notes. It is significant that on February 25, 1959, the sighting of a glowing, egg-shaped object near Hobbs, New Mexico, by Jim Dobbs, Jr., coincided with interference in his car radio. Dobbs reported to authorities and the press that the radio interference consisted of a steady succession of two dots and a dash while the object was in view.

One other report is most interesting when considered in the context of the important happenings of November, 1957. In Dante, Tennessee, a twelve-year-old boy, Everett Clark, sighted a cigar-shaped object in a field. Press notices reported that the boy was honest and delivered a straightforward report of what he had observed. Everett claimed that on November 6 he had seen a "spaceship" land in a pasture at 6:30 A.M. His parents were at work in the nearby knitting mills and when he got up to let his dog Frisky out he saw the object across the road in a field about a hundred yards away. His first impression was that he had been dreaming, and he went back into the house. Twenty minutes later when he went to bring the dog in the object was still there, and his dog was among a group of furiously barking dogs in the field near the object.

He said there were two men and two women near the ship, and when one of the men grabbed for Frisky, his dog growled and backed away. The strange man then grabbed another of the dogs; the animal twisted in his grasp and attempted to bite him, whereupon the man let him go. The boy said he walked down the road to see better, and one of the men motioned to him, but Everett did not try to approach the ship or the strangers. Finally, the four strange individuals entered the ship, apparently without opening a door, as though "walking through glass," and the ship took off.

Reporter Carson Brewer of the Knoxville *News-Sentinel* investigated the report and found a faint, cigar-shaped imprint in the grass where Everett said the object had rested. Everett apparently did not know the imprint was there, and was pointing out where he thought the people had stood when Brewer found the imprint.

These points are significant: (1) On November 2 the Russians launched an artificial satellite containing a living animal, and four days later a boy in Tennessee saw a strange ship in a field and a strange man trying to pick up a dog. (2) It appears evident that military bases were visited during November, 1957, following on the heels of the satellite launchings. It also appears that some kind of weapon or device was being tested throughout the United States—a device which inhibited the function of gasoline-driven engines. (3) An unidentified radio tone in space indicates that a foreign object capable of transmitting radio signals was in the upper reaches of earth's atmosphere; two months later the luminous track of an unidentified object traveling parallel to the path of Sputnik II was photographed in Venezuela.

9
Physical Evidence

*A Report on the Investigation of Magnesium Samples
From a UFO Explosion Over the Sea
in the Ubatuba Region of Brazil*

BY OLAVO T. FONTES, M.D.

IT IS widely known that since 1947 many people in many places have reported "flying saucers" and other strange objects in the sky. But the absence of physical evidence—such as crashed "saucers"—has been considered the best argument against the existence of such UFOs. In fact, it is difficult to recognize the reality of a flying machine so far advanced as to have reduced to near zero the probability of mechanical failure. Major Edward J. Ruppelt, USAFR, in his excellent book, *A Report on Unidentified Flying Objects,* states that the USAF had never picked up any "hardware" —whole "saucers," pieces or parts—that could not be readily identified as something very earthly.

Such an unexpected occurrence was reported, at last, near the Brazilian coast. It was said a disc-shaped object had exploded over the seashore. Fragments recovered from the explosion were supposed to have fallen, while burning, into shallow waters, which, according to the witnesses, quenched the fire and allowed recovery. I cannot vouch for the story, but only for the identity of the samples received and the details of the investigation that followed. The story of the origin of the samples will be of interest in connection with the results of the chemical analyses which were performed.

On September 14, 1957, Ibrahim Sued, a well-known Rio de Janeiro society columnist, reported a strange story which startled the readers of his column in the newspaper *O Globo*. Under the heading, "A Fragment From a Flying Disc," he wrote:

We received the letter: "Dear Mr. Ibrahim Sued. As a faithful reader of your column and your admirer, I wish to give you something of the highest interest to a newspaperman, about the flying discs. If you believe that they are real, of course. I didn't believe anything said or published about them. But just a few days ago I was forced to change my mind. I was fishing together with some friends, at a place close to the town of Ubatuba, São Paulo, when I sighted a flying disc. It approached the beach at unbelievable speed and an accident, *i.e.* a crash into the sea seemed imminent. At the last moment, however, when it was almost striking the waters, it made a sharp turn upward and climbed rapidly on a fantastic impulse. We followed the spectacle with our eyes, startled, when we saw the disc explode in flames. It disintegrated into thousands of fiery fragments, which fell sparkling with magnificent brightness. They looked like fireworks, despite the time of the accident, at noon, *i.e.* at midday. Most of these fragments, almost all, fell into the sea. But a number of small pieces fell close to the beach and we picked up a large amount of this material—which was as light as paper. I am enclosing a small sample of it. I don't know anyone that could be trusted to whom I might send it for analysis. I never read about a flying disc being found, or about fragments or parts of a saucer that had been picked up. Unless the finding was made by military authorities and the whole thing kept as a top-secret subject. I am certain the matter will be of great interest to the brilliant columnist and I am sending two copies of this letter—to the newspaper and to your home address."

From the admirer (the signature was not legible), together with the above letter, I received fragments of a strange metal . . .

The unusual story stirred my curiosity. Ibrahim Sued had never written about UFOs before. My first thought was the whole thing could be a joke or well-planned hoax. I tried to convince myself this was the obvious explanation, and to dismiss the matter, but I felt something should be done to clarify the doubts raised in my mind. I had to contact Mr. Sued to take a look at the "fragments" and find the answer I was looking for. I phoned him that same day and asked for a meeting to discuss the matter. He agreed. I arrived at his apartment four hours later. There on the table I saw the samples sent by the unidentified correspondent—three small pieces of dull-gray solid substance that appeared to be a metal of some sort. Their surfaces were not smooth and polished, but quite irregular and apparently strongly oxidized. Their appearance suggested they might be, if really metallic, pieces or fragments disintegrated from a larger metallic mass or object; in fact, the surface of one of the samples was shot through with almost microscopic cracks, always longitudinal, and even showed on one face a large longitudinal fissure running through almost two-thirds of its length, as if that piece had been disrupted under the action of some force. The others did not show many cracks or fissures, but the surfaces of all samples were covered in scattered areas with a whitish material. These whitish smears of a powdered substance appeared as a thin layer. The fine, dry powder was adherent, but could be displaced easily with the nail. It also filled the fissures and cracks on the surface of the first sample. This powder presented some similarity with the whitish powdered cinders on a chunk of burned charcoal—as if the fragments had been scorched by some fire or were damaged by too much heat. Two of these samples were later photographed still in their original form.

Mr. Sued said the material appeared to be lead at first sight—because of the gray color—but I would see it could not be lead, a heavy metal, if I felt the weight of the sample in my hands. He was right. The material was light, definitely lighter than aluminum—almost as light as paper. Amazed, I told Mr. Sued I had some friends with scientific backgrounds who might be called in to investigate the samples. He said he knew nothing about UFOs and was even convinced they did not exist. He was not curious about the samples and I could take them. Of course, he would like to know the results if something unusual was found in the analysis. I thanked him for his generous attitude, promising to keep him informed, and picked up the samples.

On examining the data I concluded they offered insufficient solid information for a definite conclusion. A few points, however, attracted my interest:

(1) Mr. Sued's correspondent seemed to be certain about the accuracy of his observations. He had identified the sighted object as a "flying disc." No more details were given. This was a good point on his side. In my psychological experience investigating UFO sightings I have learned the reliability of "saucer reports" appears to vary inversely with the detail the observer reports. The hoaxes are almost always marked by an accurate, precise description of detail, so that we feel the witness was obviously drawing on his imagination. In this incident, however, the observer did not present a vivid description of the "saucer" or of its crash. His story is simple, clear and concise, as it would be in a true case. Besides, in a case where everything was supposed to have happened in a few seconds, it is evident no more details could be expected. Apparently the thing was too rapid for the human vision to fix any detail of the object, except its general shape and trajectory.

(2) The man who supplied the samples said the phenomenon was also witnessed by others. This may give credence to his report.

(3) He was not, apparently, one of the so-called "saucer-cultists." He said he had never heard about "saucer" fragments or parts being found or about a "saucer" crash. A cultist would have a different attitude.

(4) He could be a hoaxer, but a poor one. A good hoaxer would have presented his case in a press conference, to gain publicity for himself. He would never start with a timid letter to a society columnist who ostensibly would not be interested in the matter. Most of all, he would never send the "disc's fragments" in the first letter before knowing Mr. Sued's attitude on UFOs and his possible reaction to the story.

(5) The observer identified the unknown object as a "flying disc." He did not use the popular term "flying saucer," which would be misleading because it is commonly applied to unconventional aerial objects of every conceivable shape, to anything in the sky that cannot be identified as a common, everyday object. In Brazil the term "flying disc" is used only in connection with disc-shaped UFOs—unconventional objects other than "discs" having different terms, such as "flying cigars" for anything cylinder-shaped, "fireballs" for flying spheres or burning ball-shaped objects, etc. We could be reasonably certain the witness really sighted a disc-shaped UFO if the study of the "fragments" would produce valid reason to support his report. Anyway, these considerations about the

object's shape are points to be stressed, chiefly because no details were reported on the object's structure.

(6) The man who supplied the samples was not aware, apparently, that the first man to lock down physical evidence of the interplanetary hypothesis of UFO origin, or of the reality of the phenomena, would go down in history. If he was, he would not give away his samples. Such behavior might be understood only if the sender was a mischievous hoaxer, doing what he did on purpose, or if he was really puzzled and did not comprehend the real importance of his findings.

These reasons explain my interest in obtaining the samples and making a scientific investigation of the material.

The peculiar appearance of the metallic samples (if they were really metallic) indicated they could well be "fragments" originating from the explosion of a larger metallic mass or object, and that they had been burned or scorched by some kind of fire or heat. I decided to enlist the help of chemists of considerable repute. The peculiarities of the material, as well as its obvious light density, constituted a real puzzle that only scientific investigation might solve. I kept the samples for seven days before reaching my decision to send the material to a highly qualified laboratory, one of the best in my country.

The samples (the fragments it was claimed originated in the "explosion" of the reported UFO) were turned over to the Mineral Production Laboratory, a division of the National Department of Mineral Production in the Agriculture Ministry of Brazil. The laboratory is the official Brazilian institution for the examination and analysis of mineral substances, metallic ores, metals and alloys. The samples were registered there as being of "unknown origin" and were delivered personally to Dr. Feigl, the chief chemist. I was introduced to him by a friend, Dr. Julio de Morais. I hoped this famous German chemist would conduct the investigation. However, he was doing experimental studies in organic chemistry and researches on plastics at the time, and he could not make the investigation personally. He called one of his assistants, Dr. David Goldscheim, who made a careful examination of the samples and suggested their physical appearance indicated they might be fragments of meteoric origin. But Dr. Feigl refused to accept such a possibility. "They are too light to be fragments of a meteorite," he said. "They appear to be metallic, made of a lightweight metal. But this metal is not aluminum. I am going to make a chemical test . . ."

A small chip of the material was placed in a test tube. A few drops of phosphomolybdic acid were added, plus a few drops of dilute hydrochloric acid—a qualitative screening test to identify metals. If the material was metallic a blue color would appear in the test tube (phosphomolybdic acid is easily reduced, in the presence of a reducing agent, to produce the blue-colored mixture of colloidal reduced oxides of molybdenum). No change was detected at first; but when the test tube was slightly heated, bubbles appeared on the surface of the material and the blue color was observed. Thus the material (or part of it) was really a metal of some sort.

It was decided that a spectrographic analysis should be made for the identification of the unknown metal in the sample, and to establish the presence of other possible constituents. The spectrographic method is extremely sensitive, making it possible to determine the chemical composition of a piece of metal no larger than the head of a pin. Minute traces of elements can be detected, traces so small they could not possibly be detected by any other known means. Each metal (as well as gasses and a few non-metals) has a spectrum which is uniquely its own, whether it consists of two lines (sodium) or thousands of lines (iron), and whether the element is alone or in combination. Each element, when excited under proper conditions, gives off its spectrum; and all compounds are resolved into their components.

One of the "disc's" fragments (referred to as Sample 1) was preliminarily divided in several pieces. Two of these metallic pieces weighing approximately 0.6 grams each, were sent that same day to the Spectrographic Section of the Mineral Production Laboratory. The others were returned to me, to be kept for other analyses, if necessary. The remaining two "disc's fragments," still in my hands, were also set apart for any future investigation. These were later photographed. Unfortunately, no photograph was taken of Sample 1 in its original form; this was a real oversight.

The large sample (Sample 2) showed clearly the longitudinal fissure and small cracks described previously. The smaller one (Sample 3), which also presented a few small fissures, had a peculiar curved cross-section. This unusual shape might suggest it came from a curved shell, a spheroid object or a dome-shaped device, but in view of the heat required

for oxidation it may not be significant. Both samples presented a quite irregular and apparently strongly oxidized surface. Their dull-gray color contrasted with the whitish areas
covered with the powdered material already described. This
material was presumed to be an oxide of the metal in the
samples, possibly formed when the samples were at ignition
temperature and exposed to air.

I was curious about the results of the spectrographic analysis. I knew the presence or absence in the unknown material
of any of the seventy chemical elements would be revealed
by the spectograph, and no element could be missed if it
constituted as much as the one-millionth part of the whole.
It was planned that the material should be investigated by
other methods, if necessary: (1) a standard "semi-quantita-
tive" spectrographic analysis; (2) an X-ray diffraction analysis; and (3) a special "mass spectrograph" analysis.

(1) Spectrographic Analysis

THE official analysis of the two metallic pieces taken from
Sample 1 was made on September 24, 1957, by the chief
chemist of the Spectrographic Section of the Mineral Production Laboratory, Dr. Luisa Maria A. Barbosa. A routine
exposure was made initially, to identify the metal in the
sample. One of the metallic pieces was burned in an arc
between standard electrodes in an exposure of fixed length.
The metal in the sample was identified as magnesium. Then
a second exposure, using the other metallic piece, was made,
to determine the purity of the metal and to detect other possible elements present in the sample. This exposure was made
by a special method prescribed for highly-sensitive analyses,
using a large Hilger spectrograph for more precise and reliable results. The official report on this spectrographic analysis,
signed by Dr. Barbosa, was received a few days later. (Figure
1A; English translation, Figure 1B. The conclusion was that
the magnesium in the sample was of unusual purity, with no
detectable inclusion of other elements. But since I expected
a more detailed description of the results of the analysis, I
went to the laboratory on September 30, 1957, to meet Dr.
Barbosa and request additional explanation. I tried to im-
press upon her the necessity of a more detailed report including technical data on the spectrum lines recorded on the
photographic plate. We talked for almost an hour. She said
I had no authority to appraise her work, if I were a chem-

ist I would be satisfied with her report, etc. I tried to convince her, but she refused to consider my request for an additional report. In the end I asked some questions about the interpretation of the spectrographic data. Here is a summary of the questions and answers:

Q. Did your analysis show the presence of magnesium of very unusual purity and absence of any other metallic element?

A. Yes, I identified on the film all common and uncommon spectrum lines of the element magnesium. There was no other metallic element in the sample, not even the so-called "trace elements" usually detected in metallic samples.

Q. Your report *suggests* that the metal in the sample was absolutely pure in the spectrographic sense, with a percentage of 100. Why did you not state this very interesting conclusion?

A. Because a pure metal in the spectrographic sense may still contain other possible constituents which could be present in your sample and still escape detection. The method has its limitations. Different compounds or states of combination of the same element, for instance, are not distinguishable by spectrographic analysis. Most of the nonmetallic elements are not detected by it—the exceptions are very few. Thus in this particular case it could be a mixture of the element found with any of its compounds, or a chemical combination with any of those nonmetallic elements—a salt, for example, despite the fact that the appearance of the sample suggests the element as being in its metallic form.

Q. Will you detail the spectrographic plate for me?

A. Of course. Here [showing me the film] you can see five spectra. The spectrum corresponding to the sample analyzed is the first one, at the top of the film. It shows a number of spectrum lines with different strengths, but all of them belong to the same element—they represent the spectrum of magnesium. The other four spectra were made for comparison purposes. The third is also a magnesium spectrum and corresponds to a chemically pure magnesium salt, CO_3Mg. The remaining spectra are iron, Fe, comparison spectra.

A photocopy of the Barbosa spectrographic plate was requested later and obtained.

MINISTÉRIO DA AGRICULTURA
DEPARTAMENTO NACIONAL DA PRODUÇÃO MINERAL
LABORATÓRIO DA PRODUÇÃO MINERAL

BOLETIM N.° 15 001   Em 24 de setembro   de 19 57.

       Análise espetrográfica de material indeterminado.

    Protocolo: 571/57.

    <u>PROCEDÊNCIA</u>: Ubatuba - São Paulo.

    <u>REMETENTE</u>: Dr. Olavo Fontes.

    A amostra recebida constava de dois fragmentos de aspecto me-
talico, côr cinza, baixa densidade e pesando, cada um, aproximadamente
0.6 gramas.

    <u>Resultado da análise de um dos fragmentos:</u>

    A análise espetrográfica revelou a presença de magnésio (Mg)
em alta concentração e ausência de qualquer outro elemento metálico.

                       Luisa Maria A. Barbosa
                       LUISA MARIA A. BARBOSA
                      TECNOLOGISTA QUIMICO "M"

VW.

VISTO

Substituto do Diretor

Figure 1A: Report of the Barbosa spectrographic analysis.

MINISTRY OF AGRICULTURE

NATIONAL DEPARTMENT OF MINERAL PRODUCTION

MINERAL PRODUCTION LABORATORY

BULLETIN NO. 15 001

On September 24, 1957

SPECTROGRAPHIC ANALYSIS OF UNKNOWN MATERIAL

Protocol: 571/57

ORIGIN: Ubatuba, São Paulo.

SENDER: Dr. Olavo Fontes.

The sample received included two fragments of metallic appearance, grey color, low density, and weighing, each one, approximately 0.6 Gm.

REPORT OF THE ANALYSIS OF ONE OF THE FRAGMENTS:

The spectrographic analysis showed the presence of magnesium (Mg) of a high degree of purity and absence of any other metallic element.

(signed)   *Luisa Maria A. Barbosa*
CHEMIST-TECHNOLOGIST "N"

VM/

APPROVED
(the name is not legible)

(signed) . . . .
SUBSTITUTE-DIRECTOR

bulletin of analysis-model DMA 1-412

Figure 1B: Translation of the Barbosa spectrographic analysis.

SPECTROGRAPHIC ANALYSIS
OF UNKNOWN METALLIC MATERIAL

ORIGIN: Ubatuba, São Paulo
SENT BY: Dr. Olavo Fontes
DATE: 10/24/57

The sample received was a small piece of a silvery-white metal, slightly oxidized on its surface and with a very low specific gravity. It came from the same fragment as the sample used in the analysis reported on Bulletin No. 15.001 issued by the Mineral Production Laboratory.

ANALYSIS REPORT

The spectrographic analysis identified the unknown metal as *magnesium* (Mg), and showed it to be *absolutely pure*—as it can be concluded from the study of the spectrographic plate taken with the Hilger Spectrograph. No other metal or impurity was detected in the sample analysed; even the so-called "trace elements," usually found with any metal, were not present.

A photocopy of the original spectrographic plate is shown in *Fig. 2B.* There are five spectra recorded on it.

Each one has a position which is marked by a number already registered in the film. They can be identified, from above to below, as the following:

26	Fe
28	Mg (a salt)
30	Unknown
32	Fe
34	—
36	Fe

A comparison was made between the spectrum of the unknown metal and that of a chempur magnesium salt. It showed clearly that they were identical—in fact, all their spectrum lines corresponded with each other. This demonstrated the *extreme purity* of the metal in the sample. As it is shown in *Fig. 2B.*, all lines in the spectrum of the unknown belong to the element magnesium. Even impurities that might exist in the carbon rod used as electrode (*i.e.*, traces of Mn, Fe, Si and Ti), sometimes appearing as contaminants, were not detected in this case.

A group of representative lines of magnesium was marked on

the spectrographic plate. These eight lines were selected at random, as examples. The 2852.2 (intensity: 500) is the most sensitive of the group; the others follow in sequence, arranged on the basis of their relative intensities.

(signed) *Elson Teixeira*
CHEMIST

(Fig. 2B, referred to in this report, is not reproduced in this volume. EDITOR.)

Fig. 2: Report of the Teixeira spectrographic analysis (translated).

To confirm the results of the first investigation and to obtain a more accurate evaluation of the findings, I requested a second spectrographic analysis of the material. It was made on October 24, 1957. Another metallic chip from Sample 1 was put under the Hilger spectrograph by Elson Teixeira who for fifteen years had handled spectrochemical analysis at the Mineral Production Laboratory. His experience included more than fifty thousand spectrographic determinations. He had left the laboratory a few years earlier to enter business, but he still had permission to use the laboratory's facilities. He agreed to make a second spectrogram of the magnesium sample instead of doing a report on the analysis made by Dr. Barbosa. His problem was to determine whether or not the magnesium was of absolute purity in the spectrographic sense.

He used special technical procedures to control the many variables that might influence the results (such as atmospheric contaminants, dirty electrodes, etc.) Mr. Teixeira's analysis was translated verbatim. (*Figure* 2). He had also planned a "semiquantitative" spectrographic analysis to establish the percentages of any possible impurities not detected in the previous spectrogram of the magnesium sample. But his analysis confirmed the reported absence of impurities of any kind and therefore he felt that the "semiquantitative" test was obviously unnecessary.

The spectrographic film accompanying Teixeira's analysis was sent to me.

Incidentally, the two spectrographic analyses included in this report were not the only ones made of the magnesium samples. A third spectrographic study of the material was conducted by the military. The Brazilian Army had been informed about the case, and I was contacted by Major Roberto Caminha, who requested and received a sample of the material on November 4, 1957. The military analysis was made at ITM (Military Institute of Technology), but I was not informed of the findings. It was intimated a complete investigation would be ordered by the Brazilian Army, but I was unable to confirm this information.

Another small fragment (the last piece of Sample 1) was given to Commander J. G. Brandao of the Brazilian Navy, who contacted me a few months later. No information was obtained concerning the methods employed and the results in this investigation, but there are reasons to assume a spectrographic test (the fourth) was made at the Navy arsenal in Rio de Janeiro.

(B) *X-Ray Diffraction Analysis*

SINCE the spectrochemical analysis by Dr. Barbosa indicated the metal in the samples was pure in the spectrographic sense, other tests became necessary to correct the limitations of the spectrographic method and to investigate the possibility of nonmetallic impurities in the material. The remaining fragments of Sample 1 were sent to the Laboratory of Crystallography of the Geology and Mineralogy of the National Department of internal Production—for X-ray diffraction studies. The director and chief chemist of this research institution, Dr. Elysiario Tavora Filho, is recognized for his pioneer works on crystallography since 1949, and is professor of mineralogy at the National Chemistry School. He is responsible for the results presented below. In my opinion his work is complete and flawless in every detail.

The X-ray method of chemical identification was obviously indicated to complete the results obtained with the spectrographic analysis of the magnesium samples. The advantages of the procedure are that only small quantities of the material to be investigated (only a few Mg) are required, and that different compounds or states of combinations of the same elements are distinguishable since they posses different crystal structures. It is widely used for the identification of alloy phases. If more than one variety of crystal is present in any specimen, each will produce its spectrum independently (a very important fact to remember), and the pattern will consist of superimposed spectra with relative intensities depending on the relative amounts of the phases. Thus, the constitution of inorganic and organic systems, minerals and alloy systems can be determined with accuracy through X-ray crystallography. Besides, X-rays are also applied for chemical analysis through the use of X-ray spectrometers that record the characteristic X-ray emission lines, or absorption edges, of the sample. Favorable combinations of elements permit *extreme sensitivity* in the detection of small percentages of an element in a compound or mixture (independent of the state of chemical combination), and also permit fair precision in quantitative analysis.[1]

Because the precise results of X-ray diffraction analysis, together with the advantages noted above, make it a sensitive method to determine the composition and structure of metals, it was decided to use this analytic procedure in the investigation of the magnesium samples. The conclusion that the metal was of absolute purity (in the spectrographic sense), with no detectable inclusions of other elements, was one all previous investigators hesitated to accept without confirmation by another method.

A preliminary identification of the samples by X-ray spectrometry confirmed the previous report. The metal was really magnesium—and appeared to be of unusual purity, with a precentage of about 100. Amazed by this truly incredible result, Professor Filho repeated the spectrometric examination several times—always with the same findings. He then decided to request a careful re-examination of the spectrographic plate to recheck the reported results of the spectrographic analysis. One of his assistants, Dr. Augusto Batista, was sent on that mission to the Mineral Production Laboratory. Informed about these unexpected developments, I was puzzled and failed to recognize the significance of Professor Filho's approach. He adopted a reserved attitude concerning the motivations for his decision, and I was unable to get any clue from Dr. Batista. As I was informed later, however, Professor Filho had realized the full implications of the reported absence of any impurity in the samples. The X-ray diffraction diagram matched a standard diagram of high quality that was available for comparison, printed on a card from the current X-ray powder data file (and its accompanying index volume). That "standard" diffraction pattern had been produced, however, using the available ASTM standard of purity

[1] Von Hevesy, G.: *Chemical Analysis by X-Rays and Its Application.* McGraw-Hill, New York, 1932.

for magnesium (ASTM 4-0770), which is the spectrographic analysis still showed several impurities. The conclusion was that the magnesium in the samples would be purer than the ASTM "standard of purity" for that metal. It would be a truly incredible discovery, one that could not be accepted easily. Therefore a verification of the spectrographic analysis was ordered. When he saw the reported results confirmed, Professor Filho was probably inclined to reject the whole thing at first sight. But he had no choice. As a true scientist, he could not discard the hard, cold facts of the evidence obtained in the previous analysis. So he decided to use the most sensitive procedure available at his laboratory to settle the question, if possible. He decided to make a careful and complete study of the powder diffraction pattern of the magnesium in the samples, using the powder method.

Professor Filho's Laboratory of Crystallography is equipped with the most elaborate and sensitive instruments for X-ray diffractometry and spectrometry available anywhere. A powder camera of the Debye-Scherrer-Hull type was employed. A fine-grained polycrystalline specimen of the magnesium sample was prepared. Its diffraction pattern was recorded on a special photographic film (of the cylindrical type) and that film was the object of careful examination. From the position of the lines on the film—the so-called "Debye rings"—the spacing d of the corresponding atomic planes was determined. From the X-ray picture, supplemented by other data, Filho determined space lattices, the spacing d already mentioned (interplanar distances) and the values of Θ (bonding angle). The relative intensity of each line (or arc) on the film was also measured. The pattern obtained matched the diffraction pattern of the ASTM standard of purity of magnesium referred to above (ASTM 4-0770). All lines in the film were accounted for with the exception of six very faint ones. These did not correspond to the metal. They indicated that the sample contained inclusions of an unknown crystalline substance, which was present in very small amounts.

Was it the impurity of impurities the chemists were attempting to detect since the first examination? The identification of this unknown material was the next step, for obvious reasons. But this task was going to be difficult because the unidentified component was not present in sufficient amount to give a characteristic diffraction diagram. In fact, the six reflections in the film which were not accounted for were too weak to be used. A possible method to solve this problem was to expose different films for different lengths of time, thus making possible the measurement of strong intensities on one film and weak intensities on another. However, Filho decided on another approach.

The appearance of the "fragments" suggested that at some time they had been subjected to violent oxidation over all their surfaces, which were covered with a powdered non-metallic material presumed to be magnesium oxide. This oxide, in Filho's opinion, might possibly be present *within* the body of the samples—as the unidentified constituent. A plausible theory, and consistent with the claimed origin of the samples. The oxide formed on the surface of molten magnesium exposed to air would be present within the metal as a result of oxygen diffusion through the samples at ignition temperature. A microscopic examination made by Batista showed findings that appeared to support this theory. In fact, some of the small magnesium chips (taken from Sample 1) were covered with the powdered substance at points that corresponded to the surface of the original "fragments," and showed a few cracks and small fissures also filled with the same material. In these areas the crystalline metal was shot through with fissures containing that material too. On the other hand, it is true such areas were scattered and small—most of the samples showing only the crystalline pattern of pure metal. Besides, under microscopic examination, powdered specimens showed only a kind of crystal. They did not present any visible trace of the nonmetallic inclusions. Obviously, the mixture was not homogenous: the nonmetallic component was more abundant in areas close to the surface of the original sample; it might be present within the metallic mass, but in very small amounts, possibly in sufficient amount to explain the six unidentified lines on the film. As to the grain structure of the metal itself, Batista was almost sure the samples were fragments of a magnesium casting. Unfortunately, their appearance suggested they were not from the surface of the original casting, but came from *within* the metallic mass disrupted in the explosion; as a result, no information could be obtained on the thermal and mechanical treatment involved in the production of the casting. He also verified that the heat developed in the fragments when they were at ignition temperature had influenced physical and chemical properties at the surface of the molten metal, but apparently was too brief to produce gross melting or other recognizable changes in the grain structure. The accuracy of these observations was apparently confirmed by the diffraction pattern for the magnesium in the samples.

These findings supported the hypothesis that magnesium oxide was the unknown component. Since the patterns of known materials can be used to identify the composition of an unknown constituent, the diffraction lines of magnesium oxide was studied. It was found the unidentified lines on the X-ray film did not belong to that pattern. Therefore the composition of the dry, white powder on the surface of the samples should be determined too, and a second diffraction pattern was made, using this material. As a result, the non-metallic powder was identified as magnesium hydroxide, $Mg(OH)_2$, plus magnesium in its metallic form. The hydroxide was obviously the unknown component already detected, for the unidentified lines on the first film corresponded with the diffraction pattern of this substance. No evidence was found concerning magnesium oxide, which was not present at least in the analyzed samples (from Sample 1). If a surface film of oxide was eventually formed while the molten fragments were falling through the air, or during the initial melting stage, it certainly was removed when the heated metal was cooling rapidly in the sea water. It is evident, on the other hand, the hydroxide in the samples was not a constituent of the metal in its original form, appearing as an effect of oxidation in contact with water (the fall into the sea of the burning magnesium fragments, if the story of the samples' origin is true).

The diffraction patterns recorded for magnesium and magnesium hydroxide were presented side by side in the photocopies of the original Filho films that were obtained.

The X-ray diffraction diagrams determined for each material, in comparison with the standard diagrams of the respective ASTM standards of purity, are presented in *Figure 3A*, which is a photocopy of Filho's original report on the X-ray diffraction analyses of the magnesium samples.

For those who possess the technical background necessary for an interpretation of technical data presented in the Filho diagrams, a translation of his report is presented in *Figure 3B*.

Professor Filho's promised written statement on the possible origin of the magnesium samples, in the light of the data obtained with X-ray diffraction analyses, was not received. Due to the unexpected results he found, Filho decided only numerical data should be released: written statements or conclusions of any kind could not be issued because he didn't want to discuss certain problems connected with the origin of the samples.

(3) *Radiation Tests*

THE relative density of the magnesium samples (expressed in terms of water at 4° C.) was measured at the Laboratory of Crystallography by Dr. Batista. The method used was the classical procedure involving two weighings, the relative density of the metal being determined by a simple formula (the weight of the specimen in the air divided by the loss of weight when suspended in water). A Jolly balance of the type used by mineralogists was employed.

Previous studies suggested large pieces of the metal should not be used. Their surfaces were covered with magnesium hydroxide, a denser material; areas within the crystalline metal with inclusions of this material were also observed. One of the two remaining "fragments" (Sample 2), for example, evidently contained more hydroxide inclusions than the other one (Sample 3), but the appearance of both samples indicated their relative densities would not correspond to the values predicted for magnesium.

In fact, they would represent only the average densities of samples containing unknown amounts of a denser material. To solve the problem, Batista selected a small metallic chip taken from the center of the divided "fragment" (Sample 1) for the density determination. This specimen was carefully polished until the silvery-white surface of pure magnesium showed no trace of hydroxide under microscopic examination. Such a sample should have a density of about 1.741, but a significantly higher density was found—the carefully measured density of this magnesium sample was 1.866. The procedure was repeated three times with a microbalance, and the same value was found each time.

How could this discrepancy be explained? Three possibilities had to be considered: (1) a hitherto unknown, close-packed modification of ordinary magnesium (this was not the case, because X-ray diffraction had identified the ordinary crystal structure of that metal (close-packed hexagonal) in the sample); (2) inclusion of a denser constituent in the sample; or (3) unusual distribution of the three stable, natural isotopes that make up terrestrial magnesium, *i.e.*, a dif-

Ministerio da Agricultura

Magnesio					Hidroxido de Magnesio				
Amestr. Recebida			Padrae ASTM 4-0770		Amestra Recebida			Padrae ASTM 1-1169	
d A	Intensity	hkil	d A	Intensity	d A	Intensity	hkil	d A	Intensity
4.79	* mtmtfc				4.79	mtmtfrt	0001	4.75	53
2.78	mtmtfrt	1010	2.780	35	2.78 **	mtmtfrc			
					2.71	mtmtfrc	1010		
2.607	mtfrt	0002	2.606	41	2.61 **	mtfrc			
2.458	mtmtfrt	1011	2.453	100	2.46 **	mtfrc			
2.36	* mtmtfrc				2.36	mtmtfrt	0002	2.35	100
1.900	frt	1012	1.901	20	1.90 **	mtmtfrc			
1.800	* mtmtfrc				1.798	md	1012	1.79	40
1.603	md	1120	1.605	18	1.60 **	mtmtfrc			
1.57	mtmtfrc				1.574	frt	{ 1120, 0003	1.57	33
					1.495	md	1121	1.49	17
1.473	frt	1013	1.473	18					
1.389	frc	2020	1.389	2					
					1.372	dif	2020	1.37	13
1.367	md	1122	1.366	16					
1.342	md	2021	1.343	9					
					1.310	dif	{ 1122, 2021	1.31	9
1.304	md	0004	1.303	2					
1.225	frc	2022	1.227	2					
					1.184	dif	0004	1.18	7
1.179	frc	{ 1014, 1123	1.1795	2					
1.085	md	2023	1.0851	2					
1.050	mtfrc	2130	1.0506	1					
					1.0305	dif	{ 2130, 2023	1.03	3
1.029	frc	2131	1.0296	7					
1.011	frc	1124	1.0112	3					
					1.0074	dif	2131	1.01	4
0.9753	md	1015	0.9757	2					
					0.9473	dif	0005	0.95	4
0.9259	mtfrc	3030	0.9265	1					
					0.9091	dif	3030		
0.8990	md	2133	0.8988	4					
					0.8933	dif	{ 1015, 2024, 3031		
0.8737	frc	3032	0.8729	2					
					0.8660	dif	2133	0.86	1
0.8341	mtfrc	2025	0.8337	2					
0.8280	dif	1016	0.8288	1					
					0.8180	dif	1125		
0.8173	dif	2134	0.8177	1					
0.8109	dif	3033							
					0.7860	dif	{ 2241, 2134, 2025		

Convencões:

*—Reflexão devida ao Mg(OH)₂   md—Reflexão média
**—Reflexão devida ao Magnesio   frc—Reflexão fraca
mtmtfrt—Reflexão muite muite forte   mtfrc—Reflexão muite fraca
mtfrt—Reflexão muite forte   mtmtfrc—Reflexão muite muite
frt—Reflexão forte   fraca

Figure 3A: The original X-ray diffraction report.

| Magnesium | | | | | Magnesium Hydroxide | | | |
| Sample received | | Standard ASTM 4-0770 | | | Sample received | | Standard ASTM 1-1169 | |
d A	Intensity	hkil	d A	Intensity	d A	Intensity	hkil	d A	Intensity
4.79	* mtmtfc				4.79	mtmtfrt	0001	4.75	53
2.78	mtmtfrt	1010	2.780	35	2.78	** mtmtfrc			
					2.71	mtmtfrc	1010		
2.607	mtfrt	0002	2.606	41	2.61	** mtfrc			
2.458	mtmtfrt	1011	2.453	100	2.46	** mtfrc			
2.36	* mtmtfrc				2.36	mtmtfrt	0002	2.35	100
1.900	frt	1012	1.901	20	1.90	** mtmtfrc			
1.800	* mtmtfrc				1.798	md	1012	1.79	40
1.603	md	1120	1.605	18	1.60	** mtmtfrc			
1.57	* mtmtfrc				1.574	frt	1120 / 0003	1.57	33
					1.495	md	1121	1.49	17
1.473	frt	1013	1.473	18					
1.389	frc	2020	1.389	2	1.372	dif	2020	1.37	13
1.367	md	1122	1.366	16					
1.342	md	2021	1.343	9	1.310	dif	1122 / 2021	1.31	9
1.304	md	0004	1.303	2					
1.225	frc	2022	1.227	2	1.184	dif	0004	1.18	7
1.179	frc	1014 / 1123	1.1795	2					
1.085	md	2023	1.0851	2					
1.050	mtfrc	2130	1.0506	1	1.0305	dif	2130 / 2023	1.03	3
1.029	frc	2131	1.0296	7	1.0074	dif	2131	1.01	4
1.011	frc	1124	1.0112	3					
0.9753	md	1015	0.9757	2	0.9473	dif	0005	0.95	4
0.9259	mtfrc	3030	0.9265	1	0.9091	dif	3030		
0.8990	md	2133	0.8988	4	0.8933	dif	1015 / 2024 / 3031		
0.8737	frc	3032	0.8729	2	0.8660	dif	2133	0.86	1
0.8341	mtfrc	2025	0.8337	2	0.8180	dif	1125		
0.8280	dif	1016	0.8288	1					
0.8173	dif	2134	0.8177	1	0.7860	dif	2241 / 2134 / 2025		
0.8109	dif	3033							

Abbreviations and Symbols:

*—Reflection due to Mg (OH)$_2$
**—Reflection due to Magnesium
mtmtfrt—Very very strong reflection
mtfrt—Very strong reflection
frt—Strong reflection

md—Medium reflection
frc—Weak reflection
mtfrc—Very weak reflection
mtmtfrc—Very very weak reflection

Figure 3B: Translation of the X-ray diffraction report.

ferent isotopic constitution in the magnesium of the samples.

Interpretation of the available data suggested the second possibility was the most plausible explanation. It was possible a small inclusion of hydroxide was still present in the specimen (rendered plausible by the X-ray diffraction analysis). The density measurements gave no ground for reliance on an unusual isotopic ratio. On the other hand, the powder diffraction pattern showed hydroxide was mixed with the pure metal in very small amounts—too small, apparently, to explain the high density found. This discrepancy can be resolved only with careful determinations, using several metallic chips taken from the samples. It is evident the hydroxide cannot be evenly distributed through the whole metallic mass, and tests with different samples will show different densities. If any of the density measurements corresponds to the expected value for terrestrial magnesium, the problem is solved. But if any discrepancy remains—even a small one—then a mass spectrographic analysis is necessary to study the isotopic constitution of the magnesium samples. The reasons will be discussed in another section of this report.

The magnesium in the samples analyzed, which was absolutely pure in the spectrographic sense, represents something outside the range of present-day technological development in earth science. In fact, the metal was of such fantastic purity that even to see it symbolized on paper is unbelievable. Even the infinitesimal quantities of "trace elements" usually detected by spectrographic analysis—traces so small they could not possibly be detected by any other analytical method—were not found. Thus, the magnesium in the samples was absolutely pure in the spectrographic sense—with a percentage of 100. X-ray spectrometry and X-ray diffractometry by the powder method confirmed the results of the spectrographic analyses—the metal was pure magnesium. Again, no impurity was detected to introduce irregularities in the crystal lattice. The presence of any impurity of any interstitial atoms would change the regularity of the crystal lattice, thus causing crystal imperfections that would be revealed by the X-ray method. Therefore, on the basis of the chemical analyses the conclusion was that the magnesium in the samples was of *absolute purity,* in the sense that any other possible constituents which could be present would be present in such an infinitesimal amount as to be beyond the reach of any known method of chemical analysis.

We know very little about metals completely free of impurities and imperfections, simply because they are never found in nature and, in most cases, cannot be prepared in the laboratory. It is not too difficult to refine a metal to 99.99% purity (which means there is something else besides the metal to the extent of 1 part in 10,000), but once beyond this point the going gets rough. For every 9 we tack on after the decimal point following the first two 9s, the cost increases tenfold, sometimes a hundredfold. This is so because involved, delicate and time-consuming crystallization operations are required so that the final product becomes more precious than gold.

In the study of the properties of absolutely pure metals the first problem is to secure them. As a matter of fact, the task seemed hopeless for any metal until eight years ago when the American metallurgist Walter Pfann invented the zone-refining process, which promises to be one of the outstanding developments in the story of the metallurgist's efforts to produce "super-pure" metals. With this method it is possible to produce germanium and molybdenum (also iron and titanium, according to some sources of information) of almost absolute purity. However, even with this process, everything has to be done piecemeal: metals cannot be purified continuously. This one great drawback to the large-scale production of pure metals seems now to have been overcome by a new development announced by Dr. Pfann five years ago. His new invention, based on the zone-refining method and called "continuous multistage zone refining," will make it possible to obtain pure metal in a continuous flow.

Such is the situation concerning the latest developments in the field of "super-pure" metals. A few can already be refined to approach absolute purity, but the problem still remains unsolved for the other metals, because of technical difficulties not yet solved. Magnesium is included in this latter group. In other words, to produce magnesium of absolute purity is still an impossible task. Getting rid of the last bit of impurity is *impossible,* even in the laboratory. If this postulate is correct the magnesium in the samples analyzed could not have been produced here or recovered from the explosion of a man-made missile or vehicle. It is, then, of interest to discuss the matter further for direct and indirect support of the postulate.

Magnesium occurs abundantly on earth, but never in the

pure state—always in combination. The meteorites (almost entirely composed of common silicates and nickel-iron) reaching earth may contain magnesium, but always in combination (magnesium oxides, silicates, etc.), never in the pure state. The production of metallic magnesium requires special extraction and refining methods, the most widely used being the process of electrolytic reduction of magnesium chloride derived from sea water, natural brines, potash waste liquors, dolomite and magnesite. Thermal-reduction processes are also available; they are of two types—one using carbon (the Hansgirg process), the other using ferrosilicon (the Pidgeon process)—for the reduction of magnesium oxide derived from magnesite, dolomite or sea water.

Refined commercial magnesium of a purity of 99.8% Mg (pure magnesium, ASTM: B 92-45) can be produced by any of these methods in the form of ingots, powder, ribbon, wire and extruded and rolled strips. Impurities such as iron, nickel and copper have definite tolerance limits because the quantity and state of these impurities determine the resistance of the metal to corrosion. Some elements are not harmful in large proportions, but others are detrimental even when present in minute amounts. Calcium is usually present in very small quantities, chiefly in solid solution; if present in amounts greater than approximately 0.1%, calcium occurs as Mg_2Ca. It is not harmful, and in some magnesium alloys (M1 and AZ31X), it is added to improve such characteristics as the grain size of the ingot, rolling properties and ductility. Excessive amounts, however, are considered detrimental to welding characteristics in some alloys.

In common with aluminum and many other metals, magnesium is not used commercially without alloying. Manganese, zinc, zirconium and aluminum are the chief alloying components of magnesium alloys. Magnesium-cerium and magnesium-thorium alloys are more recent developments.

Silicon is the impurity usually picked up in ordinary foundry operations and occurs generally as Mg_2Si. If present in amounts of 0.5% or more, it changes the regularity in the crystal lattice, causing defects in the magnesium crystals.

The presence of even a few hundredths per cent of manganese greatly increases the tolerance limit for iron (which is 0.017% for pure magnesium) and also for nickel.

Composition limits for commercially pure magnesium (ASTM B 92-45 for ingot and stick) are: Pure magnesium sheet, wire extrusions, ribbon, and ingot and stick for remelting: 99.80% Mg min.; impurities (max.), 0.02% Cu, 0.001% Ni, 0.20% total of Al, Cu, Fe, Mn, Ni and Si. Powder, grade C: 96% Mg min.; impurities (max.), metallic Fe 0.05%, insoluble residue 0.25%, Si 0.10%, grease and oil 0.020%, alloyed iron and aluminum as oxides 0.40%.[2]

It is evident the quantities of impurities found in commercially pure magnesium vary according to sources of production and methods employed. In any case, however, they are always present, even in the composition of the purest commercial magnesium available. It can be concluded that no commercially pure magnesium exists with a composition at all like that of the samples analyzed.

To complete the investigation on this important point, I decided to test the accuracy of the spectrograph in detecting these impurities in commercially pure magnesium. But typical samples of this metal were not available; the metal is not produced in Brazil, except in powdery or granular form. As an alternative, tests were made using chempur magnesium salts and samples of commercially pure tin and lead. All elements whose presence was predicted in each sample, even the so-called "trace" elements, were detected in spectrograms made with the same Hilger spectrograph used for the magnesium samples. The Teixeira investigation confirmed the high precision and accuracy of the instrument. It also eliminated the possibility of other constituents which could escape detection. On the basis of these studies, it is evident the person who supplied the samples could not have obtained them from any available source.

The ASTM standard of purity for magnesium (ASTM 4-0770) shows in spectrographic analysis the following impurities: Ca 0.1%; and traces of Al, Cu, Fe and Si[3]. This is the purest magnesium that can be produced by present-day processing methods and refining technologies of terrestrial metallurgy. The conclusion is that the magnesium in the samples analyzed, which was absolutely pure in the spectrographic sense, is better in quality than the purest magnesium refined on this planet and represents something outside the range of present-day technological developments in earth science.

On the basis of this evidence, it is highly probable the

[2] Townsend, R. A.: *Properties of Magnesium and Magnesium Alloys.* ASTM Metals Handbook, Cleveland, 1954.

[3] Swanson and Tatge: *J.C. Fell Reports.* NBS, 1951.

metallic chunks picked up on the beach near Ubatuba, in São Paulo, Brazil, are extraterrestrial in origin. This is indeed an extremely important and almost incredible conclusion. But on the basis of the findings of these chemical analyses there is no other alternative. As staggering as the implications may be, this appears to be the only acceptable explanation. Therefore, the magnesium samples analyzed must represent "physical evidence" of the reality and extraterrestrial origin of a UFO destroyed in an explosion over the Ubatuba region. They are, in fact, "fragments" of an extraterrestrial vehicle which met with disaster in the earth's atmosphere, as reported by human beings who witnessed the catastrophe. The gratifying aspect of this case, however, is that we do not have to depend on the testimony of witnesses to establish the reality of the incident, for the most advanced laboratory tests indicate the fragments recovered could not have been produced through the application of any known terrestrial techniques.

Further investigation of the incident will be necessary, of course, but only to complete the information already obtained and, if possible, to obtain more samples of the material for additional examinations. I had in my possession three fragments of the "flying disc." Sample 1 was used for the chemical analysis made in Brazil. Sample 2 was divided and a large piece, roughly a rectangular prism approximately 1.2 x 0.7 x 0.7 centimeters, was sent to Coral E. Lorenzen, director of the Aerial Phenomena Research Organization in Alamogordo, New Mexico. This sample can be used for other analyses, if necessary. However, if other tests are needed for a critical evaluation of the Brazilian analyses, special precautions must be taken from a technical viewpoint. The reasons are obvious. It is far more difficult to prove the "absolute purity" of a metallic sample than to show the presence of "impurities." Thus, spectroscopic tests cannot be accepted because they are based on the visual impression of the technician conducting the test—they cannot be rechecked by other observers. Spectrographic tests done in a routine manner, using standard electrodes and making an exposure of a fixed length, cannot be accepted either. A spectrum must be run on the electrodes for reference, and possible impurities in the carbon rods used as electrodes (such as traces of Mn, Fe, Si and Ti) sometimes appear as contaminants; they cannot be subtracted out on the basis of a standard assumption of purity, *i.e.,* assuming that all electrodes have the same impurity content. Many variables have to be controlled, such as atmospheric contaminants, dirty electrodes, use of different electrodes, use of different excitations techniques, etc. These are some of the corrective measures to avoid mistakes, especially in this case, in which a claim of "absolute purity" was established on the basis of chemical examinations. We need a true scientific research, not a routine examination of the samples. Incidentally, Sample 2 was not analyzed in Brazil, but there is no logical reason to suspect it is less pure than the other—the material is similar in appearance and came from the same object.

Density measurements of magnesium chips from Sample 2 must be made to resolve the discrepancy represented by the high density found in previous tests. If any discrepancy still remains a mass-spectrographic analysis is indicated, to study the isotopic constitution of the magnesium in the samples.

Magnesium has five isotopes, but only three are stable; the two others are unstable, having a very short half-life. It is a striking fact that, with few exceptions, the relative abundance of the isotopes for each element is the same once and for all. The exceptions are the elements Pb, He, C, O, N and S. Apart from these minor exceptions, in the early geological period in which minerals were formed a certain isotopic constitution appears to have prevailed over the material now accessible to our investigation. (*Figure 4* shows the isotopic abundance of terrestrial magnesium.)

Isotope	Percent Natural Abundance	Half-Life	Atomic Mass
Mg^{23}		11.9 sec	
Mg^{24}	78.6		23.99189
Mg^{25}	10.1		24.99277
Mg^{26}	11.3		25.99062
Mg^{27}		9.6 m.	

Figure 4

A higher density might indicate a different isotopic constitution in the magnesium of the samples, if the possibility of a small inclusion of hydroxide is excluded after a careful evaluation. An unusual isotopic distribution—probably a pre-eminence of the heavier isotopes 25 and 26—would be absolute proof of the extraterrestrial origin of the metal, in my opinion.

Are the relative abundances of the isotopes of each element characteristic only for the earth? We don't know. The little material we possess derived from the investigation of meteorites (which, presumably, are members of our solar system, too), shows they present the same relative abundance as the elements known in the laboratory. If this could be proved for all the planets in our solar system, and for planets in other solar systems, the possibility of metals with unusual isotopic constitution could not be discussed. With our present knowledge, however, we must be prepared to consider it in this case at least as an interesting theoretical possibility. For technical reasons such a study was not made in Brazil. A mass-spectrographic analysis may solve the problem. Or perhaps the isotopes can be identified by their microwave spectra; if so, microwave spectroscopy might serve as a quick means of measuring how much of what kind of isotope is present, to at least show if the magnesium is a naturally or artificially mixed sample.

The available evidence seems valid enough to establish that the magnesium fragments were recovered from the explosion of an aerial object of artificial origin; that this disc-shaped object was not a man-made missile, an artificial satellite or a remote-controlled device—but an aerial machine of extraterrestrial origin. The question of the place, means and purpose of the original fabrication cannot be solved with the evidence at hand. Yet a few deductions can be attempted to explain the mystery of the UFO's sudden explosion and some other important issues of the Ubatuba incident.

(1) The lack of physical evidence (such as crashed UFOs) has been accepted as the best argument against UFO reality. In fact, it is difficult to admit the existence of a flying machine so far advanced as to reduce the probability of mechanical failure to near zero or even to believe that UFOs utilized a principle of flight unknown to us. The Ubatuba incident, however, established the fact these alien craft are not free of the failure factor—they can be destroyed by unexpected failure of their flight mechanism as can any ordinary aircraft. There is still an important difference to be emphasized—UFOs never crash, as do ordinary planes, possibly because of their material and the peculiar characteristics of the particular accident itself. The Ubatuba incident suggests the effect of a mechanical failure is such that in a split

second the UFO explodes with prodigious kinetic force; there is a vivid flash followed in a few seconds by disintegration and thermic volatilization—and the object vanishes in a shower of fiery sparks. As a result, no fragments or parts of the UFO are found in most cases of accident, especially if the explosion occurs high in the sky, since the UFO would be completely burned to cinders long before reaching the ground. In the Ubatuba case there were two fortunate circumstances to change the usual sequence of events. First, the disc-shaped UFO was very low in the sky at the moment of the accident. Second, the explosion was over the sea, yet close enough to the shore to permit recovery of fragments dropped in shallow waters. If the burning metallic debris reached the ground, it would certainly be entirely consumed by the fire. As it happened, the magnesium fire was smothered; the water quenched the burning and allowed the recovery of "physical evidence."

(2) There are, or were, two well-known uses of magnesium that unfortunately convey a wrong impression with regard to its inflammability. At one time magnesium was known to the general public only as the powder or ribbon used by the photographers to produce a brilliant flash of light. More recently the magensium incendiary bomb has confirmed the popular idea of extreme inflammability. Both the photographer's ribbon and fire bomb are special cases, however, and must not be taken as indicating the properties to be expected in the engineering applications of magnesium. Magnesium powder and ribbon burn easily because in a free atmosphere the temperature may be quickly raised to a temperature well above that used for normal melting operations in the foundry. Normally the ignition of magnesium depends on the mass. Fine powder burns readily; components of normal masses as used in engineering cannot be ignited by any normal accidental method. The conclusion is that in the Ubatuba incident the explosion shattered the magnesium container (the UFO's shell) and then ignited the fragments of the object's disintegration. On the other hand, it is true that water usually is ineffective to extinguish a magnesium fire. Burning magnesium uses outside oxygen, and at the high temperature of this reaction it will also burn in the oxygen of the water, setting the hydrogen free.

There is, however, one exception to this general rule, which explains the Ubatuba case. It is possible to stop the reaction by suddenly supplying a great mass of cold water, thus taking away the heat more rapidly than it is being produced. When this happens, we may find a certain amount of magnesium hydroxide on the surface of the metal (instead of the oxide), which acts protectively. There was magnesium hydroxide in the Ubatuba samples, and no oxide was found—evidence that the UFO's metallic debris was still at ignition temperature when it reached the sea.

There is nothing theoretical or imaginary in all this. The deductions are inherent in the evidence itself. Such evidence gives us a clear picture of what happens when the flight mechanism of UFOs of the type seen over Ubatuba is suddenly put out of operation by an unexpected engine failure. It suggests an explanation for the lack of "physical evidence" in similar cases reported, and explains why this "physical evidence" was present in the Ubatuba case.

(3) Magnesium is the lightest structural metal. Its extreme lightness and good mechanical properties explain the ever-increasing use of magnesium alloys in the aircraft industry. A more recent application is its use in the manufacture of artificial satellites. Sputnik I was made of a magnesium-aluminum alloy. The Vanguard's shell is magnesium-coated inside and out with gold (.0005-inch thick) and covered on the outside with layers of chromium, silicon monoxide, aluminum and silicon monoxide (total thickness of the multilayered shell: 1/33 inch). The gold coating and outer layers were added because magnesium cannot maintain the temperatures needed for the proper functioning of instruments inside the satellite. Its high thermal conductivity dissipates heat rapidly.

Pure magnesium, on the other hand, has a low structural strength and is not used in aircraft or missiles. Similarly, it could not be the chief constituent in an interplanetary vehicle of another culture. In fact, pure magnesium serves no conceivable mechanical purpose in competition with other available materials—at least apparently. In spite of this, the evidence available in the Ubatuba case is that *"flying discs"* (at least the type involved in the explosion) are made of magnesium of very unusual purity. Metals of other kinds possibly existed inside that UFO, but were not found. The small magnesium pieces picked up near the beach apparently came from the object's shell. They suggest that shell was made of magnesium of absolute purity, *i.e.,* with a material of low structural strength. We can't explain this fact yet. The intrinsic properties of absolutely pure metals are not known.

More and more it is being realized in chemistry and metallurgy that trace elements have enormously potent effects. For instance, really pure iron has a strength a hundred times as great as that of commercially pure iron. Titanium, which is almost as strong as structural steel and as light as aluminum, fails miserably if it is contaminated with as little as .02% of hydrogen. Accordingly, absolutely pure magnesium with perhaps undreamed-of properties may be, perhaps, the metal of the future. Some day when we shall be privileged to study its properties we will know why it is used in "flying discs."

Another possibility—if the extreme purity of the metal had no special purpose but only expressed the advanced technology of its production—is that the Ubatuba UFO was not manned. It could have been a small, automatic, remote-controlled device launched by spacecraft in the earth's atmosphere to pick up scientific data. Several of these objects containing scanning instruments might be released from the same craft and controlled from a distance. In such a case, extreme lightness would be far more important than structural strength. Our own artificial satellites clearly show this possibility.

(4) To ignite magnesium it is first necessary for the metal to reach its melting point—650° C. (1202° F.). In the Ubatuba incident this high temperature was reached instantly at the moment the UFO exploded. "It disintegrated into thousands of fiery fragments," reported the witness, "which fell sparkling with magnificent brightness. They looked like fireworks despite the time of the accident, noon . . ." This is a perfect description of a magnesium fire, of burning magnesium fragments with their brilliant actinic light. Such a report offers a clear idea about the amount of thermic energy released in the explosion. Certainly it was not a common explosion.

The mystery of that sudden explosion probably will never be solved. It may have been produced by the release of some self-destroying mechanism to prevent the machine from falling into our hands and thus giving us the chance to learn its secrets. There is also the bare possibility of an atomic explosion. We have some evidence that UFOs are powerful radioactive sources[4] in certain cases. The Campinas inci-

4 Ruppelt, Edward J.: *A Report on Unidentified Flying Objects* (Chapter 15). Doubleday, New York, 1956.

dent[5] indicates that they may use atomic engines of some sort which might blow accidentally. But then we would expect the debris to be contaminated, highly radioactive. However, use of a Geiger counter and an atomic scaler to determine whether the magnesium fragments register an extraordinary amount of radiation gave negative results. There is a third possible cause for the disaster, the most interesting possibility in my opinion—a sudden failure in the UFO's flight mechanism. The Ubatuba incident involved a body moving at high speed and apparently in trouble, almost crashing into the sea, then a controlled maneuver to avoid the crash at the last moment, the object making a sharp turn upward—and then the explosion. This sequence suggests the high-speed maneuver was fatal. The UFO propulsion system, already too overloaded, was unable to withstand the tremendous strain of that sudden reversal of course, and ceased to operate.

Recent evidence (two incidents in France: at Vins-sur-Caramy on April 14, 1957, and at Palalda, near Montlucon, just eight days later) strongly suggests that UFOs are capable of creating electric and magnetic fields of extreme intensity, fields so powerful iron objects placed inside the fields acquire long-lasting magnetic properties.[6] Fields of such a magnitude evidently must be connected with the UFO's flight mechanism, possibly as a means of propulsion. But we do not know how they are utilized. Many scientists have rejected the possibility that UFOs could be spaceships, on the ground that any solid body moving through the earth's atmosphere at the reported extremely high speeds would burn up. Recent experiments, however, indicate heated air around an aerial machine or missile can be deflected electromagnetically. This might explain the electromagnetic fields referred to above. On the other hand, other scientists have questioned the so-called means of propulsion and the reported sharp turns made by UFOs (as reported in the Ubatuba case). Some scientists have claimed such sharp turns would rule out the possibility UFOs are piloted craft, or even aerial machines of any kind.

It has been suggested that an artificial gravity field would

[5] Fontes, Olavo T.: "We Have Visitors From Outer Space," *APRO Bulletin,* July 1957.

[6] Michel, Aime: *Flying Saucers and the Straight-Line Mystery* (Part 5). Criterion Books, New York, 1958.

solve those problems. It is interesting to note that two physicists at a recent meeting at the American Physical Society claimed to have produced a measurable gravity field with a device consisting of electromagnets mounted on a rotating disc.[7] If such experiments are confirmed, we may be on the way to duplicating the performances of the UFOs. At any rate, the very strong electromagnetic fields detected in connection with the UFOs seem somehow related to an artificial gravity effect of some sort. Unfortunately, we still don't know what gravity is, though we can describe what it does. The strong interactions (electromagnetic forces and nuclear forces) are certainly fascinating, but it is the relatively ultrafeeble interactions of gravity and inertia that have us earthbound. The science of gravitics, electrogravitics and electromagnetism is still groping in the dark; we are just beginning to study the complex problems involved. However, if "force fields" can be used to neutralize the gravitational pull of the earth and to propel a vehicle to reach the planets, then such fields could act also on the air molecules surrounding a fast-moving UFO in the dense lower levels of the atmosphere, dragging the adjacent molecules of air along with the object at speeds varying with their proximity to the object's surface. Such an effect could protect the UFO against overheating, even at enormous speeds. In fact, the heat produced by friction, instead of being concentrated on the surface of the UFO, would be dissipated in this thick layer of air carried along with it. Now, what would happen if the mechanism creating the "force field" failed unexpectedly? The "force field" evidently would vanish instantly. If the speed is very high, as in the Ubatuba incident, these three stages blend in a sudden and violent explosion: (a) the "force field" collapses, the surrounding air ceases to be carried along and the thick layer of air around the UFO disappears as well; (b) moving at speeds between Mach 4 and Mach 8, the UFO strikes against the motionless and elastic barrier of air with tremendous kinetic force, especially if it is hypersonic at the time, and its equilibrium temperature changes instantly from normal to white hot; thermic disintegration is a matter of seconds; (c) with a vivid flash and sometimes a noise like a thunder, the craft explodes in flames or dissolves in a shower of sparks.

[7] "Science Suggests Answers to UFO Performances," *UFO Investigator*, 1:8, December 1958.

(5) This theory, that UFOs can control the so-called "boundary layer," making it very thick and turbulent by an artificial gravity field, has been suggested by Lieutenant Jean Plantier of the French Air Force in his recent book on the UFO's propulsion system.[8] Plantier's theory would explain how UFOs are protected against overheating even at enormous speeds. Also it would explain the mechanism of that sudden explosion destroying the Ubatuba UFO. To accept his hypothesis, however, it is necessary to prove by experiments that a rotating electromagnetic field can produce a measurable gravity effect, or that the strong interactions—in the form of "force fields"—can somehow be used to neutralize the gravitational pull of the earth and propel a vehicle to the planets. The development of such a theory requires a body of data not yet available to us and obtainable only through long-term research. The only thing we know now is that UFOs seem to be capable of creating electric and magnetic fields of high magnitude around themselves.

In my opinion, these electromagnetic fields suggest another explanation making unnecessary the existence of an artificial gravity field around the UFOs. Recent developments in the field of hydromagnetics seem to indicate that the heating effect on the surface of a rocket or missile can be avoided by using magnetic fields. The possibility was discussed by Dr. W. F. Hilton, chief aerodynamicist of the Armstrong-Whitworth Aircraft Company in England.

From a study of thermonuclear work on the "pinch effect," we decided to try the effect of magnetic fields on the hot flow from our company's shock tube. The basis of this interaction is the very great heating of air behind the shock wave from the front of the vehicle. This heating causes the air to become partially ionized into electrically charged particles, and these particles in rapid motion past the vehicle have the nature of an electric current. They are, therefore, susceptible to deflection by means of a magnet. So far our results have been very encouraging, and we have been able to provide quite definite deviations with a small electromagnet powered by a 12-volt battery. Whether this

[8] *La Propulsion des soucoupes volantes par action direct sur l'atome.* Mame Édition, Paris, 1958.

effect will lead to a practical contribution to reentry remains to be established.[9]

In a recent report to the American Rocket Society, Princeton University physicist Dr. Russell M. Kulsrud stated that the new field of "hydromagnetics" (formerly called magnetohydrodynamics) might help solve the missile reentry problem.[10] In nuclear fusion devices (H-bombs, for instance) magnetic fields are used to keep electrified gases away from the walls of a container long enough for the nuclear reaction to take place. The same principle, he said, might be used to deflect hot gases generated by devices plunging into the atmosphere. Dr. Kulsrud, who is working on the Princeton plasma-physics Project Matterhorn, also said that the science-fiction concept of using invisible "force fields" to repel incoming objects was becoming a reality in hydromagnetics.

Hydromagnetics deals with the reaction of "plasma" fluids to high magnetic fields—strong enough to control charged particles moving in a "plasma"—and smaller electric fields. In the "pinch effect," the flow of an electric current through a gas generates a strong magnetic field which at once contains the gas and brings it up to high temperature by compressing (that is, pinching) it. In my opinion, ionization and magnetism combine to produce a hydromagnetic effect on the air in rapid motion around a fast-moving UFO—i.e., energized ions, atoms (or positively charged nuclei) and free electrons in the air are contained in a magnetic field. Thus contained in the magnetic field, the ionized air will not touch the surface of the object. In the particular UFO case a magnetic field produced independently of the electric current that heats the gas in the pinch effect was necessary (a pinch-effect current was not needed because the very great heating of air behind the shock wave already made it partially ionized into electrically charged particles). This could be obtained by an externally applied, rapidly pulsating magnetic field. The charged particles moving across the field would experience a deflecting force and proceed to gyrate in circles about the lines of magnetic force. An electric current would flow through the air along the magnetic surfaces. The power dissipated by the resistance of the gas would go into ionizing and heating the air, as well as into producing some ultraviolet

9 *UFO Investigator*, 1:1, August-September 1958.
10 *UFO Investigator*, 1:8, December 1958.

and visible radiation. This might be called "ohmic heating." (it is the ohmic resistance of the gas that generates the heat on passage of the current). Unlike a pinch-effect current, this ohmic-heating current will not produce any contraction or compression of the ionized gas. As a result, the strong magnetic field around the UFO would hold the gas firmly in place and almost constant in volume. Such a magnetic field must be "force-free," *i.e.*, capable of maintaining its form through a balance of purely magnetic forces. It is already proved that a force-free magnetic field is possible in a toroidal shape.

In fact, there are magnetic fields (according to the German astrophysicists A. Schluter and R. Lust) that possess certain field configurations which are "force-free" in the sense they do not tend to expand or distort their shape. If we assume a set of wires wound into a metallic object in such a manner as to produce a three-dimensional magnetic field, the object would have a longitudinal field into the coil (inside its walls), seeking to expand, and a circular field running around it, seeking to contract. In short, these fields would balance so that no inward or outward force exists. The trouble would come at the end of the system, for the compensation would break down there and the force-free configuration consequently would be disturbed.

A way out is suggested by the torus or doughnut—a system without end. It seems obvious that in a disc or saucer-shaped object the "coil" bends in a circle to form a closed but endless system. In the resulting toroidal or doughnut-shaped magnetic field the lines of force become circles and the path of each charged particle is a helix. Yet such a toroidal field is not stable enough, due to the effect of particle drift. In fact, as a result of curvature, the strength of the magnetic field is greater near the inside than it is near the outside. This inhomogenity of the field alters the helical path of charged particles. The result is that the charged particles drift across the field, the positively charged ones collecting at the top of the tubular field and the electrons at the bottom. This drift is bad enough in itself, but its indirect effect will be catastrophic. The resulting separation of electric charges produces a large electric field which will completely disrupt the particle paths, throwing the entire gas into the surface of the UFO—due to the fact that a steady electric field imposed across a magnetic field produces no current at all in a fully ionized gas, but drives the gas particles in a direction at right-angles to both the electric and magnetic fields. The UFO would be destroyed in the process.

There is a simple solution for this drift of charged particles across a toroidal magnetic field. By one means or another the magnetic field can be twisted around its circular axis, giving the lines of force a helical form like the strands of a rope. In this twisted toroidal field the effect of particle drift is much reduced. Oppositely charged particles will still show some tendency to drift apart, with an accompanying separation of charges, but now the charges can leak back along the lines of force. Any difference in electric charge along a line of force will thus be eliminated, and a steady confinement of the ionized air now becomes possible. The necessary twist can be imposed on a toroidal field in a number of ways. Passing an electric current along the lines of magnetic force in a torus will do it, but such a current would require pulsing every few seconds. Another way is the method in which the toroidal field is twisted by interaction with an additional transverse magnetic field (generated by a set of helical windings in which the current flows in opposite directions in adjacent groups of wires).

It is my opinion hydromagnetics would explain the UFO's apparent immunity to air friction and suggest a possible power source. It is postulated that ionization and magnetism produce a hydromagnetic effect on the air surrounding a high-speed UFO which avoids any contact between the gas and the object's surface. There is, first, the very great heating of air behind the shock wave from the front of the vehicle, causing the air to become partially ionized into electrically charged particles, and these particles in rapid motion past the vehicle have the nature of an electric current. The interaction of an independently produced magnetic field, possibly created by an externally applied, rapidly pulsating magnetic field, holds the electrified particles in circular orbits. This force-free field is probably a twisted toroidal magnetic field (or a special field configuration with similar properties). The deflected particles are kept away from the UFO's surface; the charged particles and atoms collide only with each other, and the plasma becomes fully ionized. A circular electric current flows into the doughnut-shaped plasmoid thus formed around the object. This plasmoid acts as a "cushion" of high magnetic-field pressure between the object and the surrounding atmosphere (like an invisible "force field"), but does not touch the surface of the UFO—which moves inside of it in a kind of "aerodynamical vacuum." The strong force-free, rotating magnetic field holds the plasmoid firmly in place and constantly (or almost so) in volume around the object. The ohmic-heating current (unlike the pinch-effect current of thermonuclear experiments) produces no contraction or compression of the ionized gas confined in the externally applied magnetic field around the UFO. It is obvious, however, that the air does not remain steady and motionless during ohmic heating; in fact, the ionized gas is expected to develop violent activity during the process. The object's own motion, plus the effects of electric and magnetic forces involved, introduce complications which make the activity quite different from ordinary turbulence. Ultraviolent and visible radiation certainly are produced as a side effect. In addition, the "co-operative activity" of charged particles in the heated and ionized gas can produce many other effects, some of them not yet understood—such as the production of radio-noise bursts similar to those observed from the sun. Disturbances of the hydromagnetic type can also be expected, as well as the appearance of "runaway" electrons that no longer can be confined and strike the object, producing intense X-rays (this tendency is probably reduced with a twisted field).

It seems reasonable to expect that a high magnetic field strong enough to form and maintain a plasmoid around a fast-moving UFO through a balance of purely magnetic actions would protect UFOs against their friction at any speed, thus avoiding any heating effect. Also, these effects correspond with many of the unexplained phenomena reported in connection with UFOs. But magnetic fields are, of course, invisible and lines of force are purely imaginary constructs. How can we "see" them on UFOs? A way out is suggested by the Zeeman effect, which certainly would be detected in the spectrum of light emitted from UFOs at night. Available empirical evidence suggests careful research of the theory. Fields of the magnitude we have been discussing are probably strong enough to dominate the motion of charged particles within atoms, to cause some crystals to contract, to make a conducting metal extremely resistant to electrical current or opaque to infrared radiation, and perhaps to produce a measurable "gravity field" effect, too.

In the case of a UFO moving at low speed, or halted in mid-air, the heating of air particles is possibly not enough to generate a plasmoid around it—only the magnetic field would exist. If necessary, however, magnetically confined plasmas might be generated by a rotating part in the object (a spinning ring, for instance), by rotation of the object itself around its axis, or with the help of special "plasma jets" on the object firing doughtnut-shaped bursts of plasma. In the near-vacuum outside the atmosphere these plasma jets also might operate as a possible propulsion source. On the other hand, it seems evident that if the object is moving at high speed in the dense lower levels of the atmosphere, the sudden collapse of the force-free field and plasmoid would result in its thermal disintegration in a matter of seconds. The mechanism, similar to the one discussed in connection with Plantier's theory, could certainly explain the mystery of the sudden explosion which destroyed the Ubatuba UFO.

(6) We are beginning to probe the new frontier of the so-called "thermal barrier" as our planes approach thermantic (Mach 3 to Mach 4) and superthermantic (Mach 4 to Mach 8) speeds. There is also the missile and satellite reentry problem. In the thermantic region (1325 to 2650 mph), stagnation temperatures (air's original temperature plus the heating caused by friction with the moving surface of a plane) range from 250° to 1500° F., varying from 1200° to 6300° F. or more in the superthermantic region. However, the picture is much less severe in the relation to equilibrium temperatures (those in the metal on the surface of the airplane). In the thermantic region, for instance, they get up to only 900° F. but this is still heat, and plenty of it). At superthermantic speeds the problem becomes far more difficult. Tomorrow's airplane may glow red and give off enough heat to heat four hundred average-sized homes when reaching its equilibrium temperature at 180,000 feet at a speed of Mach 8. To solve the problems involved we are making an endless search for better and better heat-resistant materials and cooling systems.

On the other hand, the available evidence suggests the problem of the "thermal barrier" was solved by the intelligences behind the UFOs. These unconventional aerial objects can move across the earth's atmosphere at velocities between Mach 4 and Mach 8 or more, with apparent immunity to the heating produced by friction with air molecules. Are they made with heat-resistant material better than Pyroceran of Inconel-x? This is apparently the obvious explanation despite the fact the extremely high speeds reported in certain cases would be enough to burn up even the best heat-resistant material in the universe. Cooling systems are useless if the speeds are high enough.

The physical evidence in the Ubatuba incident provides a different answer for the question. It indicates clearly materials of high heat-resistance are not the key to the "thermal barrier" problem. It is obvious an object made of magnesium (a metal of low heat-resistance) could never stand the overheating at the unbelievable speed it was moving when first seen over the sea. The magnesium shell would lose its mechanical strength quickly and burn in a few seconds— even at speeds far below the one reported. Yet the Ubatuba "flying disc" did not show any sign of overheating at any time before the explosion, despite its enormous speed. This is a very important point. As no trace of any protective coating was detected in the recovered fragments, it seems evident something invisible existed around that UFO to protect its magnesium shell against air friction. When that protection disappeared, thermal disintegration within a few seconds was the observed result.

Whether or not that something protecting the UFO against overheating at high speeds was an artificially thickened and controlled "boundary layer" (Plantier's theory) or a hydromagnetic effect producing a kind of "aerodynamic vacuum" (my hypothesis) remains to be established. At any rate, the conclusion is that our present approach to the problem should be carefully reevaluated. Our endless search for better and better heat-resistant materials and cooling systems may show good results for some time yet, but it will not win this new frontier for us. A different approach should be tried, for it seems that more practical and efficient solutions can be found. On the basis of the evidence available on the Ubatuba incident, it is my opinion the key to the problem is just before our eyes—every time a UFO is sighted . . . .

Thus concludes Dr. Fontes's report. Only a few additional facts are required to bring it up to date.

Soon after receiving the samples from Dr. Fontes, APRO submitted a portion of a sample to an Air Force spectrographic lab for analysis. An "emission spec" was requested. The following day the emission spectrograph operator reported that he had accidentally burned the entire sample without obtaining an exposed plate. He requested another sample. APRO declined.

Our next venture fared little better. A piece of Sample 2 was submitted to an Atomic Energy Commission laboratory. A density test was performed which involved creating a solution in which chips of the metal would neither float nor sink. This solution (a mixture of bromo benzine and bromoform) was found to have a density of 1.7513 grams per cc., a little high but near normal for terrestrial magnesium (1.74 grams per cc.). The experts concluded that this small deviation was the result of a small inclusion of oxide in the chips and was insufficient grounds for belief in an unusual isotopic ratio, and that "the sensitivity of mass spectrographic determinations is such as to make such an examination completely unprofitable."

A technician (who requested that his name be withheld) ran an emission spectrograph test which showed the presence of several trace elements, as follows: iron—between .01 and .1%; silicon—between .01 and .1%; aluminum—between .01 and .1%; calcium—between .0001 and .001%; copper—between .0001 and .001%.

The instrument used was an Applied Research Laboratories two-meter grating spectrograph with a dispersion of five angstroms per cc. The technique used was the standard "semiquantitative" method prescribed for a magnesium matrix by Harvey, using standard electrodes. The resulting film returned with the report showed five irrelevant spectra, the magnesium spectrum and an iron spectrum for comparison. There was no separate spectrum of the electrodes, and it was not possible to determine whether the detected impurities were in the electrodes or in the sample. The impurities, however, are those normally found in standard carbon electrodes. The complete test was, in Texeira's opinion, "completely valueless from a scientific standpoint." A metallographer who examined the remaining portion of Sample 2 came to the conclusion the sample was a portion of a casting which had not been worked mechanically since it had originally "frozen" from the molten metal; the experience it passed through, which led to the oxidation noted, apparently having been too brief to allow gross melting or other recognizable changes in the grain structure.

One thing seemed clear—we were not likely to obtain satisfactory results simply by sending out samples and having faith; furthermore, our supply of the metal was dwindling alarmingly. After due deliberation, the staff decided that an attempt should be made to have the metal examined by a qualified laboratory with APRO and USAF advisors participating. This seemed the best way to insure no important aspect of the problem was overlooked. Accordingly, a letter was addressed to ATIC, with a copy to the press to insure prompt attention—but to no avail. We received only a routine request to forward the purported material to ATIC at the Wright Air Development Center. We then attempted to establish liaison with ATIC, but they declined to answer our letter. We could only conclude that the USAF was not interested in any real answers, or already had obtained full details (and possibly samples of the metal) through classified channels. Our correspondence with the Air Force had one satisfying result, however. The resulting UPI news story brought the matter to public attention in Brazil. As a result all aspects of Dr. Fontes's report were verified in press and TV interviews with the principals.

The identity of the witnesses to the original incident remains unknown. In an attempt to locate them, Dr. Fontes and Joao Martins canvassed the beach area in the neighborhood of Ubatuba. Eventually they located a fisherman who remembered a group of vacationers from an inland town who told of the incident and displayed pieces of a gray substance to support their story. He could remember nothing else of any value except they were excited and talked eagerly of their experience. This information might only serve to deepen the mystery, except for this fact: During 1958 when Dr. Fontes was in the midst of his investigation of the strange metal he was visited by two members of a Brazilian intelligence agency. These two individuals at first made veiled threats as to what might happen to him if he continued his inquiry into matters that "did not concern him." When it became apparent that Fontes could not be coerced into silence, they appealed to his "better judgment" to cooperate with them and turn all his notes and the strange metal over to them.

It is my opinion that the original witnesses may have reported their experience to some official agency and that they thus lost their metal samples and were encouraged into silence. Another conclusion may be that official agencies learned of the incident in the same way Dr. Fontes did and contacted the witnesses through Mr. Sued. One researcher questioned the validity of the case on the basis of the lack of witnesses, and also claimed the British are able to produce pure magnesium. Inasmuch as names of scientists and

Plate 1: *A series of four photographs of an object taken by Helio Aguiar, a draftsman, on the highway near Itapoan, Brazil, on April 24, 1959. In his photo analysis, John Hopf points out that the apparent size of the object increases from view No. 1 to view No. 3, indicating that the object is approaching the camera. In views 1 and 2, he goes on, we seem to be looking at the bottom of the disc. From view No. 3 to view No. 4 the altitude of the disc has increased so that the water is no longer visible in the last view.*

Plates 2A-2E: *Photographs of a "flying disc" taken by photographer Ed Keffel and first sighted by reporter Joao Martins on May 7, 1952, in the vicinity of Barra da Tijuca, Brazil, at 4:30 p.m. (See p. 192.) The following captions describing this sequence are taken from* Aerial Phenomena Research Organization Special Report No. 1 *by Dr. Olavo T. Fontes, M.D.*

Plate 2A: *In the first photograph the object looks like an airplane facing the camera.*

Plate 2B: *The second photograph shows a side view of the disc, which is slightly tilted upward, turning its lower surface toward the camera. The top cupola cannot be seen from this angle.*

Plate 2C: *The third photo in the sequence presents a bottom view of the disc, which is now closer than in the preceding ones and consequently larger in size.*

Plate 2D: *This photo presents a top view of the flying disc, which indicates that the object suddenly reversed its position in space and is now tilted downward so that only the upper side is visible to observers.*

Plate 2E: *The last photograph in Keffel's sequence shows the disc in an almost vertical position. It is far more distant than in photo No. 4 and is also very low.*

Plates 3A-3D: *Photograph of an object over Trindade Island taken by Almiro Barauna on January 16, 1958, at noon. (See Chapter 11 and also Figure 6 in the text for full details.)*

Plate 3A: *The object is seen approaching Trindade Island, which is off the coast of Brazil.*

Plate 3B: *The object was flying over the center of the Island, behind the "Galo Crest," at low speed.*

Plate 3C: *After disappearing behind "Desejado" Peak, the object reappears closer than before.*

Plate 3D: *The object leaves the area of Trindade Island, disappearing out over the sea.*

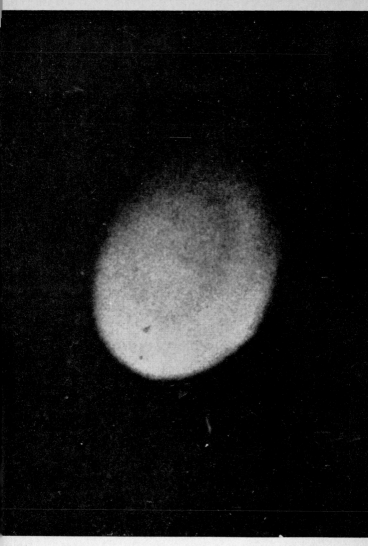

Plate 4: *Photograph of an object taken by an official of a Rio de Janeiro bank on December 9, 1954, as it hovered over the Army Munitions plant at 11 p.m. The photographer wishes to remain anonymous but is personally known to Dr. Olavo T. Fontes, APRO's Brazilian representative.*

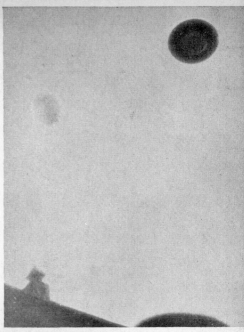

Plate 5: *Photograph of an object taken by Yukuse Matsumura outside his residence at 1687 Hama, Isogo-ku, Yokohama, Japan, at 10:47 a.m. on January 17, 1957.*

Plate 6: *Miss Ella Fortune took this photograph of a huge object as it hovered over the north range of the White Sands - Holloman Air Force Base, New Mexico, test complex at 1 p.m. on October 16, 1957.*

Plate 7: *Photograph of a typical bell-shaped Unidentified Flying Object taken on April 2, 1966, in Melbourne, Australia, by an Australian engineer who asked that his name not be used. The photo was turned over to Peter Norris, president of the Commonwealth Aerial Phenomena Investigation Organization. The object is seen hovering over a house whose pink roof its lower edge apparently reflects. (This was seen more clearly in the color version of this photograph.) The object is apparently made of highly polished metal and is similar (or identical) to objects seen all over the world. (See p. 252.)*

laboratories supposedly involved have not been forthcoming, APRO feels the burden of proof is on the doubter, and to prove his case he must produce samples of 100%-pure magnesium manufactured prior to September 1957.

10
Aftermath

FACTS gleaned from the November flap indicated that a third satellite was shunted into orbit around the earth shortly after Sputnik II was launched, and this or a similar object was photographed in Caracas, Venezuela, by Dr. Luis E. Corrales, an engineer in the Ministry of Communications there. At 6:10 P.M. on December 18, 1957, Corrales exposed a photographic plate to capture on film the luminous path of Sputnik II. In addition to the path of Sputnik II the developed plate showed another luminous streak exactly parallel to it and about one-seventh its length. The blown-up negative was studied extensively by Dr. Corrales and other qualified scientists, and the following statement was released to *El Universal* for publication in the December 19 issue:

It cannot be a double exposure, for the stars also would have registered double images on the plate, and they didn't. It cannot be an internal (camera) reflection, for the path isn't the same size as the one left by the sputnik. It is not a scratch on the plate, for examination by magnifying glass reveals that it is a precipitation of the emulsion on the photographic material, which is accomplished by light alone. The camera photographed something we can't identify . . . if the luminous trail running parallel to the satellite's trail is the path produced by another body, and it became luminous during a short period of time, we would be making a hypothesis hard to prove.

The layman's reaction to such a photograph is that the object was a meteorite or other celestial body. But in the photo the path of the object includes a short jog, indicating there was a flight-path deviation or correction during the time it was luminous. It would not be possible for a meteorite to exactly parallel the path of a satellite and then correct trajectory in this manner. The object photographed by Corrales was intelligently controlled, capable of altering course—and it was tracking the satellite.

With the first of the year came several sightings of the Saturn-shaped objects which had begun to haunt South America. At noon on January 16 photographs were obtained of an object which closely resembled the descriptions of the Saturn-shaped UFO seen on several occasions in the vicinity of the Trindade Island navy installation. (*See plates 5A–D.*) The Brazilian Ship *Almirante Saldanha* was riding in the waters off Trindade, preparing to participate in International Geophysical Year projects. Almiro Barauna, official photographer of the expedition, spotted an object and took four exposures before it sped out of sight. Others on the ship had also seen the object and Barauna developed his film immediately in the ship's darkroom in the presence of others. The prints which showed an oval object with a Saturnlike ring silhouetted in the sky above the island, were published by the Rio de Janeiro newspaper *O Jornal,* and International News Service later gave the pictures worldwide coverage.

But the best was yet to come. In the ensuing months Brazilians began to wonder why their country was chosen for such particularly close observation. Although many sightings were made in January through March, in December a particularly sensational report came out of the small village of Ponta Poran, near the frontier of Paraguay. The March, 1959, issue of the *APRO Bulletin* featured a carefully documented account by Dr. Olavo Fontes of a series of incidents in that area. Prefacing the account—"This immense plateau, covered by a forest which has given its name to one of the states—Mato Grosso—may be the region where the first secret UAO (unconventional aerial object) base on this planet was located. For it was the scene of the most fantastic chapter in UAO history so far on record"—Fontes then relates the following events of the night of December 21, 1957.

Mrs. Ivonne Torres de Mendonca, her three children, her servant, Miss Bruna, and her young driver, Marcio Goncalves, were traveling by jeep from her farm to the village of Ponta Poran. In places the road ran almost parallel to the frontier of Paraguay. Low-hanging clouds covered the sky and night had come early. Suddenly at 6:30 P.M. far away to the south Mrs. Mendonca spotted a large ball of light about the size of the full moon. It appeared to be close to the ground but she knew it couldn't be another car as there were no other roads in that area. The little party drove on as they discussed the possible identity of the thing. The light then started moving rapidly in their direction, and they realized it was not one but two spherical, luminous objects flying side by side. The objects approached the jeep silently, gradually increasing the gap between each other so that when they were near each object was flying along a side of the road. They followed a horizontal course but oscillated from one side to the other in a strange wobbling motion and appeared to spin on their own axes. Then one of them stopped in mid-air and dived toward the ground—stopping a few feet above it and about sixty feet from the jeep. The other object kept maneuvering in circles above the jeep, occasionally getting uncomfortably close. The outlines of the objects could not be seen clearly because of the intense light they emitted, although it was apparent that the objects were shaped like a spheroid encircled by a ring at the equator—similar to the planet Saturn. Both were of the same size and of two colors—the upper hemisphere and the ring a fiery red, the lower hemisphere surrounded by a bright silverwhite glow. The objects were extremely bright and intermittently sent brilliant jets of light toward the jeep.

All of the group were frightened; the road was deserted and they did not know what to expect next. One child, Fernando, was almost paralyzed with fear; the others had begun to cry. Mrs. Mendonca instructed Marcio not to stop the car, and he began to drive faster. But the eerie objects stayed with them, sometimes very close, sometimes increasing their distance from the jeep. At times one object would get ahead of the jeep and shine a brilliant light on the occupants, while the other followed closely behind, apparently observing them. At other times one object would fly above them and direct beams of light at them, while the other dived toward the jeep at high speed. Marcio had difficulty controlling the vehicle.

This strange chase lasted for two hours until the little party reached Ponta Poran. Only twice during the nightmarish experience did the jeep stop—once to take stock of the situation and once to see if the objects were interested in a motionless vehicle—they were. Each time the jeep pulled to a stop the reaction of the objects was instantaneous—they would both dive at high speed; one would hover, throwing a beam of light on the ground while the other would approach the illuminated spot. It did not land—it appeared to hover motionless above the ground and its brilliancy would decrease; then the jeep's occupants got their first real look at the object. It appeared to be a huge metallic sphere, about fifteen feet in diameter, encircled at the center by a large apparently rotating metallic ring. The observers saw no doors, windows or portholes; there was no sound, no heat, no odor.

When the jeep began to move again the objects followed, and when the jeep approached the town the objects moved away. But when Marcio stopped to refill the gas tank, the weird globes made another appearance, "landing" again, but this time remaining near the ground for about fifteen minutes, then climbing into the sky and apparently keeping watch until the jeep arrived in Ponta Poran. There Mrs. Mendonca looked for the objects, but they were gone. Later, she and some of her group returned to where the last landing had taken place and found an odd luminous haze floating in the air above where the object had hovered. They watched it slowly dissolve in the faint wind blowing from the north; and they saw one of the objects disappearing into the west, in the direction of the frontier.

But this was not all. On February 19, 1958, Mrs. Mendonca, her son Fernando, her farm overseer, a farm worker and Goncalves had another similar experience (They were interviewed at great length and their reports tallied in every detail. The report of the incident was strongly supported by a second group of observers including Athamaril Saldanha, a civilian pilot and chief of the Institute Nacional de Mate at Ponta Porna, his wife and two sons and Dr. and Mrs. Eraldo Saldanha.) They left Ponta Poran at 4 A.M. for Mrs. Mendonca's farm. At Porteira Ortiz they spotted a reddish light in the sky. The windless night was dark and there was no moon, but the sky was cloudless and full of stars. Goncalves was the first to see the unidentified object, and he called it to the attention of the farm supervisor who had been unbelieving about their first experience. The supervisor merely laughed and said, "That's just the planet Mars." But his smile froze as he watched the "planet" approach silently but swiftly until it was fairly near and then begin its side-to-side descent. It hovered just above the road in front of the jeep, its red light replaced by a dazzling silvery glow. Mrs. Mendonca noted that it was exactly the same type of objects she had viewed two months previously, but there was only one of them this time. She ordered the driver to turn the jeep around, and they started back to town. The object made no move to interfere, but followed them for some time. Then it passed the side of the jeep and climbed abruptly just before they arrived back in town. It continued to track the jeep from high altitude over the town, and finally stopped over the Brazilian Army headquarters in Ponta Poran, where it stayed motionless for half an hour.

Meanwhile, Mrs. Mendonca ran through the quiet streets, knocking on doors, and a small crowd gathered in the street, including Dr. Athamaril Saldanha, Dr. Eraldo Saldanha and his wife Ione and Mrs. A. Saldanha and her two sons who joined the group some minutes later. They watched the object for fifteen minutes until someone suggested they do something to make the object show its hand. It apparently was only observing the people. Mrs. Mendonca's group and the Saldanha party boarded two jeeps and headed for the edge of town. The object appeared to follow them. The two vehicles stopped at Porteira Ortiz; the object stopped, too. But instead of coming close, this time it started to climb vertically; then it stopped, and with the first rays of the sun it climbed to an even higher altitude and stopped again. Viewed through binoculars, in the sunlight the object resembled an aluminum ball. At 6 A.M. the object moved suddenly, shooting straight up at tremendous speed and vanishing.

The third incident in the Fontes report took place on February 19, the night after Mrs. Mendonca's second experience with the glowing globes. Professor Cicero Claudino da Silva, law student Mustafa Esgaib, Alegario Campos, and Dr. Joao Manuel Vasquez decided to investigate the Mendonca claims, for the whole town had been buzzing about the weird incident that morning. They left Ponta Poran in a station wagon, taking the same road on which the other incidents had taken place. At 10:30 P.M. they arrived at Porteiro Ortiz and stopped the car so that the headlights were shining in the direction of the frontier. They did not have long to wait. A reddish light in the sky to the west appeared and started toward them, increasing in size and brilliancy as it flew in an odd, side-to-side oscillatory motion. It came so close to the car that the ground around it was brilliantly illuminated for a few seconds. The men became panicky but stood their ground. Then they realized that a rear-action maneuver was taking place—another similar object was approaching from the other side of the car. They jumped into the car and raced back to Ponta Poran. The object stayed put, swaying back and forth gently. Back in town the frightened men told what they had seen and it was decided that a caravan of cars go immediately to Porteira Ortiz and fully investigate the objects. Several cars took off for the spot; they flashed headlights and spotlights for hours, but nothing happened. They went again the next night in a caravan of cars—but with the same results.

One night less than three weeks later, Marcio Goncalves, his girl friend, his younger brother and other friends drove out on the Ponta Poran road. Between two small wooded areas Goncalves stopped the jeep and the boys went looking for a "flying saucer" with their flashlights. It was about 10:30 P.M. Goncalves and his girl friend in the car suddenly saw a bright object hanging over the thicket ahead of them. The boys had spotted the thing, too, and they ran for the car, shouting, "The saucer—the saucer!" With unexpected suddenness the object shot straight toward the running youngsters. The boys were quick, however, and they reached the car ahead of the object.

Then everything lighted up as bright as if it had been daytime. But the light was blood-red. Goncalves said his hair stood up on the back of his head. They were directly under the thing—it was larger than their car and seemed to be made of polished metal; it appeared to be so near they could have struck it with a short pole. Goncalves, fearing the object might come down on top of the car, started the jeep and headed back toward town.

But the UFO wasn't through playing. It followed them, flying just behind the jeep and about nine feet above the ground. The jeep and the surrounding road area were illuminated by the bright glow emitted by the object. No noise or heat came from it. Goncalves drove at breakneck speed over the narrow, rough road. The chase lasted about fifteen minutes, until the jeep reached another thicket where the road passed through the woods. Goncalves hoped the object couldn't fly under the small trees. He was right, for they watched the object pass behind the trees and disappear. Thinking the object had left, they relaxed. But when they left the protection of the woods they spotted it hovering over the thicket, higher in the sky now, as though the object was waiting for them to reappear. The road curved toward a hill a few hundred yards away. The object dived at high speed, not toward the jeep but straight toward the top of the hill, well ahead of the vehicle. Then it descended over the hill, stopping on the ground in the middle of the road. It blocked their way. The jeep had started to climb the hill. Goncalves was panic-stricken. The object had cut off escape toward town, he could not go back. He made his choice—he kept going. The jeep picked up speed and the young people prepared for the inevitable crash.

Then a strange thing happened. As the car climbed the hill its headlights were gradually raised until the beams of light hit the UFO directly. To the amazement of everyone in the jeep the object began to wobble violently, then shot straight up into the air as though it was running away. Goncalves kept the accelerator pressed down. They passed the point where the UFO had sat, and they kept going. They passed just under the object, but it did not interfere with them. Minutes later the object began to follow the jeep again, but at a distance. After ten minutes of this, it changed course and climbed vertically. Its light went out at about three hundred feet and it vanished into the darkness.

The fifth and final incident included in Dr. Fontes's July 1959 report, *Shadow of the Unknown,* documenting incidents of UFOs chasing cars, took place on February 24, 1958, about twelve hundred miles from Ponta Poran. (Dr. Fontes had investigated still another report at Ponta Poran, but the principals in the case refused to be interviewed.) Dr. Carlos Jose da Costa Pereira, a lawyer in SENAI's National Department, Manoel Mendes and a friend, Antonio de Araujo, were driving between Nazare and Salvador, in Bahia. Between these two towns lie two small villages, Santo Antonio de Jesus and Conceicao Almeida. At 3:05 A.M. somewhere between the two villages, their car began coughing and missing and then abruptly the motor stopped dead. The men attempted to locate the trouble, but to no avail. The next inhabited spot was some distance away, and they decided to sleep at the edge of the road and in the morning do something about the car.

It was then that they spotted a huge luminous object hovering overhead. According to Dr. Pereira's report, "It glowed with a strange light which seemed fluid, between silver and blue. At first it was only a light, but as it approached we were able to detect what appeared to be a solid body behind the glow. The object seemed to be two hemispheres on top of each other, between them a luminous disk or ring spinning at high speed; it was the source of the brilliant glow surrounding the whole object." The object came silently toward the car until it was about two hundred and forty feet from the observers and about ninety feet above the ground. Then it descended in a curious manner as though it were a falling leaf. It steadied itself at about nine or twelve feet above ground, and the three men were able to discern its contours very clearly. The bottom was smaller than the top hemisphere and it was slightly flattened underneath. Its luminosity spread in a curtain of light suspended between the UFO and the ground below.

The frightened driver, Mendes, got back into the car. The other two, however, decided to investigate, and walked toward the strange object. As they approached the illuminated area (about twice the size of the UFO which appeared to be about 60 to 75 feet in diameter) the object suddenly took off in a vertical climb. It stopped at about six hundred feet, and made a tight circle in the sky, its luminous focus on the ground rotating around itself. Then the UFO stopped again and tilted forty-five degrees. In this position the rotating ring was more easily viewed and Dr. Pereira got the impression that it was notched like a cogwheel whose indentations appeared to be oblique in relation to the edge of the ring. Minutes later the object began to move again, in a series of high-speed maneuvers across the sky, sometimes moving vertically, sometimes in tight circles around the car and sometimes in straight lines in different directions. In the straight-line maneuvers it moved "more rapidly than lightning," becoming at times a small dot of light in the sky in a split second. Then for a second time the object executed the "dead-leaf" descent, stopping about 9 to 12 feet from the ground. When the observers tried to approach it, the object took off vertically at high speed and was gone. The time was 4:35 A.M.

At 6:30 A.M. the object appeared for the last time, at a low altitude, silvery in color and with no glow. It was motionless, tilted to one side; then it suddenly shot up at tremendous speed and vanished in a split second. The men attempted to start their car. To their surprise the motor functioned smoothly, with no further stalling, and the car made the rest of the trip to Salvador without trouble.

Several things about this and the Ponta Poran incident deserve close scrutiny. One is the striking similarity in the descriptions of the object in these incidents and the one photographed at the Trindade Island naval base. Mrs. Mendonca's first experience with the "Saturn-shaped" object preceded the Trindade sighting by almost a month, negating the possibility that her experience was inspired by the later sighting. The ensuing sightings in Ponta Poran strengthen Mrs. Mendonca's report of her first experience. Her farm overseer had been a skeptic until the second experience—when he was initiated. Gonclaves's account was verified by his companions. The object seen by Pereira matched the description of those seen at Ponta Poran, although it appeared to be considerably larger.

Another interesting point is that although the objects on the lonely road near Ponta Poran maneuvered very close to the cars, flying above, beside and behind them, there was no evidence of cars being stopped by the objects. In the Pereira incident, however, the car was stopped first and the UFO spotted later. Recalling the Stokes incident, we note that the cars were stopped although the object was apparently a considerable distance from them. Most researchers of the November flap believe that the car-stoppings were merely a by-product of the propulsion of the strange air machines. Mr. Lorenzen was the first to suggest, in all seriousness, that if we take into consideration the foo-fighter's study of planes in the latter part of World War II the later close-range observations of aircraft and even close-range observation of cars by the UFO, it would appear that a weapon had been devised to disable their propulsion systems, and that the weapon was being tested on different types of vehicles under various conditions, weather included.

Dr. Fontes's *Shadow of the Unknown*, Part II: "Friends or Foes," includes only three incidents, all of which indicate the use of at least one and possibly two weapons. They are noteworthy here as the final link in the chain of evidence indicating hostile visitors from outer space.

On the night of August 14, 1957, a Varig C-47 cargo ship took off from Porto Alegre Airport in Rio Grande do Sul,

Brazil, en route to Rio de Janeiro. At the controls was veteran pilot Commander Jorge Campos Araujo; his co-pilot was experienced Edgar Onofre Soares. At 8:55 P.M. the plane, over the state of Santa Catarina, had passed Joinville five minutes before. At 6300 feet Soares spotted a luminous object far to the left of the aircarft. He decided it was not another aircraft or an astronomical body. They were flying a 10-degree course, and although there was a thick layer of clouds below the plane at about 5700 feet the sky above was absolutely clear and they had a visibility of some eighty miles. Suddenly in a fast maneuver the object was ahead of the plane, then crossed to the right side, following a horizontal trajectory. It stopped for a moment and then abruptly went into a dive and was out of sight in the cloudbank below. Besides the commander and co-pilot, radio operator Rubens A. Tortilho and stewards Jose D. S. Machado and Alfonso Schenini also observed the strange craft. All said the object was saucer-shaped with a cupola or dome on top. The dome glowed with an intense green light and the flattened base showed a less intense yellowish luminosity. Although he could not accurately estimate its speed, distance or size, Commander Araujo ventured his guess that the object's speed was at least supersonic and probably several times that of sound.

Araujo radioed a report to the Varig office at Congohas Airport in Sao Paulo. A few days later word leaked out and when a Sao Paulo reporter interviewed the witnesses the case became headline material throughout Brazil. The Brazilian Air Force did not comment, didn't even attempt to debunk the account.

But more important was the rest of the story: the complete account had not been made public. After Commander Araujo landed at Sao Paulo Airport, a friend (a former pilot who was traffic chief for another airline at the airport and who was also a close friend of Dr. Fontes) found Araujo and his crew seated at a table; something seemed to be wrong, for they were silent and preoccupied. When he asked what the trouble was and Araujo related their experience, he made light of it, saying: "After all, it was only a saucer not a ghost." Then Araujo told him the remainder of the story: When the object had reached the right side of the airliner, the engines of the plane began acting up, coughing and missing, and the lights in the cabin dimmed and almost went out —it seemed that the whole electrical system of the plane was going to collapse. A few seconds later the UFO dived into the clouds, and everything became normal again. This was the reason for the crew's reflective silence. Their plane had played "sitting duck" for an unidentified flying object.

Another case, which took place over Ararangua, Santa Catarina, at 7000 feet on the morning of November 4, 1957, was reported by Commander Auriphebo Simoes, a well-known Brazilian UFO expert, who interviewed Captain Jean Vincent de Beyssac, the chief witness, and published the full report in the January-February 1958 issue of *The Flying Saucer* which he edits. The flight began on the clear and starlit evening of November 3 when the Varig C-46 cargo ship took off from Porto Alegre Airport bound for Sao Paulo. At about 1:20 A.M. the ship flew above a layer of stratus. Suddenly de Beyssac sighted a red light to the left of his aircraft. He watched curiously and joked to his co-pilot that at last they were seeing a real flying saucer. When the thing appeared to grow larger, de Beyssac decided to investigate. He started to put his plane into a left bank, but just before he pressed his rudder the object jumped a 45-degree arc on the horizon and became larger. De Beyssac started pursuit and was about midway on his left 80-degree turn when the object became even brighter and suddenly he smelled something burning inside his ship—all at once his ADF, right generator and transmitter "burned" out. The "thing" disappeared almost instantly, while the crew looked for the fire. De Beyssac turned on his emergency transmitter and reported the incident to Porto Alegre control; then he turned his ship around and headed back to Porto Alegre, where he landed an hour later. After submitting a full written report he went home and got soused. On the same day Varig Airlines issued an order forbidding pilots to tell the press about their sighting of UFOs.

The third and last report was a top-secret military sighting which took place forty minutes after the de Beyssac incident. In revealing the incident, after he had investigated and verified it, Dr. Fontes felt that if sufficient people knew the actual status of the UFO situation, particularly those incidents indicating hostility, there might be hope for a defense. In his words: "Civilian scientists and technicians working in every country might help to find new weapons and defenses before it is too late. . . ."

It was a quiet moonless tropical night and the army garrison at Itaipu was peacefully asleep, two sentries at the top of the fortification going about routine tasks in a relaxed manner. A new "star" suddenly burst into brilliant life among others in the cloudless sky over the Atlantic. The sentries watched with detached interest until they realized it was not a star but a luminous flying object coming straight toward the fort. They realized it couldn't be a plane for its speed was tremendous. Within seconds the UFO was over the fort; then it stopped abruptly and slowly drifted down, its strong orange glow etching each man's shadow against the illuminated ground between the heavy cannon turrets. It hovered about 120 to 180 feet above the highest turret and then was motionless. The sentries, their eyes wide with surprise, seemed glued to the ground, their tommy guns hanging limply in their arms. The weird object was large, about the size of a big Douglas, but round and disk-shaped and encircled by an eerie orange glow. It had been silent as it approached, but now at close range the two men heard a distinct humming sound coming from it. The weird object hovered overhead and nothing happened for about a minute.

Then the nightmare. . . . Something hot touched their faces. One of them said later he thought he heard a faint whining sound at the time. Then an intolerable wave of heat struck the two soldiers. One of the sentries said later it was like a fire burning all over his clothes, the air filled with the UFO's humming sound. Blind panic seized him; he staggered, his only conscious purpose to escape from that invisible fire which seemed to be burning him alive. He gasped and beat the air before him; then he blacked out and collapsed to the ground. The other sentry had the horrible feeling that his clothes were on fire. He began to scream desperately, stumbling and crying like a trapped animal. He did not know what he was doing, but somehow he managed to skid into shelter beneath the heavy cannons. His loud cries awoke the garrison. Inside the installation everything was confusion, men and officers trying to reach their battle stations.

Suddenly the lights throughout the fort collapsed—the electrical system which moved the turrets, cannons and elevators failed; the intercommunication system was dead. Someone switched on the emergency circuits, but they failed to function. And then the electric clocks set to ring at 5 A.M., began their clamor—at 2:03. The fort was helpless. Confusion changed to widespread panic, soldiers and officers running blindly along the dark corridors. Then the lights came on again and every man ran to face the enemy attacking the fort. Some were in time to see an orange light climbing vertically above the fort and then moving through the sky at high speed. One of the sentries was on the ground, still unconscious. The other was hiding in a dark corner, mumbling and crying.

Both sentries, badly burned, were put under medical care. One of them was a severe case of heat syncope; he was still unconscious and showed obvious signs of peripheral vascular failure. Both had first-degree and deep second-degree burns of more than ten per cent of the body—mainly on areas covered by clothing. The sentry who could talk later was in deep nervous shock and it was many hours before he was able to tell his story. The nightmare had lasted for three minutes.

On the next day, November 4, the fort commander, an army colonel, issued orders forbidding discussion of the incident, even with relatives. Intelligence officers came and took charge, working frantically to silence everyone. The fort was put under martial law and a top-secret report was submitted to HQ. Days later, American officers with the U.S. Army Military Mission arrived at the fort with officers of the Brazilian Air Force to question the sentries and other witnesses. A special Air Force plane took the two injured sentries to Rio de Janeiro, where they were completely isolated behind a tight security curtain in the army's Central Hospital.

Three weeks after the incident Dr. Fontes was contacted by an army officer who was at the fort on the night of the incident. He related the story reported here. Fontes was unable to get to the soldiers at Central Hospital. Two months later the sentries were still at the hospital, but it is unknown where they are now. Fontes was not satisfied with the report he obtained from the officer (his first report to me came only three weeks after the incident). With his usual meticulous method he was checking it out. After a year of work he was not able to corroborate the incident except to establish that the two badly burned Itaipu soldiers had been in Central Hospital. In May, 1959, fully twenty months after the Itaipu incident, Dr. Fontes finally located and interviewed three other officers who had been present that night. Their story corroborated that of his first informant in every detail.

In a short paper entitled *UFO Weapons—Comments on*

Technical Aspects Involved, Dr. Fontes set out to establish a few facts and their probable meaning. This dissertation is quoted here in part:

The evidence at hand indicates that UFOs possess means of creating in the ignition systems of automobile and aircraft internal combustion engines secondary currents powerful enough to destroy the synchronization of spark-plug action and thus stall the engines; that they can interfere at will with radio transmitters and receivers, electric-current generators, batteries, telephone lines and, generally, with all electrical circuits; and that these "electric effects" are not merely side effects of the powerful electromagnetic fields that exist around UFOs, but the result of purposeful interference of a weapon used as a means of defense or attack.

These effects are independent of the proximity or any movement of the UFO, and sometimes (as in the Itaipu incident) they appear to be provoked entirely by the behavior of the witnesses. Such a weapon is very efficacious, since the great majority of man-made machines are either electrical or depend on an electrical ignition system. In the Arujo and de Beyssac incidents it was used against airplanes, but produced no biological effect on the crews. In other cases, however—chiefly in France[1] —the witness reported that they were "electrified," "paralyzed by an electric current" or felt a "sensation of heat." But such a heat was not enough in any case to produce the biological effects described in the Itaipu incident.

Existing evidence suggests that such a weapon is not an alternating magnetic field in itself, but a high-frequency, long-range electromagnetic beam of some sort, *i.e.,* a radio-electric wave concentrated into a narrow, powerful beam. After a careful analysis of the data I came to the conclusion that this weapon might be a microwave ionizer—a generator of odd-shaped microwaves that ionize the air where they strike. They would make the air a high-resistance conductor; nothing more than that. And if ionization can make air a high-resistance conductor then an ionizing beam would make a high-resistance short between the power terminals of a battery. In the electric charge a battery carries, that short would

[1] See *Flying Saucers and the Straight-Line Mystery* by Aime Michel.

grow hot; so would the battery, hot enough—given sufficient time—to boil the solution inside it. A microwave generator with enough power would short-circuit anything within its range—electrical instruments (as in the de Beyssac incident), or motors with electric systems (as in the Arujo incident); or it could momentarily paralyze every bit of electrical equipment in a plane, ship, grounded vehicle or building (as in the Itaipu incident). Such a microwave device also might be used as a scanner. In this case it might explain the so-called "spy beam" sometimes mentioned in connection with UFOs. This appears to become visible near the focal point in radar, photography or the human eye. Jets have sometimes flown through such radar "ghosts," while others have appeared on films as discs, ovals or cones.

The "heat wave" which burned the two sentries at Itaipu represents another problem. It was not a side-effect of the weapon which produced the "electric effects"—these came at least one minute later, when an all-over alarm had been caused by the soldier's shouts. Besides, the heat produced by an electrical device would be diffuse and less intense, similar to that obtained through diathermy, in which case the victim would report a tingling on the skin and a raising of hairs. It is clear that a different kind of weapon was used against the soldiers. What was it?

It is known that the temperature rise of any volume element of matter may be brought about by two different mechanisms: (1) A readily accessible surface is kept elevated in temperature and as a result of conduction there is heating of the deeper parts; (2) Heat may be developed in the volume itself (in our case, a human body) by physical energy being conducted through it and converted into heat. The first is exemplified by the application of a heating lamp or hot packs, the second by diathermy. But in none of these would the heat produce the "feeling" of burning clothes, nor would the burns be worse on skin areas protected by clothes—as with the two sentries. This effect is unique and can be termed "structural" heating, produced only by ultrasonics. This is due to the fact that the longitudinal ultrasonic oscillations are transformed into transverse waves (shear waves) at interfaces between mediums of different acoustic impedance as, for example, between the clothes and the skin. These resulting transverse waves are more rapidly absorbed than the longitudinal ones, with a subsequent increased heat development at interface areas.

This ability of ultrasound to produce a unique thermal effect, not duplicated by any other available modality, through differential heating at interfaces between different substances and differences in absorption capacity has been demonstrated and accepted. Only an ultrasonic beam could produce the peculiar characteristics of the "heat wave" that struck the Itaipu sentries. There is no alternative.

The presence of an ultrasonic weapon can explain the sudden "heat wave" encountered by military pilots in the pursuit of UFOs. For example, early in 1954 a test pilot for the French Fouga Aircraft Company of Pau in the Lower Pyrenees trying to approach a UFO hovering near the city was forced to turn away because of the intense heat that built up in his cockpit. This ultrasonic weapon seems to be a short-range device used only at close range. It might destroy aircraft if a powerful ultrasonic generator is used—through the phenomenon of resonance. If the driving frequency of the beam coincides with the natural one of the vibrating body (the metallic structure of an aircraft, for instance), then a maximum motion or vibration occurs.

Cases have been recorded in which such vibrations reached proportions where large structures were destroyed. In the case of an airplane the molecular cohesion of its metallic structure suddenly would be disrupted; instantly all metallic parts of the plane would disintegrate into thousands of small fragments. The plane would explode, as if hit by an invisible internal force—an explosion without fire. The nonmetallic pieces or objects would not be affected by the sudden disintegration. The shredded condition of the plane would be the chief clue that such an ultrasonic weapon was used. Confirming evidence would be the bodies of the crew members killed in the crash.

An ultrasonic scanner, *i.e.*, an instrument to meter the nature of the terrain below, may also be used by UFOs. The constant stream of reflections of the ultrasonic signals (microwaves or shortwaves might be used, too) channeled into computing equipment at precisely the right time for comparative analysis may provide sufficient data to obtain a complete picture of the planet's outer crust. Such a device could explain the strange behavior of animals and birds—chiefly dogs—when a UFO is sighted in their proximity. The ultrasonic vibration emitted by the UFO, which bypasses the ear and directly stimulates the brain, could play on the organism the way a musician plays on his instrument—creating emotional moods that strike too deep for an untrained animal to resist. Dogs would be especially sensitive.

Although Dr. Fontes went into more detail, the foregoing excerpt furnished APRO with clues to other puzzles. The Desvergers incident, for instance, contained a puzzle even the Air Force couldn't explain. However, within the context of Fontes's theory of the ultrasonic device, the charred grass roots are no longer so puzzling.

The mysterious crash of an Air Force plane in which UFOs were involved was the front-page story of the May, 1959, *APRO Bulletin*. At 6:29 P.M. Wednesday, April 1, 1959, a C-118 transport with a crew of four took off on a local training flight from McChord AFB, Tacoma, Washington. About one hour and fifteen minutes later the pilot radioed: "We've hit something or something has hit us"; then he called "Mayday," the international distress signal, and reported that he was headed back to the base. Some time later came the final cryptic message: "This is it." The C-118 crashed five miles southeast of Sumner, Washington, between Sumner and Orting, at about 8:19 P.M., about thirty minutes after the "contact" message. Members of the Aerial Phenomena Research Group of Seattle did not see the wreckage, but they notified APRO that those who did had commented that the plane was "shredded almost beyond belief—smashed to bits." Three bodies were found—two nearly buried in the ground.

A series of incidents in the immediate area are significant: (1) At 7 P.M. a series of aerial explosions shook the northern Seattle area; (2) At 7:20 P.M. the entire Seattle area shook from a tremendous aerial explosion and damage was reported; (3) At 7:45 P.M. Sam Snyder of Graham, Washington, near the crash area, said his wife and a friend witnessed a brilliant glow through the timber in the direction of the crash scene; after dying out, it was followed by a second glow which soon disappeared (this glow or a similar one was seen by the Seattle-Tacoma International Airport tower controller just before the pilot reported his aircraft in trouble). During the early hours of darkness mysterious lighted objects were seen in the sky from Kent (about twenty miles north of the crash scene) to Carbonado, about eight miles southeast of the crash scene, as well as in the Mount Rainier area. Sighting of these mysterious objects in the Orting area was confirmed on April 2 in a telephone conversation between Orting's chief of police and the PIO at McChord Field. The latter, however, said the objects were parachute-dropped flares, part of an exercise at Fort Lewis near the air base. Fort Lewis news chief Delwood denied that such an exercise was in progress on the night of the crash. Witnesses in the Sumner area stated none of its four engines were running when the C-118 passed over their area. They also said that two parachutelike glowing objects were following the transport, part of whose tail assembly was missing (a large portion of the horizontal stabilizer was found later in the hills on the north side of Mount Rainier). Mr. and Mrs. Bill Jones of Orting reported seeing three or four parachutelike objects in the air as the plane passed near their home. The Air Force had no comment regarding these objects. For some unknown reason, the plane did not attempt to land at McChord. Instead, it turned away from the field, still flying at a very low altitude, struck trees on Crocker Heights, damaging number four engine and tearing open the wing tank which caught fire and turned the plane into a flying torch.

At 10 P.M. another series of explosions shook the Seattle area. About ten o'clock on the morning following the crash an anonymous telephone call was received by APRG members in Seattle: "Radar at McChord AFB picked up UFOs prior to the crash." The public information officer at McChord would neither confirm nor deny this report.

On Saturday, April 4, a group of APRG investigators went to the Orting-Sumner area to investigate reports of UFOs seen in the area prior to the crash. Fred Emard, Orting's chief of police, had advised them by telephone that he would be glad to furnish them with information regarding the mysterious flying objects, but he would like them to come to Orting so he could "see who I am talking to." Upon their arrival they found him in conference with an Air Force colonel. After they had waited about fifteen minutes the chief saw them and announced he had nothing to say to the members of the group. The entire area of the crash scene was under semi-martial law. Troops were moved in from Fort Lewis to interview residents of the area and instruct them not to discuss the crash. In Robert Gribble's words, "The citizens of the Sumner-Orting area are silent and scared. They know something is wrong, but they can't put a finger on it. The unlawful suppression of freedom of speech which occurs in cases like this is hard to believe and easy to dismiss as exaggeration when it happens to someone else. Where in the past many APRG members were reluctant to believe such stories, they have now experienced such censorship firsthand. The impact of the realization that such things can and do happen in this free country of ours is far from pleasant."

Gribble's words echoed my own when the full impact of the events of November, 1957, finally struck me—"the shredded condition of the plane," ultrasonics. To a UFO researcher accustomed to working with dates, places and specific similarities in descriptions the three Brazilian incidents fit into the pattern of activity which commenced after the sputnik launching. The C-118 case is but one additional case we found out about; how many other such disasters were covered up by official censorship we do not know.

Activity before the launching of Sputnik I had been mainly in South America. On November 2 "glowing eggs" landed on roads near Levelland, Texas, stopping approaching vehicles. Scarcely hours later the site of the first A-bomb explosion was visited. Seventeen hours later it was visited again. Early the next morning a plane flying a routine cargo flight over Brazil was attacked by a strange disc-shaped object. Forty minutes later the Itaipu fort was immobilized. The first time I read the Itaipu account it brought to mind certain information passed on to me a year before, but which we had never been able to confirm or discount. According to my informant, on a Saturday night in the early part of November, 1957, an army camp in Texas was visited by a glowing disc-shaped object which came down and hovered above the buildings. Tanks were vectored in, training their armaments on the object. Suddenly the men in the tanks came scrambling out—it had become unbearably hot in the tanks. At a USO dance in a nearby building the lights went out.

Shortly after receiving Dr. Fontes's last report, I was outlining its contents to an APRO member. His face lit up and he asked, "Do you suppose that could have been what happened at Sandia Base a couple of years ago during that saucer scare?" He had heard that on at least two separate occasions the power at Sandia had failed for no particular reason, though it was rumored each time that a UFO had been in the vicinity when the power failure had occurred. The described disc activity in New Mexico was in the vicinity of military installations. Did this pattern hold true elsewhere during November, 1957?

It cannot be doubted that a device which brings about the effects described by Dr. Fontes is being used; that these effects are no accident is a certainty. The strange objects have reconnoitered military installations on many other occasions, but in my 19 years of active UFO research the first detailed account of such happenings I was able to ferret out were the reports of the three which took place in November, 1957, in Brazil.

11
Incidents at Trindade

IN the early part of January, 1958, the *Almirante Saldanha* of the Hydrography and Navigation Division of the Brazilian Navy left Rio de Janeiro bound for the island of Trindade. The trip was routine, and the ship remained anchored in the waters off the island for several days.

At 12:15 P.M. on January 16, when the ship was preparing to depart from Trindade, someone on deck shouted and pointed to a strange object in the sky. The airborne object had the shape of a flattened version of the planet Saturn. It sped toward the island, hovered momentarily and then left in the direction from which it had come, speeding east.

Almiro Barauna, a member of the Icarai Club for Submarine Hunting, had been invited aboard the *Almirante Saldanha* by the Navy to take underwater photographs. At the time the object was sighted, Barauna was on deck with his camera. Despite the confusion on deck Barauna was able to get four good exposures of the object. (*See plates 5A-D.*) He later made the following statement to the Rio newspaper *Jornal Do Brasil:*

Suddenly Mr. Amilar Vieira and Captain Viegas called me, pointing to a certain spot in the sky and yelling about a bright object which was approaching the island. At this same moment, when I was still trying to see what it was, Lieutenant Homero, the ship's dentist, came from the bow toward us, running, pointing to the sky and yelling about the object he was watching. Then I was finally able to locate the object by the flash it emitted. It was already close to the island. It glittered at times, perhaps reflecting sunlight, perhaps changing its own light—I don't know. It was coming over the sea, moving toward the point called the "Galo Crest." I had lost about thirty seconds looking for the object, but the camera was already in my hands, ready, when I sighted it clearly silhouetted against the clouds. I shot two photos before it disappeared behind Desejado peak. My camera was set at a speed of .125 with an f/8 aperture, and this was the cause of the overexposure error, as I discovered later. The object remained out of sight for a few seconds, behind the peak, reappearing larger in size and flying in the opposite direction. It was lower and closer than before and moving at a higher speed. I shot the third photo. The fourth and fifth shots were lost, partly because of the speed at which the object was moving, and partly because I was being pushed and pulled about in the excitement. It was moving in the direction from which it had come, and it appeared to stop in mid-air for a brief time. At that moment I shot my last photo, the last on the film. After about ten seconds the object continued to increase its distance from the ship, gradually diminishing in size and finally disappearing into the horizon.

In the questioning of Barauna it was learned that the object made no discernible sound; it was dark gray in color, appearing to be surrounded, mostly in the area ahead of it, by a kind of condensation of a greenish, phosphorescent vapor or mist; it definitely appeared to be a solid object; and its flight was an undulatory movement across the sky—"like the flight of a bat." After the sighting, Barauna said, "The ship's commander and several officers from the garrison wanted to see what I had got in the photos. As I was curious, too, I decided to develop the exposed film at once, aboard

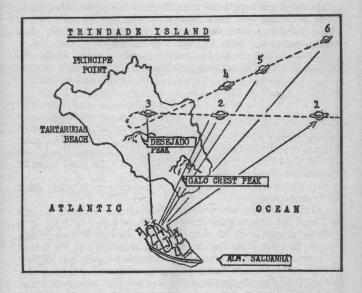

Figure 5: The ALMIRANTE SALDANHA *was anchored close off Galo Crest Peak. Photographer Barauna was in the stern of the ship. The UAO was first seen over the ocean, coming toward the island. The first photograph was taken when the object was in position 1, flying at slow speed. The second photograph was shot when the object was behind Galo Crest. The third photograph was taken a few seconds after the saucer made a turn near Desejado Peak. The fourth and fifth photographs failed to register the object which was now flying at high speed. The sixth photograph was taken as the object was moving away, close to the horizon; it disappeared a few seconds later. (See Plates 5A–D.)*

THE four photographs taken by Almiro Barauna on January 16, 1958, are without a doubt the finest record of a UAO to come into my hands. Although there can be no question as to their authenticity, due to the circumstances under which they were taken, I have made a careful study of the 8 x 10 enlargements sent to me. I am satisfied that these enlargements and the blowups from them which I made for publication in the *APRO Bulletin* show all or nearly all the detail that was visible in the negatives (APRO could not obtain the negatives).

The data, previously published in the *Bulletin:* CAMERA: Rolleiflex Model E, f2.8 lens. EXPOSURE: f8, 1/125 second. TYPE OF FILM: Not stated. TIME: 12:20 P.M. WEATHER: Bright overcast.

Six exposures were made in fourteen seconds, as determined by subsequent tests with the same camera and photographer. Two of these (exposures four and five) did not show the object, since the photographer's aim was upset by the confusion on deck.

I have carefully weighed this data against the actual appearance of the photographs and have reached these conclusions:

(1) The general appearance of the sky, water, rock detail, etc., indicates that they were taken on an overcast day.

(2) The density and contrast of the object is that of a *solid* object at a considerable distance from the camera under such lighting conditions. This was checked by comparison with many similar distant photographs of conventional aircraft taken under overcast conditions. This comparison also indicates a likely size of 120 x 24 feet as deduced from the studies and tests made by the Brazilian Government.

(3) The object is *not* luminous or cloudlike as in many other UFO photographs.

(4) The used shutter speed of 1/125 second would be enough to "stop" an object going several hundred miles an hour if it were far enough from the camera, as this one was. It is interesting to note that the outline of the object is quite sharp in the second and third photographs where it had slowed down, but slightly blurred in the first and fourth photographs, where it was going at a higher speed and the shutter setting was not high enough to freeze the motion. Greater distance would also contribute to the effect.

(5) I see *no* evidence of a vapor trail or luminous halo as reported by some witnesses. This may not have registered, due to overexposure of the sky background.

(6) Had the shutter been set at 1/250 or 1/500 second we would have had a much sharper set of pictures; however, Mr. Barauna should be complimented on his alertness and self-control in getting photographs as good as these under such trying conditions. Had he stopped to reset his shutter speed we might not have this valuable evidence.

Figure 6: Analysis of the Trindade Island photographs, by John T. Hopf, commercial and aerial photographer and APRO photographic analyst. For the Trindade photographs see Plates 5A–D.

the ship. The processing was done under the supervision of
several officers, including Commander Carlos A. Bacellar.
There was no photographic paper on the ship, so only the
negatives were seen while still aboard. They were seen and
examined by the whole crew, however."

Two days after the return of the ship to Rio de Janeiro,
Commander Bacellar appeared at Barauna's residence and
asked if he could see the enlargements made from the negatives. He took them to the Navy authorities and returned
them two days later, and congratulated Barauna. Later Barauna was asked to appear at the Navy Ministry, where he was
questioned by high-ranking staff officers. At the first meeting the officers asked for the negatives. They were sent to
the Cruzeiro do Sul Aerophotogrammetric Service where
they were analyzed, and Barauna was told the negatives were
found to be genuine, definitely excluding the possibility of a
trick or falsification. On the second visit time tests were
performed—Barauna worked with his Rolleiflex, taking shots
at the same time intervals he had used to photograph the object, while three officers with stop watches recorded the time
intervals. Based on charts of the island they concluded that
the object was flying between 900 and 1000 kilometers per
hour (about 600-700 miles per hour), and its size was determined to be about 120 feet in diameter and about 24 feet
high.

Questioned about the official report, Barauna said that
he had seen a thick dossier which the officers consulted constantly during his interrogation. He was informed that his
pictures, mixed with others, had been shown to witnesses
for identification. His photos were selected as those which
caught the object at Trindade.

Rio de Janeiro's *Ultima Hora* on February 21 reported
that at least a hundred individuals had witnessed the sighting
of the object and that the four Barauna exposures were obtained within fourteen seconds. Barauna was quoted in *O
Globo:* "At the end of the meeting, the chief intelligence
officer said he was convinced my photos were authentic. He
showed me another photo which had been taken by a Navy
telegrapher sergeant, also at Trindade. A box camera had
been used. The photo showed the same object seen in my
pictures. They told me it had been taken before my arrival
at Trindade Island."

Subsequent stories on the IGY pictures (as the Barauna

photos were to be designated) indicated Brazilian newspaper interest was high. A Brazilian Air Force retired captain, J.T. Viegas, was the first witness to confirm Barauna's report, in the *Diario Da Noite* and *O Jornal* on February 22. He said the object appeared as a flattened sphere encircled at the equator by a large ring or platform. He also stated that the pictures were taken to Navy headquarters where, together with a picture of a flying saucer sent from the United States, they were projected on a screen. The American picture was part of a military report on sightings in the United States. Also on February 22 the *Diario Da Noite* reported Commander Paulo Moreira da Silva of the Hydrography and Navigation Service in the following careful statement: "The object sighted in the skies of Trindade was not a weather balloon, nor an American guided missile. I cannot yet give my conclusions, for the data are being analyzed in a secret evaluation at the Navy Ministry. I can tell, however, that the object was not a meteorological balloon— for the one we had launched that day was released at 9 A.M., two hours before the appearance of the object in the sky. The balloon was tracked until it burst at the proper altitude. Besides, while the object was encircled by a greenish glow, our balloon was of a red color."

The Brazilian press recorded interviews of many witnesses to the sighting, both military and civilian. The case of the IGY pictures remained on the front pages of Rio de Janeiro's newspapers for fully seven days.

Dr. Fontes became interested in the IGY pictures, cognizant of the fact that such pictures would be photographic proof of the reality of the so-called "flying saucers." He began a systematic collection of the newspaper interviews and other information after he was alerted about the IGY pictures on February 4 by a friend in the Navy who, formerly skeptical about UFOs, had been convinced by the IGY pictures. On the evening of February 14 Dr. Fontes went to the Navy Ministry to be shown the four Barauna shots and a fifth one. At the time Fontes did not know that the fifth picture by another photographer was taken at an earlier date than the Barauna collection. Practically everything he learned on this visit was later confirmed in the press when the pictures were made public.

On February 27 and 28 a congressional investigation was

launched to get to the bottom of the situation, and the text
of the official inquiry was published in all Rio papers:

The Navy Ministry is requested to answer or explain
the following items of the inquiry presented by Representative Sergio Magalhaes on February 27, 1958, and
approved by this House: (1) Whether it is true that the
crew of the *Almirante Saldanha* witnessed the sighting
of a strange object over the Island of Trindade; (2) Considering that the official statement released from the
Navy Minister's office recognizes that photos of the
strange object were taken "in the presence of members
from the crew of the *Almirante Saldanha*," it is asked
whether an investigation was made and whether the reports from the Navy officers and sailors involved were
recorded; (3) In the hypothesis of a negative answer the
Navy Minister is requested to explain the reasons on
which he has based his inclination to attribute no importance to the fact; (4) If it is correct that the photos
were developed in the presence of officers from the
Almirante Saldanha and that the picture showed the
image of the strange object since the first examination;
and (5) If the negatives were submitted to a careful examination to detect any photographic trick contrived before the sighting; (6) Why the information was kept secret by Navy authorities for about a month; (7) Whether
it is correct that other similar phenomena were observed
by Navy officers; (8) Whether it is correct that the commanding officer of the Navy tow ship *Tridente* witnessed
the appearance of the strange object called a "flying
saucer."

The appearance of these strange aerial objects known
as "flying saucers" has attracted the world's interest and
curiosity for more than ten years. For the first time, however, the phenomenon is witnessed by a large number of
members from a military organization, and the photos
of the object receive the official seal through a statement released to the press by the Navy Minister's office.
Yet, as the problem affects the national security, more
information is necessary to clarify the facts. There is
some controversy in the information divulged through
the press, but the Navy apparently has no intention of
releasing the complete report to stop the confusion and
inform the public. Furthermore, in spite of the Navy
Minister's office declaring (officially) that a large number
of people from the *Almirante Saldanha* crew had sighted

the strange object photographed over the Island of Trindade, there was no request for the witnesses' reports or any other measures, as the chief of the Navy high staff admitted when interviewed by the press.

Aroused newspaper reporters rival intelligence officers when it comes to digging up facts, and they managed to dredge up the secret Navy answer to the House of Representatives; this was published on April 17, 1958, by the Rio de Janeiro *Correio Da Manha, O Jornal* and *Jornal Do Brasil*. The report pointed out that investigation hadn't started with the Barauna incident. Several other sightings had been made by civilians, sailors and officers on different occasions during December, 1957, and January, 1958, and these accounts indicated the presence of strange objects in the air over Trindade Island. The Navy's analysis of the Barauna incident and evaluation of the Barauna photos concluded: "Personal reports and photographic evidence of certain value indicate the existence of unidentified aerial objects."

It has not yet been determined who gave the Navy report to the newsmen, but it is a matter of record that the President of Brazil turned over the pictures to the press. APRO was to verify the contents of the report, however, for Dr. Fontes saw the document in the hands of friends in the Navy. In his carefully documented report to the APRO he included the first sightings at Trindade that were made before the Barauna incident.

Trindade is a small rocky island in the middle of the South Atlantic Ocean between the Brazilian coast and the African continent, more than six hundred miles off the coast of Bahia. It was used as an American and Brazilian anti-submarine base during World War II. Abandoned after the war, it was reoccupied in October, 1957, when a Brazilian Navy task force built an oceanographic post and meteorological station there for the International Geophysical Year (IGY) research. In early November instrument-carrying meteorological balloons were released there daily to study high-atmosphere conditions.

On a clear sunny day in the latter part of November the first UFO was sighted at Trindade. A balloon had been launched. Commander Bacellar was inside the radio station and everything seemed normal. But suddenly the signal frequency changed unexpectedly. Commander Bacellar sent a man outside to inform the theodolite operators that the balloon's instruments must have been prematurely parachuted. The technician came back seconds later, very excited, informing Bacellar the instruments had not yet been dropped. But Bacellar said, "That is impossible. I am listening to a new signal. What's going on out there?" The technician answered, "I don't know, sir, but they say there is another object in the sky near the balloon. . . ." There, high above the station, hovering near the balloon, was an ovoid object, silvery-white in color. Suggestions that the object might be Venus were immediately discarded—the elevation and azimuth of the object did not coincide with that of the planet. The balloon burst at the proper time and the unconventional object stayed in sight for three hours, eventually disappearing upward and out of sight.

The second sighting took place on December 25, but was considered to be of no consequence because the witness, a laborer, was deemed an unqualified observer. He described the object as silvery in color, round, with an angular diameter comparable to that of the full moon and flying silently at great height. On December 31 came the third sighting. The same or a similar object passed over the island again at 7:50 A.M. The silvery, circular object, with the apparent size of the full moon, crossed the sky silently at about six thousand feet. This time it was reported by five workers, a sailor, the island's doctor and Navy Lieutenant Inacio Carlos Moreira. On the following day, January 1, 1958, at 7:50 A.M. a bright point of light flashed over the sea at high speed. It described a 90-degree trajectory before vanishing into the horizon. In the middle of this trajectory it glowed brightly for a few seconds similar to a mirror reflecting sunlight. The object was viewed by the whole garrison, and workers and sailors reported that it was the same object they had sighted on previous occasions. January 2 was the date of the fifth sighting, but this sighting was only of a few seconds duration. On the same night, however, the Navy tow ship *Triunfo,* traveling off the Bahia coast four hundred miles from Trindade, was circled for almost ten minutes by an unknown aerial object. The crew witnessed the round object which was encircled by a weird orange glow and maneuvered at high speed with sudden changes of course and right-angle turns. At times it briefly hovered motionless, sometimes close to the ship.

Then on January 6 a released weather balloon was being tracked from the ground. The sky was blue and clear with no haze, and there was only a solitary cumulus cloud almost overhead. Commander Bacellar was inside the radio cabin tracking the balloon's slow ascent by the signals emitted from its radiosonde. Suddenly the signals gradually began to diminish in intensity, fading away as if the transmitter was moving outside the ground station antenna's range. There was no change of frequency; in fact, the signal's frequency didn't change even when the instruments were supposed to be automatically dropped by parachute—the balloon's transmitter became silent. Commander Bacellar went outside to investigate. Everything appeared normal—the balloon was high in the sky and still climbing, slowly approaching the cumulus cloud overhead at fourteen thousand feet, the height at which the balloon's instruments were to be jettisoned.

Then a strange thing happened—the balloon appeared to be sucked suddenly toward the cloud, entered it and was lost to sight. The balloon reappeared ten minutes later and resumed its ascent, more rapidly now, for it was without instruments. The balloon had gone into the cloud with its full instrument load and had reappeared without it. The instruments were never found; observers did not see them come down. But soon after the balloon reappeared another object left the cloud. A silvery object, the color of polished aluminum, came slowly from behind the cloud, moving in a southwest-to-east direction. Bacellar watched the object through a theodolite; it appeared to have the shape of a half-moon, and it altered its course finally, moving from east to west.

This sighting was reported in the Rio de Janeiro press on April 17, 1958 (*Correio Da Manha, O Jornal* and *Jornal do Brasil*), and on May 17 in the magazine *O Cruzeiro*. All details were included except the facts of the radiosonde signals and the missing instruments; these were first made public by Dr. Fontes in the *APRO Bulletin* in January 1960.

A seventh sighting reportedly took place just a few days before the arrival of the *Almirante Saldanha*. The object came in very low over the island, flashed toward the meteorological post at high speed, slowed abruptly and hovered for a brief moment above Desejado Peak, then moved again in a zigzag course and was gone into the horizon at tremendous speed. The object was described as resembling a highly polished flattened spheroid with a large ring circling its equator. The ring appeared to be rotating at high speed, and the object made no sound as it flew. It was surrounded by an eerie greenish glow which almost disappeared while the object was hovering and becoming brighter when the object moved.

Witnesses described the object as two or three times the size of a DC-3, and they said it appeared to be intelligently controlled. Investigation by Dr. Fontes revealed that the object was photographed by a Navy sergeant (Fontes believes it is the fifth picture he viewed when he visited the Navy Ministry).

These seven sightings and the Barauna incident in sequence unfold this interesting picture:

(1) A former war base is reactivated. As soon as men and equipment are moved in unconventional aerial objects scout the area;

(2) At least one and possibly two of these objects are photographed;

(3) There is the indication that an unconventional object interfered or possibly absconded with meteorological instrumentation equipment from a balloon launched at the base;

(4) The Brazilian Navy, following the pattern set by military authorities in other countries, attempts to suppress the information on the sightings;

(5) Pressure from the press and the public brings about the publication of the photographs and most of the details of the sightings.

Despite all this, only one photograph and very few of the details necessary to complete the picture were carried on the press wires in the United States and elsewhere. Why?

12
More Keys to the Puzzle

A REPORT which arrived at APRO headquarters in October, 1959, was one of the most detailed observations of an unconventional aerial object we have yet received. Our first knowledge of the Gill sighting came from a short Associated Press item published mainly in the west and east coast newspapers. The incident had taken place in a remote area of New Guinea where the Boianai Anglican Mission is located. The full report was forwarded by our Australian representative, Peter R. Norris, a brilliant young Melbourne lawyer. The principal sighting was preceded by several others. Thirty-eight witnesses were recorded, twenty-seven of whom signed statements examined by Norris. He also interviewed the principal observer in the case, the thirty-one-year-old Reverend Father W.B. Gill of the Boianai Mission.

After sightings by natives, medical personnel and mission helpers on June 21, UFO interest was high on Boianai. On Friday, June 26, at 6:45 P.M. a bright white light came in from the northwest and at 6:50 Father Gill called others to observe the object, which was approaching rapidly; at 6:52, as carefully recorded by Gill, the object was approximately five hundred feet from the observers. At 6:55 an object on top of the disc-shaped thing began to move, and what appeared to be three glowing men began moving about on top of the craft; then they disappeared from sight. At seven o'clock two of the men appeared again, only to disappear at 7:04. Gill said that at 7:10 a cloud ceiling covered the sky at about two thousand feet. Four men showed up at 7:10, then a thin, blue electric spotlight appeared and the men disappeared again. Two minutes later two of the human-appearing creatures reappeared in the blue light. At 7:20 the spotlight and the men disappeared again, and the craft entered a cloud. At 8:20 the same or another object appeared and Father Gill called to others as the object appeared to approach; it was not as large as the first object but it seemed closer. During the next hour and a half no less than four separate objects were seen approaching the Mission, coming in and out of the clouds, all apparently proceeding in orderly fashion. One was the large, manned craft with elaborate superstructure, the others were smaller, disc-shaped, with no apparent protuberances.

The following details were noted but not written down at the time of the observation: Cloud heights were determined in relationship to the highest point visible on surrounding mountains. Because the objects were often below the clouds and their glow gave off a wide halo of light reflected on the clouds, it was determined that the objects descended below two thousand feet altitude. The color of the objects was a dull yellow or pale orange; in motion they were very bright. When they finally left the vicinity of the Mission at 9:30 the color changed from a thin white to deep red and then to blue-green. A rough sketch of the object, observed between 6:55 and 7:22 P.M. by thirty-eight witnesses, showed the object as an inverted saucer with a "deck" projecting above the outer rim and four sticklike legs on the bottom. The "men" sketched in on the deck appeared from the waist up and a shaft of blue light was projected upward by parallel dotted lines.

The sighting of Saturday, June 27, proved to be the most important of the Boianai area. At 6 P.M. a large object was sighted by one of the mission workers, apparently in the same position as the object sighted the evening before. He called Father Gill who called other personnel outside to observe the strange craft. Although the sun had set, there was sufficient light for about fifteen minutes for the observers to clearly see four men who appeared shortly after the object was first spotted. Two smaller objects were hovering near—one above the hills in the west, the other directly overhead. On the large craft two of the figures seemed to be bending over and raising their arms as though adjusting or setting up something which was not visible to the observers. Father Gill impulsively raised his arm and waved. To his surprise, one of the figures on the strange craft returned his greeting. Then Ananias, one of the mission workers, waved both arms high over his head and two other figures on top of the craft did likewise. Both Father Gill and Ananias continued to wave and all four strangers imitated their gestures.

Darkness began to close in and Gill sent Eric Kodawara for

a torch; with it he directed a series of long dashes toward the UFO; after a minute or two the object made several wavering motions back and forth. The men on the ground continued to wave and flash the torch as the object seemed to grow larger, apparently approaching them. After about thirty seconds it ceased and came no closer. Two or three minutes later the figures lost interest in the party on the ground and went back to what they had been doing and then disappeared "below deck." At about 6:25 two figures appeared to carry on what they had been doing, and the blue spotlight came on twice in succession for a few seconds. During this time the two other UFOs remained stationary at high altitude. At 6:30 Father Gill went in to dinner. When he came back at seven o'clock the large object was still visible but seemed to be farther away. Gill left to attend church services. At 7:45 when evensong was concluded the sky was cloud-covered and visibility was limited—the UFOs apparently were gone.

Except for minor observations during the following months, no other incidents occurred on Boianai. Father Gill, who subsequently went to Australia, was closely questioned there by Mr. Norris. In our exchange of letters which followed his report, Mr. Norris emphasized the Reverend W. B. Gill's very objective account of the observation. During the time he spent getting the facts about the sightings from Father Gill he came to realize his honesty and sincerity; he considered the Gill series of sightngs to be one of the most important ever recorded. In all, five teachers, two medical assistants and many natives, besides Father Gill, witnessed the major sighting. There can be no doubt that they saw material objects and that the "men" on the objects were real beings of some type.

One question remains: What were those craft and their occupants doing at Boianai? The answer was not clear at the time, but some light has since been shed on the problem. It is obvious that the occupants of the large ship had no interest in the people on the ground and were merely satisfying curiosity when they waved to them; they soon lost interest and went about their business, whatever it was. No attempt at a real contact was made; they did not come back. It is conceivable that their ship was in trouble and repairs were being made. There are many possible answers, of course—many avenues of conjecture. However, the most important aspect of this series of sightings is that unconventional aerial objects, obviously not originating on earth, were seen simultaneously by a large number of reliable observers.

During this time South American countries were experiencing a flap of sorts. Bernardo Passion, our representative in Argentina, forwarded several routine reports of the usual disc- and cigar-shaped objects performing incredible maneuvers at equally incredible speeds in the skies over Argentina. One incident was significant, however, for it confirmed our conviction that the objects were experimenting with a device which inhibited the use of electrical equipment. On June 22, just four days before Father Gill's history-making sighting, a luminous spherical object passed over a wide sector of Salta near the San Bernardo hills. At 8 P.M. eyewitnesses watched as the object flew north-to-south and every light in the city went out. The blackout lasted for several minutes, after which everything went back to normal.

When this information, reported in Salta's *El Tribuno,* arrived at APRO headquarters it rang a bell; it was so similar to something we had investigated in the past. I searched the master file of APRO *Bulletins* for a similar incident. In the September, 1953, issue I found what I was looking for. Weird flashes of bright yellow light along the middle fork of the Kaweah River near Moro Rock, California, had baffled residents and Sequoia Kings National Park officials. Park Superintendent E. T. Scoyen announced to the press that the phenomena had occurred four nights in a row during the week prior to July 24, 1953. On the night of the 24th Scoyen himself observed the strange sight. Sitting on the terrace of his home in Ash Mountain, he was startled by a yellow streak of light which lit up the canyon near Moro Rock. The light appeared to be traveling from north to south at a very high speed. About ten seconds later a huge yellow ball, which appeared to Scoyen to be about a thousand feet in diameter, rose from that point. Other individuals had reported seeing similar flashes on the preceding Tuesday, Wednesday and Friday nights. Some of the witnesses said the light appeared to have a ball on the leading end, and all agreed on the bright yellow color and the direction of travel. Fern Gray, telephone operator at park headquarters on Ash Mountain, added the information that all the drops on her switchboard *were mysteriously knocked down during the Friday-night flash.* Scoyen ruled out explosions or meteors because of the regularity of the appearances as well as the fact that the objects seemed to be low and made no sound.

The third incident which involved seeming interference with electrical equipment took place on August 17, 1959, when power employees in Uberlandia, Brazil, experienced an unexplainable power failure. The report probably would not have been submitted to APRO for quite some time if the hostile UFO theory had not been seriously considered. After the Itaipu incident, which also involved a power failure, Dr. Fontes and I began to consider the possibility of predicting future actions by UFO occupants. As I have outlined in an earlier chapter, there were indications that the capabilities of our defenses, weapons and transportation were being closely examined by the uninvited visitors. Following the incidents in the United States in the fall of 1957, as well as those in Brazil in the early months of 1958, I began to look for areas in which obvious military reconnaissance had not been completed. It is a well-known fact that in addition to military bases the aggressor takes into consideration the basic needs of the victim, such as his water and electrical power sources. Prior to the summer of 1959 the discs had successfully halted automobiles, trucks and planes. However, to our knowledge, they had not ever caused the immobilization of a steam or diesel engine. I suggested to Dr. Fontes that trains, dams, locks and power plants would probably be the target for future UFO visitations—that a geographical and military reconnaissance of the whole planet had been undertaken which would not be complete until our power and water supplies were mapped.

In a letter commenting on my prediction Fontes said I had apparently hit the target with my guess—he had just received the details of a reported UFO reconnaissance of a power station in Minais Gerais, Brazil. On the night of August 17, 1959, the four automatic keys at the Uberlandia station suddenly turned off, simultaneously disconnecting the power to all trunks. Baffled technicians at the station hurriedly checked their instruments but found nothing wrong— the trouble had to be at the power trunks or at the four substations. Before the chief engineer could call the substations on the battery telephones his telephone began ringing. The caller at a substation about forty-five miles from the central station reported that all keys at his station had been disconnected simultaneously. He also reported that a "flying saucer" had passed overhead just as the keys switched off. After receiving a warning against drinking on the job, the technician told his superior that he would soon find out for himself, for the object was following the trunk line and was headed for the main station.

The chief at the main power station himself switched on the automatic keys—he flipped two and nothing happened; he flipped the third and all three automatically turned off again. At that moment there were shouts outside the building. The power station is on a hill overlooking the Uberlandia Valley. The whole valley was illuminated by an eerie glow from a very bright round object high in the sky. Approaching the main station at high speed, the object's path followed the trunk line connecting the substation, which had just reported in, with the main station. The UFO silently crossed above the station and disappeared over the horizon; thereafter the keys automatically turned on and everything returned to normal. The time between the two sightings was two minutes, the distance between the two places approximately forty-five miles and the speed of the object about fifteen hundred miles an hour. Analysis of the incident indicated that the object did not have the configuration of a jet or other aircraft and that the speed was much faster than that of operational jets in Brazil. The possibility that the object might have been a meteor had to be discarded because of its apparent size and speed (much too slow). We concluded that the object was indeed an unconventional aerial object under intelligent control.

The year 1959 waned with few reports of outstanding sightings. The Gill sighting was still causing much comment among UFO researchers, however. In January Mr. Norris informed me that RAAF officials had told Father Gill he had observed merely exceptionally bright planets, but they admitted they could not account for the huge ship he had seen at close range. We had expected a disclaimer of some sort, and in the case of a churchman we were sure no attempt would be made to cast reflection on his honesty. Therefore it had to be a "misconception" of conventional objects—planets. Not surprising, but wholly ridiculous.

At 10:05 on the evening of August 13, 1960, Clarence Fry, deputy sheriff and jailer at the Red Bluff prison in California, observed an oval, pale-yellow glowing object, with a flashing red light on each end and squarish white lights along the side, come out of the west-southwest. Later, at 11:45, highway Patrolmen Stanley Scott and Charles Carson, in a patrol car about eighteeen miles north of Red Bluff, spotted a similar (or the same) object in the eastern sector of the sky. The object, which appeared to be hovering between 200 and 1000 feet above the ground, occasionally moved up and down, rotating a slowly sweeping red beam of light. The patrolmen gave chase, driving up and down the country roads in an attempt to get close to it. They estimated their proximity as less than two miles at the time they first sighted the object. Several others, including Fry and some prisoners whom he marched out onto the front steps of the jail, also observed the object. At about 1:45 A.M. the next day the object appeared to be approached by a similar object from the south, and both disappeared on the eastern horizon.

Data which came to light later included the following: The patrolmen experienced excessive radio static during the observation. Scott reported to APRO in a signed statement that there had been complete radio failure on their and other frequencies for forty-five minutes about two hours before they sighted the object. After the sighting Scott and Carson sent out a radio alert. Three deputies who heard the alert sighted the object and took up the chase, but soon were outdistanced. The San Francisco *Chronicle* reported that one Air Force official the paper had contacted said he was convinced something was seen but that it "sounded more like something made on Mars than a government product."

Scott, in a telephone conversation with me on August 19, said he had been told by Red Bluff radar station personnel that the object had been picked up on radar there after he had sent out the radio alert. Several days later Major Malden, commanding officer at the Red Bluff station, said their radar had not picked up the object. Subsequently the Air Force official explanation was that the object observed by Scott, Carson and others, which appeared huge, glowing, with porthole-like lighted portions on its side and with sweeping red beam at one end, was merely a refraction of the light of the star Aldebran and/or the planet Mars.

It is important to note that neither Mars nor Aldebran had risen during the two-hour sighting, and that while it was in sight the object did considerable maneuvering and exhibited itself over a good portion of the eastern sky. A reputable astronomer noted that atmospheric refraction does not exceed the order of one-half degree, even at the horizon. Another fact: observers reported that the night was clear with temperature about eighty degrees. Scott reported that the moon rose over the eastern horizon while he and Carson watched the object in the east. The moon exhibited no abnormality, thus negating any possibility of the object being a mere aberration of the light of an astronomical body. The Air Force explanation is completely without foundation. It is an "explanation" —nothing more; it "explains"—but it does not identify.

Two days prior to this sighting a most sensational one took place near Boulder, Colorado. Our first hint of it was a news clipping, and we directed a very competent APRO member in the area to make a complete investigation. Brownlow V. Wilson had written for the *Bulletin* and Mr. Lorenzen and I had discussed with him aspects of the UFO situation on several occasions. If the sighting was real Wilson would be the one to make that determination. These are his findings:

Ray Hawks of Boulder was working a farm tractor in secluded Left Hand Canyon, west of Boulder. Hearing a muffled explosion which seemed to come from above, he looked up and shortly a round object dropped vertically through a cloud, stopping about 650 feet away and some 200 feet above the ground. The object wobbled a little as it stopped, as a coin wobbles when thrown upon a table. Hawks noted that the object appeared as two concave discs joined together and about one-fifth as deep as its diameter. The disc was not shiny; rather it had a dull gray color. Around its perimeter and a little inside from the edge were a series of shiny metal plates with a small gap between each which could be seen on the undersurface as it descended and on the upper edge as it came to rest in the air.

Hawks became aware of an intermittent hum similar to an electric motor out of phase and idling, which seemed to come from the interior of the disc. One of the plates was oozing a "royal blue" smoke. Then to Hawks's amazement he observed that the plate giving off smoke began to recede into the object, "just like you might tilt the windshield of an automobile prior to taking it inside the car." Then an elongated hole could be seen in place of the plate. Next he saw what appeared to be a new plate which was worked into place from within, and he distinctly heard a click at the end of the operation. The intermittent hum increased in intensity, until it "increased a whole octave" and attained a very high pitch. At this stage the disc appeared to be surrounded by a sort of shimmering field which resembled heat waves. Then the disc suddenly took off vertically at very high speed and disappeared from view.

When Hawks first sighted the UFO he was working the

shovel loader on his tractor; as the disc came closer the engine stopped. He thought he had continued the lifting operation after it was fully elevated, which would have killed the engine. He reached down to restart his engine, but the starter was dead. Hawks said he wasn't frightened and that the disc took only about fifteen minutes for the whole operation.

Later, when Hawks had returned to the same area (after the sighting had been publicized in the local papers), he was surprised to find an Air Force helicopter there. A colonel and a major got out while a captain remained in the aircraft. After a brief conversation the colonel asked him to tell the newspapers that the saucer would be back again on the 20th. Hawks refused, saying people would think he was crazy. The colonel said this pronouncement would help prevent panic. (Such a suggestion could serve a definite purpose. In other instances when witnesses said they expected the saucers back on a certain date, their original observations were discarded as probably hoaxes when the saucers failed to show up. Whether or not these "predictions" were suggested by Air Force personnel we do not know, but Hawks's testimony indicates that at least this method of discrediting an observation had been used once and could have been used before.)

Although 1960 and 1961 have not provided many UFO sightings, some interesting incidents took place which tend to discredit official statements. A repetitious denial of sightings by "responsible individuals" (such as astronomers) is an old standby of the explainers. "Experts Puzzled" headlined an article in the May 30, 1961, Melbourne *Sun* describing a fantastic sighting in the Australian skies by competent observers:

> A photograph of a strange object seen glowing with bluish light in the night sky near Gundagai this week has astronomers puzzled. The photographer was among a party of five who kept the object in view for more than two hours. At one stage the object slowly eclipsed over four-fifths of its area as if a straight black curtain was drawn across.
>
> Naval rating Stephen King, an electrical mechanic, took a four-minute exposure shot with a high quality camera. "It was five times as bright as any star," he said later. Members of the observing party agreed unanimously that what they saw was not a planet, the moon, a weather balloon or a "stooging" aircraft.
>
> Astronomers at Mount Stromlo Observatory have not

been able to solve the mystery. The strange object was seen on May 7 when King and the other four were returning to HMAS Harman near Canberra, from Melbourne. All are stationed at the naval establishment. King said they first saw the glow at 4:20 A.M., when they were about ten miles from Gundagai on the Yass Road. He last saw it at 6:25 before they reached Canberra. King said he did not report he had taken the photograph because he thought it would not be taken seriously.

He took the negative to a professional photographer in Canberra who made a print. What the picture showed caused amazement in scientific circles. King and his co-observers were surprised that the print showed three separate glowing areas, of the strangest shapes, and not the regular shape they saw. However, the photographer—well known commercially in Canberra—examined the negative under a powerful microscope. The shape reported by the five—generally circular with a "nose" effect pointing earthward—then became visible.

"There's no mistake about it—it is there on the film," the photographer said.

Assistant N.S.W. government astronomer Mr. Robertson said, after having seen the photograph: "I don't know what it could be. I can't explain it at all."

Here, obviously, is an astronomer with the intelligence and humility to admit that he doesn't know everything. Refreshing.

This incident was described in full, with the photograph, in the July 1961 *Australian Flying Saucer Review,* the official publication of the Australian Flying Saucer Bureau, ably edited by Peter E. Norris of Melbourne, Andrew Tomas of Brighton-le-Sands and Carl Lehmann of Brisbane—all competent, discerning individuals who have investigated and published some of the best evidence in support of the reality of UFOs.

Some startling information was contained in a regular report from APRO's Venezuelan representative, Horacio Gonzales Ganteaume. In September, 1961, a huge "fireball" maneuvered above the boat of five fishermen, on the southern part of Lake Maracaibo. The fishermen, frightened out of their wits, threw themselves into the water and swam toward shore. Four of them managed to reach the shore, but the fifth did not turn up. The survivors swore they "never saw anything like it in our lives."

At 10 A.M. on Monday, May 22, 1961, an ovoid aluminum-colored object flew silently over the rolling hills of Santa Teresa del Tuy, sixty kilometers from Caracas, and landed on a hill near the site of earth-moving operations in the Paraiso del Tuy area. The object was seen by more than twenty people, among them engineers, topographers and a police officer. They said it wove a path in and out of the hills, dodging trees and flying at a low speed. It stopped in the air over a stretch of "gamelote" grass. One of the observers, Dr. Rino del Negro, leaped into his jeep and followed the path of the object, catching up with it just in time to see it duck behind a hillock. As he reached a bend in the road he saw the object taking off to vanish again behind some hills farther in the distance. On reaching the spot later, he was surprised to find that the tall gamelote grass was flattened toward the ground in a roughly circular area about sixty feet in diameter. Answers to inquiries by Ganteaume indicated that three similar objects had been observed traversing the same route the day before. Vicario Dante, resident topographer and ex-lieutenant in the Italian anti-aircraft corps, also saw the object. He told Ganteaume that it was neither plane, helicopter, balloon, rocket nor other known flying machine, and seemed to be moving in a sort of white cloud with fuzzy edges.

These are all very interesting details, but the incident is only one of hundreds of similar cases in APRO files. One detail, however, makes this incident outstanding. Ganteaume investigated and found the flattened grass; he photographed the area, and further examination showed that *the roots of the grass appeared to be burned*. Let's recall the West Palm Beach scoutmaster case in which laboratory examination showed while the roots of grass above which a UFO had hovered were burned, the grass spears appeared to be normal.

A special report from Ganteaume involved Adolfo Paolino Pisani, a government topographer in Merida, Venezuela. In January, 1961, driving along the Andean highway from La Victoria to El Vigia, he could see the highway stretching out before him; the sky was clear. Aware of a truck approaching from the rear, he pulled his jeep off the highway to allow it to pass. Suddenly a brilliant metallic disc with the appearance of polished blue steel swooped down at incredible speed and crossed perilously close to the hood of the truck. The object rose immediately into the sky and was lost to sight within seconds. What shocked Pisani, however, was that when the disc rose above the truck, *the vehicle also rose a few feet in the air and overturned in the direction of the object.* Fortunately there was a sandbank where the truck overturned and the vehicle found a comparatively soft landing place as it rolled over, its wheels in the air. The driver was the only occupant and escaped with minor scratches and nervous shock. Both went for help to get the truck righted.

The details of this case were kept confidential by the Venezuela National Guard and by Pisani who did not want any publicity because of the usual fear of ridicule. He confided the details to his cousin Dr. C. E. Paolini Pisani and to Dr. Franco Puppio Leon, both Caracas lawyers. Impressed by Pisani's nervous state and the potentially dangerous aspects of the incident, and knowing of Ganteaume's interest and activities in the UFO problem, they gave Ganteaume permission to make the report public.

One 1961 UFO incident to come to the attention of APRO and which was subsequently investigated concerns the observation of a large, gray-colored, disc-shaped object which hovered south of Utah Central Airport near Salt Lake City on October 2. What began as a routine takeoff for Waldo J. Harris, a pilot of Salt Lake City, turned out to be one of the most exciting and perplexing events of his life. At noon Harris was preparing for takeoff when he sighted the object to the south. At first he thought it was another plane, and he was surprised to find the object still in the same position when he became airborne. Curious, he changed his heading and flew toward what appeared to be a large disc hovering with a rocking motion at an altitude of between 6500 and 7000 feet. Harris radioed the airport that he had sighted what he thought to be a "flying saucer" and was going to get a better view. He estimated the distance between himself and the object at about five miles. Seven other individuals on the ground also saw the object. One, Virgil S. Redmond, had just landed his plane and reported that the object was not there when he came in for his landing. The other six observers were Mr. and Mrs. Jay Galbraith, operators of the airport; Clyde Card and Duane Sinclair who were preparing for a flight; Robert Butler, an employee of Ute Aeromotive based at the field; and Russ Woods, an airport employee.

They all made use of a pair of binoculars and agreed that the object hovered with a rocking motion and resembled a zeppelin at times; when it moved it achieved fantastic speed. Harris, meanwhile, attempted to close in. As he approached he realized he had misjudged the object's altitude, for it was at eye level at six thousand feet. He headed toward it and got a good view of the object's top portion as it tipped toward him, clearly silhouetted against the mountains to the south.

After receiving the initial report, I called Harris. The conversation was most informative; some of the facts not published in the newspapers included the details that the object had the appearance of "sand-blasted" aluminum. There were no clouds or ground haze, and visibility was excellent. Judging from the actual distance of the hills to the south, Harris estimated that the object was about five miles south of the field when spotted and that he got within three miles of it before it moved away. The departure was strange: it began a vertical climb and then headed south. It appeared to be about fifty feet in diameter and five to ten feet thick at the center. There were no protrusions, portholes, wings, etc., and it had the appearance of two shallow dishes joined together at the rim. Harris followed the saucer when it began its flight and observed it as it suddenly halted and hovered at a point almost directly above the Lake Omni station; then it moved straight up and began to move west at an extremely accelerated rate of speed and disappeared in a few seconds. During the chase Harris maintained communication with both Utah Central Airport and the Provo airport. In addition, he relayed information to the Federal Aviation Association communications tower at Salt Lake Municipal Airport.

When I talked to Harris most of the furor was over and the Salt Lake City *Deseret News and Telegram* had published the Pentagon's opinion of the sighting. As usual, the spokesman for the Pentagon Air Force contingent was not named and the conclusion was a familiar one: Harris had seen either a research balloon or the planet Venus. The newspaper quoted Harris's statement in reaction to the explanation; it was that of an experienced, competent pilot who had reported in good faith his observation of an unidentified flying object. After pointing out that the object had been gray, discshaped, moving against the wind, etc., Harris said, "I'd like to talk to that Pentagon spokesman."

The evidence against the Air Force explanation of Harris's observation came from the U.S. Weather Bureau itself. In the Salt Lake *Tribune* October 3 issue describing the sighting the Weather Bureau announced that the prevailing winds measured by a weather balloon at 10 A.M. (two hours before the sighting) were clocked at two miles an hour, from the southeast. If the object had been a balloon, it would have moved toward the airport, not away into the south and then west. The description of the object by several people besides Harris, plus the object's physical position in relation to the southern horizon, belies the Venus explanation.

Harris was eventually interviewed not only by Air Force Intelligence but by two Navy commanders and several lesser officers from the Twelfth Naval District Intelligence Branch, San Francisco, who flew to Salt Lake City to question him. There was no ridicule nor levity; they told him they felt the object was real. This was no news to me for I had known for approximately four years that both the Army and the Navy had been carrying on their own UFO investigations.

Data gathered for 1960 and 1961 support my contention that ignorance and fear play large parts in this hoax. Perhaps authorities do not want to "go out on a limb" and make a definite statement about something as fantastic as UFOs. This might be accepted as a reasonable attitude except for the possible danger involved—not just from the discs but from the very philosophy of fear which generates the attitude.

The public has often made the mistake of asking the wrong people for answers. A strange object is seen in the sky. When we think of the sky we think of astronomy and astronomers, so we ask the astronomer. But what is his responsibility? He is familiar with the sky and celestial objects such as planets, meteors and stars. But is he qualified to identify an unconventional aerial object? The most logical answer he can give us is whether or not the object is astronomical in nature. If he is honest and possesses some humility he will readily admit his inability to identify that which, within the scope of his knowledge, is impossible to identify. If we ask a military man he will interpret the observation within the scope of his own knowledge of conventional aircraft, and if the object is a rapidly moving light or "ball of fire" he will think of astronomical objects and "tentatively" identify the object as astronomical in origin. So we are back to astronomy and in the same old vicious circle again. Round and round we go—

The American public has been grossly misled because it has failed to give sufficient thought to the mystery. Why is a respectable citizen publicly branded an incompetent or a liar because he sees something out of the ordinary? And who is qualified so to brand him? An unnamed spokesman in a military uniform? So many times I have heard skeptics say, "He should know—he's in the Air Force, and he says they don't exist!" But who is *he?* Most of the official statements on UFOs have no name behind them. Is the military "observer" subject to a psychological "will-not-to-believe" because a new idea would threaten the little security of his own immediate world? Does the overlord of the world's finest and fastest aircraft want to believe that there are material machines in the skies about him which make his own craft look like tricycles by comparison? Is the man in the military service necessarily immune to the emotional blocks which would prevent him from believing the competent observations of colleagues to whom he would entrust his own life?

I have talked to many Air Force pilots who have not seen UFOs and ridicule the idea that they exist or that they could be interplanetary if they did. I have also talked to many Air Force and Navy pilots who have seen UFOs and are convinced by what they saw with their own eyes; they didn't believe *before* their experiences but were convinced by the weight of evidence before their eyes. Both groups wear the uniform of their country and are the best in the world—intelligent, well-trained, objective observers. Which group is right, which is wrong?

The military man is unable to make an objective evaluation of UFOs by his own dedication. The Air Force is charged with the defense of this country against air attack; this includes the supervision of the manufacture of its planes and the training of competent pilots to use them. Faced with aircraft with which he cannot possibly cope, it is easier for an Air Force man to assume that it was only a delusion or an atmospheric phenomenon—at least this assumption affords some temporary comfort in the "solving" of an insoluble problem. Similarly an astronomer, faced with data indicating that other intelligences have traversed space and know a good deal more about the universe than he, may find it expedient (albeit intellectually dishonest) to reject the evidence. This, I believe, is part of what has happened in the mystery of the unidentified flying objects. Facts have been discarded, both by the military and the public, in favor of false security.

Recently I received a letter from a man whose expert eye-witness testimony regarding a plane crash had been accepted.

He asked me why, then, his testimony as an expert witness was not accepted in the evaluation of a UFO sighting several years ago. The UFO he said he had under observation for several minutes was "identified" as a conventional object. I could not give this man the whole answer; it does not merely consist of a word or two. It is not censorship, it is not stupidity, it is not ignorance; it is a combination of many elements. But I firmly believe that the UFO problem should be taken out of the hands of the Air Force and turned over to a group of competent civilian scientists who have no ax to grind and no emotional barriers against the idea of superior beings and superior aircraft. And this group should include competent pychologists.

13
The Pattern and Its Meaning

IN 1958 Dr. Olavo Fontes in Brazil offered the theory of a pattern he had found in a sweeping but careful survey of UFO sightings over an eleven-year period. Fontes said that the UFOs are hostile and that the visitations of eleven years fell into a pattern indicating military reconnaissance. At first I was doubtful, probably a result of my natural prejudice against such a conclusion. But I started a search of the file material, and going back through reports, *APRO Bulletins* as well as other UFO research periodicals I was again and again faced with a lack of a "pattern." During 1947 through 1950 the lack of any standardization in the reports was obvious.

But Fontes had an answer for that. According to his theory the saucers started their reconnaissance in 1947 after the explosion of nuclear devices on earth. Their apparently helter-skelter observations in the first years was due, he said, to the lack of preparation. They sent what they had in the way of exploratory ships—discs, big and little; cigar-shaped ships, big and little; globes with and without rings; rings;

double rings; etc. This was what had puzzled civilian researchers for so long; why so many different kinds? The colors of the objects varied, too; some researchers conjectured that the variety of colors may have been a means of identification for the occupants, and others theorized that the colors were directly connected with the different propulsion systems being utilized.

But this did not answer my questions; Fontes's explanation for the absence of standardization in the reports was plausible, but I wanted more. My search was rewarded by a story in *Look* for July 1, 1952. The article, "Hunt for the Flying Saucer," was headlined by a map showing flying saucer report concentrations. The bulk of the sightings had been made in the vicinity of or on vital defense installations, according to the map, which was based on sightings gathered by the Air Force up to early 1952; clearly, the discs had engaged in a general military reconnaissance of the United States in 1948 and 1950. The mass of early sightings in 1947 indicated geographical surveys. Then, as Fontes put it, "In 1952 a new kind of operation had started. A very detailed and methodical reconnaissance of our aerial and terrestrial defenses was the most important part of the new survey." The most memorable of these, of course, were the mysterious objects which registered on radar scopes in the vicinity of Washington, D.C.—the "Washington blips."

On the night of July 20, 1952, radar at Washington International Airport showed the presence of unidentified objects over the city. Reams of newspaper copy were devoted to descriptions of the objects and the furor they were causing throughout the country. The fear-stricken were certain Russia was daringly testing a secret weapon over our capital. Rather hopefully, others said they were our own revolutionary aircraft; their hopes were soon deflated when it was pointed out that the air space over the Capitol, verboten even to airliners, would not be a likely place for our test hops.

During one of these saucer "invasions" a young pilot was brought to a Washington, D.C. hospital suffering from shock. He had vectored his jet in on a UFO and became panicstricken when his communications system suddenly went dead. The Air Force was fully aware of what close contact with UFOs could mean—it had the record of three Navy planes in similar trouble two years before over North Korea. Possibly this was the reason the jets failed to reach Washington in time to intercept the UFOs—no need letting too many pilots find out about the dangers involved.

Everyone was talking about the saucers and excitement was running high. The newspapers reported that the Air Force had alerted jets to intercept and shoot down the discs, whereupon Air Force spokesmen said the jets had been ordered to intercept, but not to shoot. At the height of the Washington flap General Samford called a press conference and insinuated that the saucers were nothing to worry about; he dubbed them reflections from ground lights on cold air sandwiched between layers of warm air in the upper atmosphere. The Menzel theory—otherwise known as the hot-air theory— was introduced. The public was already well-indoctrinated, for an article dealing with Dr. Donald Menzel's explanation for the saucers had appeared in the June issue of *Look*. The sedative had been concocted (by happenstance?) ahead of time, and was administered to an unsuspecting public. The people believed—some of them. What they did not know was that an inversion sufficient to create the firm images on the radarscopes did not exist on any of the nights Washington was visited. This was later confirmed by an Air Force weather expert.[1]

The year 1952 had two recorded events which went down in UFO history—the first authentic UFO photographs and the first landing, or near-landing, of a UFO. The pictures by photographer Ed Keffel were first published in the Brazilian magazine *O Cruzerio*. They were taken at a considerable distance over the waters near Rio de Janeiro and showed a disc-shaped object with a tiny cupola on top. (*See Plates 1A–E.*) The near-landing took place in a palmetto thicket near West Palm Beach, Florida, and was observed by D. S. Desvergers. With the exception of the sighting of a huge green-colored "monster" in West Virginia and a few lesser sightings, 1953 was quiet. But 1954 was another story when the "little men" appeared in large numbers for the first time. The observations of these small beings was, for the most part, confined to Europe and South America. They ranged in size from 3 to about 5 feet, according to witnesses. The European "little men" are discussed in Michel's book, *Flying Saucers and the Straight-Line Mystery,* and I cover

[1] See *Flying Saucers from Outer Space* by Donald Keyhoe.

a representative group of the "South American variety" in Chapter 6 of this volume.

The South American "little men" fell into three general size groups: the 3-feet-tall hairy midgets, the 4-feet-tall human-appearing creatures and the 5-or-more-feet-tall average-size men with or without space suits. From the testimony of witnesses the midgets usually collected rocks and soil, while the other two size groups engaged in gathering botanical and geological specimens. The animal-like midgets reacted quickly and violently to interference or interruption; the manlike creatures avoided contact, preferring to run away rather than be observed.

In the 1952 file I found information about a rumored pair of earth satellites. In later years these satellites were the subject of much conjecture, specifically in the books of Donald Keyhoe. Now, I decided, I was on the right trail. The satellites, Dr. Fontes writes, could serve as ecological and biological laboratories to filter and study information and specimens arriving from smaller ships operating within the earth's atmosphere. Considering this in conjunction with the recorded reports of "little men" engaged in the collection of flora and fauna, the picture began to make sense. It is no more logical that the comparatively small ships in the "little men" incidents housed a laboratory than it is reasonable that these craft made trips to their home planet far away in outerspace. A satellite was the logical explanation.

In 1952 a young meteorologist told me that in 1948 at Wright Air Development Center (then Wright-Patterson Air Force Base), when he had stopped off en route to California, a buddy of World War II days had showed him space suits ranging from 3 to about 5 feet in height and diagrams of a circular ship which bore a strong resemblance to a "flying saucer." He said that people who laughed about flying saucers were going to get a big jolt some day—these suits had been taken off the bodies of men who had apparently perished in the crash of their saucer-shaped ships. If true, this story indicates that the "little men" were known to officialdom at an early date.

The unexpected flap of 1957 caught civilian researchers completely unawares. According to the estimated two-year flaps, which coincided with the near approaches of the planet Mars, we were not due for another major influx until the fall of 1958. But a coincidence was obvious—the November, 1957, flap almost immediately followed the launching of the first earth satellite. When the Russian Sputnik II went up in November it took a back seat; the saucers suddenly became prime newspaper copy—for the first time since 1952 when the iron curtain of military secrecy on UFO sightings first rang down. Although the United States had its share of sensational sightings and the populace was fully aware that something extremely unusual was taking place, official statements subdued any possibility of general belief in the reality of the discs. It was not until months later, when hundreds of reports had been scrutinized, that even the researchers had a full picture of what had happened.

Through APRO's worldwide membership and contacts we learned that the discs were prominently seen during a flap in the Orient in the fall of 1956, and were also busy there in the spring of 1957, moving to South America and to Venezuela in particular in April. The United States, which had comparatively few sightings in 1957, suddenly experienced a rise in UFO reports when Sputnik I was launched. Although the general public was not made aware of it, because of the hands-off policy of the press, reports from members which flowed into civilian organizations indicated that a flap was in progress. Routine, close-range study of South American countries and the Far East had been the order of the year for the occupants of the discs until the unexpected launching of the first earth satellite. Few instances of stalled cars had been reported prior to November 3, but thereafter reports came in daily, and chiefly from the United States.

A properly equipped satellite circling the earth at a few hundred miles could easily detect the presence of another satellite. The presence of UFOs over the United States immediately after the Sputnik I launching hinted that they were looking for its source—the United States was one of the world powers capable of such a feat. But the discs weren't in too much of a hurry; after all, the first earth-launched satellite was no great accomplishment to them. However, Sputnik II's launching barely days later, with its living cargo, probably was cause for excitement among the occupants of the discs; it could mean that they had underestimated our progress in rocketry and space exploration. The next day a glowing object landed several times on the roads surrounding Levelland, Texas, within an approximate 4-mile radius of the town. Hours later in the early morning of November 3 another object, whose description matched that of the Levelland intruder, scouted the northern sector of the White Sands Proving Ground Range. At 8 P.M. the following evening another report of a glowing object in the same vicinity was made by a military guard duty. Each of these sightings involved military men in jeeps. It was not learned whether the ignition or lighting systems of the jeeps had been affected by the object, but if the sightings fitted the pattern of the others there is a good chance they were.

During the next few days a Holloman AFB electronics engineer reported the failure of his car among others as a huge glowing object passed over the highway near Orogrande, New Mexico, and autos were stopped at various places throughout the country—a truck in Tennessee, a car near Modesto, California, etc. By November 15 an unnamed Air Force spokesman at the Pentagon had quelled the "hysteria," calling the engineer incident a hoax, and the sighting influx had subsided. But not so in South America. The busy objects continued to clutter up the skies over Brazil and Venezuela. The object at Levelland on Saturday night and Sunday morning, the object at White Sands Sunday morning and Sunday night, at Orogrande Monday afternoon, tracking an airliner over Brazil Monday night, on Tuesday morning the attack on the fort—possibly the same object in all instances.

On the morning of November 4 a blazing orange disc-shaped object attacked a military installation in Brazil, badly burning two soldiers. Hardly a hallucination—the lights went out, the power failed; the burns were real, so was the darkness. In Texas the same thing happened, but no one was burned—they just got a little warm. The Itaipu fort incident was hushed up and classified secret, and it is possible that other incidents took place at approximately the same time and are not known to civilian researchers because they too concerned the military and are classified. Seemingly all isolated instances, but was that isolation deliberate? Or is there a purpose and a pattern, even in the United States sightings? I believe so. A moderate-sized American town "beseiged" by an object which stopped traffic. A test to evaluate a device to halt panic-stricken flight of the natives when the day of contact comes?

By December 1 the discs had deserted the United States; the month was strangely lacking in reports. The strange objects were all but completely absent for about two weeks, although activity continued in South America. In January the famous IGY picture was taken near Trindade Island. The object had been seen many times before the photograph was obtained. In December the incidents along the frontier of Brazil and Paraguay began, apparently an attempt to discourage spectators—the discs were very busy with something in that area.

So, Olavo Fontes's theory was substantiated by the general sighting curve for eleven years. First, geographical surveys, then military reconnaissance, then surface sampling of botanical and geological specimens. The "green monster" of West Virginia, long believed to have been a diving-bell mechanism for exploration, was probably one of the first landing attempts. Later, our visitors ventured forth in space suits, and eventually without artificial aid—the little men of 1954.

Many attempts have been made by researchers to interpret the sightings of the fall of 1957. The most logical and likely conclusion is that the visitors, possibly from some satellite base beyond the earth's atmosphere or bases on the moon, detected the presence of the first earth satellite (possibly a detection system had been devised when they first observed our attempts at rocketry in 1948 through 1950). It is certainly obvious that the saucers were not coincidentally concerned with the missile range which exploded the first atom bomb in 1945—they have revisited it not infrequently. The presence of a living being in the second satellite launching was very likely detected, and the search was on to pinpoint the origin of the satellite. The Florida launching sites as well as the New Mexico Army-Air Force missile range in the Tularosa basin were closely scrutinized. After a few days of excitement, during which several general areas were visited, quiet reigned. No great number of ships were seen, as they had been in previous years and in the fall of 1956, during the close approach of Mars. The sightings seemed to involve only the small expeditionary force which had been busy in South America prior to the satellite launchings or a few ships from their main base, possibly the moon.

During that November flap, however, there were two definite accomplishments: (1) a weapon was tested against the automobile, a prominent method of surface locomotion; (2) another weapon was tested against two military installations. Based on the testimony of the airline pilots who encountered the discs over Brazil in early November, another accomplishment may be added: the testing of an antiaircraft device.

The immediate explanation to come to mind was that the object's propulsion simply interfered with the ignition system of the automobiles. Later investigation of similar car-stopping incidents in Brazil, however, indicated that the halting was deliberate. The craft in the Ponta Poran incidents flew above, behind and beside the cars with no apparent effect on them; only in one incident was the car stopped. Another possibility is the "scanner" device mentioned by Fontes—was the car-stopping device merely investigating the automobiles, and was the stopping of cars only a side effect? In the Ponta Poran incidents the objects were as close to the vehicles as they were in the Dr. Pereira case—why was one auto scanned and not another?

Not knowing the intent of superior air machines and their occupants, my first impression of the Itaipu report was that the object just happened to stop at a fort and that its propulsion had a bad effect on the already terrorized soldiers. Further investigation and study proved this not to be so. The object was first sighted when it appeared as an orange-colored star in the sky. It came directly toward the fort, hovering just a short distance from the soldiers. In the Texas army camp affair the object also seemed purposeful in its flight. In either case if the object's crews merely wanted to hover for a few minutes, why pick a brightly illuminated army installation? It seems obvious that the occupants of the discs knew these places were army installations; it is too coincidental that two army installations were attacked in this manner within so short a period of time. Also, we have no evidence that towns, cities, prison compounds, etc., were similarly visited, though any of these would bear a general physical resemblance to an army installation at night from a vantage point in the sky.

The objects knew where they were going and what they were going to do. In the Texas camp incident the object hovered over the barracks, and though people watched it they were not affected in any way. Nothing sensational happened until the tanks came upon the scene—tanks are weapons; and the Itaipu soldiers carried guns as they watched the discs. The tanks and the soldiers experienced the effect of the ultrasonic device; no one else. That the Itaipu object *accidentally* came to the fort and came down in the immediate vicinity of the guards also quite by accident cannot be accepted. It hovered for some seconds before the heat device was used—the soldiers were able to get a good look at it before the heat forced them to cover. Having accomplished the rout of the soldiers, the object could have taken off to lose itself in the sky. No one would have believed such a tale from the soldiers, except a very few who knew the facts. But as though to leave solid evidence of its visit, the object used some device to black out the whole installation (and deter any attempt to retaliate). A warning? It is easy to rationalize; rationalization is a common foil to common sense and logic. In these instances, however, it is not possible to rationalize that the objects meant no harm, unless one throws the facts out the window.

I have shown, in a survey of known facts and reports since the inception of the UFO mystery, that the objects are not just random phenomena—they adhere to a pattern. Their activities indicate that the earth has been the subject of a geographical, ecological and biological survey accompanied by a military reconnaissance of the whole world's terrestrial defenses. I have shown that they are aware of our attempts at space travel and the launching of artificial satellites. Evidence is ample that they have tested their weapons against our automobiles, planes and defenses. There must now be an interpretation of these facts. They came in numbers in 1947—two years after the explosion of the first three atomic bombs. Their survey started almost immediately thereafter; and was pursued as though the plan had been carefully worked out. Major activity took place in the latter part of 1957—immediately following the launching of the first earth satellites. Prior to that they had been busy investigating military installations in South America; after an apparent search for the launching site of the satellites in the United States and Australia (and possibly Russia) they returned to the area they had been occupied with before— South America. They were doing something in a remote area of Brazil and would brook no interference. Thus, the Ponta Poran incidents. Moon bases, satellite bases—earth bases?

Summing up the obvious pattern of UFO activity for nineteen years, it is apparent that a psychic projection cannot account for all of it. Psychic projections on the part of hundreds of thousands of people would not fall into a pattern which indicates military reconnaissance, biological and ecological survey and, finally, hostility. Nor would psychic projections furnish us with photographic and physical evidence. And while it is tempting to discuss the psychological needs that are fulfilled by the acceptance or rejection of theories, that would involve material sufficient for another larger volume.

I do not, and cannot, claim that I have all the facts. I have, however, presented sufficient facts to indicate a pattern and support a theory which up to now are the only logical explanations of the facts. The warning has been sounded. It is now left to the people of the world whether they want such momentous events and their ramifications to be the secrets of a choice few on whom a great decision will necessarily rest. We must ask ourselves—will we permit a few to make the decisions for billions? How can we be sure that they know all there is to know or that they will have the best interests of mankind at heart?

It is time the people know the whole truth so they can participate in this decision. This is not a matter of the "big three" of the "free world" against an *earthly* interloper. We are confronted with a species which is obviously many years ahead of us in technological development; our next war may not be fought among nations; it could very well be all nations fighting as brothers against a common foe from outer space.

14
Further Confirmation

THE July, September and November issues of the 1960 *APRO Bulletin* featured a serialized article by Dr. Fontes on orthoteny in Brazil. During a period of two hours, between 6 and 8 P.M. on the night of May 13, 1960 residents in the states of Pernambuco, Paraiba, Bahia, Rio Grande do Norte, Ceara, Piaui and Maranhao observed the low-flying passage of strange sky objects.

Ceara experienced the most visitations, including an object which followed a farmer driving a herd of donkeys to Paracuru. It was described as round with no protrusions and absolutely silent; gray in color, it sported a bright blue light topside and was occasionally motionless in the air. The farmer observed the object at 6:30 P.M., while a small fishing boat far off the coast drew the attention of a dark object which seemed to come down upon the ship from nowhere. Making no audible sound, the object continued to lower itself until it was an estimated three hundred feet above the ship, whereupon it began to emit a strong blue glow which illuminated the vessel. The thing hovered for about three minutes and then moved away in the direction of Paracuru.

At 7 P.M. more than a hundred excited residents of Paracuru watched a disc-shaped object maneuver and occasionally hover over the central part of the city. It appeared to be a smooth dark gray with a strong blue light at the top and had a diameter of about sixty feet. At 4 A.M. the next day small, pale-looking humanoids were seen near two disc-shaped objects which landed on the beach near Paracuru. A farmer, Raimundo dos Santos, coming from his farm about eight kilometers away, saw the craft and the men who appeared to be talking to one another. They noticed dos Santos and beckoned to him, but dos Santos turned and ran for help. He returned with men, but they found only the marks on the sand where the two discs had landed.

Students of the UFO mystery have long recognized Aime Michel's contribution to UFO research. His book, *Flying Saucers and the Straight-Line Mystery*, embodies the discovery of a pattern of visitations which could be used as a guideline by other investigators. Few examples of orthoteny during various UFO influxes have been found since Michel's theory was published, but no example so competently illustrates the phenomena of orthoteny as Dr. Fontes's report, submitted to us in July, 1960, which carefully outlines and explains the portent of orthoteny. The term, by Michel's own definition, means "stretched in a straight line." Michel found that locations of UFO sightings on a given day when plotted on a map of France showed a definite tendency to follow straight lines. When sightings for a given day were unusually numerous a *network* of such alignments could be discerned. Michel also observed that these alignments tended to cross at common points of intersection which he called "stars" (where three or more lines crossed one another), and to meet and end at terminal points called "apexes" (where two or more lines met and ended). Each network for a given day had a principal nexus point where many lines crossed, and the phenomenon reported at these points was uniformly a large cloudy flying cigar or cigar-shaped UFO. In addition, wherever the big cigar was seen *standing still* in a vertical position, that point invariably proved to be the principal star of the day's network. Michel's most interesting discovery was the fact that the straight line plotted on the map *did not necessarily correspond to the uninterrupted trajectory of a single object: observations along a line were not as a rule arranged in chronological order* (where they were, the distances involved were usually short). Also, *the reported direction of movement almost always corresponded with an orthotenic line passing through that point* from which the UFO's trajectory had been observed. If the ground witnesses were not directly on the orthotenic line, they always located the object observed in the air in the direction of that line. Objects on the ground were the best aligned observations. According to Michel this phenomenon of straight-line alignments is ephemeral, seldom lasting more than twenty-four hours—the "changeover point" apparently coming in the later hours of the night.

As Fontes reports, the network of alignments in the Brazilian case confirms beyond doubt the pattern found in the French observations of 1954. The Fontes report won such acceptance among UFO researchers and scientists in Brazil that the leading magazine *O Cruzeiro* in its January 28, 1961, issue published his findings and conclusions, including a map illustrating the orthotenic lines for the evening of May 13 and his evaluation of orthoteny, specifically the Brazilian orthotenic pattern.

Fontes carefully points out the major characteristics of northeastern Brazil, which must be considered. The area is one of the most backward, undeveloped parts of the country—in striking contrast to the east, southeast and south. Local industry is scarce, due to an inadequate supply of water and electric power; local roads, with the exception of federal highways, are very poor; the people are illiterate; and the area is generally lacking in mineral wealth and military installations. At first glance such a region would have little to offer an invading force, but these characteristics support the contrary view: Northeastern Brazil is essential for aerial communication and ocean navigation between four continents, yet it would not be easily defended in the event of an invasion. Terrestrial communication with the north is blocked by the dense tropical forest in the Amazon region, contact with the south and southeast is only by a few federal highways and the southwest is reached only by the Sao Francisco River. Also, the few heavily fortified installations in the area are concentrated along the coast, around the state capitals of Fortaleza, Natal and Recife; military defenses in the interior are few and scattered and there are no radar network or missile bases. Fontes found one common denominator linking all thirty-three points plotted on the map: besides being population centers, *all these places are communication centers of strategic importance*. In the event of invasion the entire communication network would be completely paralyzed through the northeast as well as with the rest of the country.

Eight completely different ships in reconnaissance were observed simultaneously at 6 P.M. on May 13, although further study suggests that forty-two were probably involved. The operation was obviously a large-scale reconnaissance, carefully planned and coordinated, each craft cognizant of its part in the program. "It is interesting to note," Fontes writes, "that the network of alignments included the location of major highways, railroad arteries, dams and locks, power stations and water reservoirs throughout the region; but excluded the three important military centers in the area: Fortaleza, Natal and Recife." It is important to recall that these three installations were among the many military bases visited during the 1954 UFO sightings in Brazil.

The following is the most frightening part of the Fontes Brazilian orthoteny report:

The pieces of the puzzle seem to fall together into one very clear pattern. A task force of alien spaceships (cigar-shaped UFOs) will come down at night over the northeast. The mass landings will probably be made in the state of Ceara, inside the triangular area limited by Choro, Quixada, Cajazeiras, Campos Sales, Mombaca and Quixeramobim—possibly around the town of Iguatu. Cigar-shaped UFOs hovering over these points will be the dispersion centers for a number of smaller machines which will spread out toward points of strategic importance at the network's periphery. Their patrolling activities will give complete aerial protection and block terrestrial communication with the landing area. Cigar-shaped UFOs placed over Redencao and Macaibas will counteract any attack from the bases at Fortaleza and Natal. UFOs over Petrolina and Juazeiro will cut the Sao Francisco River in two and block the federal highway and railroad artery from Salvador; another railroad block will be established at Bonfim. Air control will be taken and completed; terrestrial communication will be entirely paralyzed at many points inside and outside the landing area. Shiploads of "men" and equipment will be landed in just a few hours. Defense will be disorganized, scattered and hopeless. The block of communication will create a terrible situation. Weeks will pass before military reinforcements can be brought in from other regions of the country. Air traffic obviously will be wiped out in the first hours. Radio communication will be disrupted, power plants paralyzed, etc. Outside the landing area no one will suspect what is happening there until it is too late. There is no need to tell more. The reader can imagine the rest by himself.

The natural reaction to such a conclusion perhaps is to scoff. But the facts speak for themselves—the alignments and the geographic and industrial picture of the area are not a product of wishful thinking or irrational fear. Considered together with the reports of UFOs interfering with automobiles, electrical power plants and aircraft, this conclusion is wholly rational, unemotional and accurate.

I noted certain similarities between the geographic and industrial characteristics of the six-state area in Brazil and the area in the United States composed of western Texas, New Mexico, eastern and southern Arizona, Colorado, Wyoming, Utah and Montana. The southernmost region has a dry, difficult climate not suitable for farming, and only within the last twenty years has it developed industrially to any extent. This area has been valuable as a site for research bases, but communication and land-travel networks are sparse. The closest defense base to western New Mexico is Fort Bliss in El Paso, Texas. The road between El Paso and Alamogordo (and Holloman AFB) was scouted by an egg-shaped glowing object which stopped cars in November, 1957. Other unidentified flying objects gave the area between El Paso and Santa Fe (from Lubbock, Texas, to eastern Arizona) a thorough going-over during the week of November 2-9. Additional sightings mostly of low-flying objects were recorded in Wyoming, Colorado, Arizona and Montana during the fall influx.

Living in Alamogordo when landed unconventional objects and low-flying unidentified aircraft were observed hour by hour in that period of 1957, I was able to view the situation firsthand. I felt at the time that the reconnaissance may have been to search out the origin of the first and second earth satellite. Since then the area of New Mexico, western Texas, Colorado, Wyoming, Montana, Utah and eastern Arizona has undergone another extensive reconnaissance. During the night hours of September 28 and 29, 1960, a little over four months after the reconnaissance of northeastern Brazil, objects were sighted landing and in the air. (Because of the overriding fear of ridicule many observers, including Air Force personnel, reported directly to APRO, shunning official channels. Many good observations, which would be of invaluable aid in determining whether or not an orthotenic pattern was present, were never reported. This is the big obstacle civilian research organizations have faced since the inception of the mystery in 1946. But APRO still hopes to attract the attention and win the confidence of many more observers and thus obtain the details of the November, 1957, and September, 1960, sightings before they are forever lost to objective research by the blurring of time.)

During the evening of October 4, 1960, the observation at Cressy, Launceton, Australia, of a large cigar-shaped object accompanied by at least five smaller disc-shaped objects received considerable attention in the Australian newspapers. At 6:10 P.M., minutes after Cressy residents reported a mysterious explosion, the Reverend and Mrs. Lionel Browning spotted a gray, cigar-shaped object while looking through the rectory window at a rainbow in the east. Mrs. Browning saw the object first and pointed it out to her husband. There were four vertical bands along the side of the object, and at the bow end a rod with what appeared to be a small propeller at the end jutted out. The wind was loud and no sound was heard above it. The speed of the object was estimated by the Reverend Browning at about five hundred miles an hour, and it traveled in a straight path toward Western Junction. After about a minute of steady movement the ship stopped in mid-air, hovering over the Panshanger Estate, about three miles away. The Brownings watched the object for about another thirty seconds and then were surprised to see five or six small disc-shaped objects appear out of the clouds above and behind the larger craft. The discs were traveling very fast and the Brownings compared their movement to "flat stones skipping along the water." The small objects stationed themselves beside the larger ship within a half-mile radius. The minister said they were about thirty feet in diameter, but he was not certain of his estimate. "After several seconds," the Reverend Browning reported, "the large object, accompanied by the smaller objects, reversed the way they had come." The large ship, he said, did not maneuver to return into the cloud—the rod end was the last part of the ship to enter the rain cloud. The object returned to the cloud faster than it had emerged and was gone from sight within thirty seconds. Browning said he believed the large object was going toward Western Junction under cover of heavy rain, and "it appears the ship sailed on for some seconds unaware that it had shed its protection."

The Reverend Browning reported the incident to Launceton Airport officials immediately after the sighting, but he did not make the sighting public for a week because of its sensational nature. APRO's Australian representative, Peter Norris, conducted the investigation for APRO and concluded: "The Reverend Browning is a most affable and genial gentleman. I have no doubt as to his reliability." Browning confided to Norris that his sighting impressed him greatly; it opened a whole new dimension of speculation. Browning was also interviewed lengthily by Royal Australian Air Force intelligence officers, who tape-recorded his testimony, after Mr. Duthie, a member of Parliament and a personal acquaintance of the Reverend Browning, had Australian Minister for Air Osborne instigate the interview. To this date no explanation for the Browning case has been forthcoming from Australian officialdom.

About three weeks after the detailed Browning sighting (the minister emphasized to Norris the precision with which the "homing" of the small objects to the "mother ship" took place) a ground-shaking, ear-splitting explosion took place in the Cressy area at 10:30 P.M. on October 29. J. Metcalfe, who was watching television at the time, said he felt a peculiar sensation of "airlessness" just before the explosion. "The windows started to rattle and it really felt as if the house was being lifted off its foundations—but there was only one explosion," he said. Metcalfe went outside where he and neighbors Mr. and Mrs. T. Saltmarsh observed a fading red glow to the northeast. Mr. and Mrs. K. G. Woodward saw an orange-colored ball hovering above Western

Tiers, a little to the south of Poatina, at the time of the explosion. Mr. Woodward said the ball seemed to stay in the same position but swelled and shrank in size. "My wife and I watched it for a minute and a half or a little longer. Then it seemed to go out rather than move away. I would suggest it was about two hundred feet above the Tiers," Woodward stated. "As soon as it disappeared we both felt a most peculiar sensation, as if there was pressure all around us." Then came the terrific explosion; at first Woodward thought an air freighter may have been in the area and the orange ball was its exhaust, but he phoned the Department of Civil Aviation at Launceton Airport and received a negative answer. J. D. Robson, who also reported hearing and feeling the explosion, had experienced a similar phenomenon at about the same time as the Browning sighting on October 3.

Taking into consideration the 1959 sighting by the Reverend Gill and the 1960 sighting by the Reverend Browning, the conclusion is in order that activity in the New Guinea-Australia-New Zealand area has been almost as intense as that in South America. It also appears that for the first time since 1957 the objects were making low-level appearances, and more frequently.

The evidence presented in this volume must be evaluated and a logical interpretation put upon it before we can begin to feel that anything has been accomplished. I have attempted to interpret the meaning behind the nineteen-year reconnaissance of the earth by unconventional aircraft, but now an extensive study of human acceptance and motivation is necessary.

We have heard the various arguments against the idea of interplanetary or interstellar travelers visiting our planet. Scientists have pointed out that although man is tugging at the edges of space and "flying saucers" from outer space *may* visit us some day, this does not necessarily mean they are doing so now. This logic seems to indicate that although we accept the reality of alien spaceships *some day*, we will not do so until man himself has conquered space. This reasoning does not, however, alter the evidence of nineteen years.

In his book, *Flying Saucers and the U.S. Air Force*, Colonel Lawrence Tacker quotes various scientists to bolster his own conviction that UFOs are nothing but hoaxes, misconceptions of conventional objects, etc. He gives the impression that no reputable astronomer has observed an unconventional aerial object. This is simply not so. Among many recognized scientists who have reported seeing UFOs are Dr. Clyde Tombaugh, discoverer of the planet Pluto, Robert Johnson, chief of the Adler Planetarium in Chicago, as well as astronomers at the Majorca Observatory off the coast of Spain and at Mount Stromlo, Australia, to name a few. The strata of astronomers who chorus that astronomers never see UFOs ("Don't they like us?" they say) are ignoring facts. Their observations are mostly confined to the telescope which covers a very small area (only a few degrees) of the sky; an observer utilizing the naked eye has the advantage of a larger percentage of the entire sky. If an astronomer observing a distant planet, star or nebula were to experience a fraction of a second of obliteration of his target he would probably chalk it up to the chance flight of a bird, etc. The mathematical chances against a UFO flying between the telescope and its observation point are astronomical. The argument is not valid.

Colonel Tacker further suggests that meteor trackers or observers at "most" observatories do not report UFOs and therefore they don't exist. I suggest that trained astronomers seldom spend much time at the telescope and meteor tracking is left to amateur astronomers and volunteer personnel who would not necessarily qualify as "trained observers" by Tacker's own definition. Too, we must consider the possibility that meteor-tracking personnel would not report the sighting of unconventional aerial objects to superiors who are on record as not believing in their existence. APRO files contain at least one incident involving the sighting of a strange object by the camera crew of an observatory. It was not reported because the observatory chief had publicly stated his disbelief in the existence of UFOs. "You can't fight the politicians," one man said. Just how long are these politicians safe from the barrage of real evidence?

The UFO issue entails many opinions, theories and assumptions. Everyone connected with it, whether in civilian research or official investigation or the average person who reads occasional accounts of UFOs, will readily admit it is a highly controversial subject. Few, however, have given much thought to the reason for this controversy. During the major part of the short span of man's known existence it has generally been assumed that he is the only intelligent species in creation. Only during the past decade has this view been subject to radical revision. The assumption that man is unique is mainly a result of religious doctrine not necessarily corroborated by Scriptures. Discoveries in science since 1945 indicate that there are other worlds, and mathematical chance indicates that some of these worlds may be populated. Theorizing further, it is not difficult to logically assume that some of these populations are intelligent. We must eventually come to the question of whether or not these hypothetically intelligent races are humanoid or resemble humans. Philosophers and scientists alike reason that because of the obvious pattern of celestial bodies in the universe there probably is a general pattern where plant, animal and intelligent life is concerned. Although there is considerable doubt that humanoid creatures exist on any planet other than earth in this solar system, it is likely that intelligent life on planets in other solar systems will follow the same evolutionary pattern as that of man on earth, and those intelligent beings will resemble man to a great extent.

Professor George Wald, Harvard University biologist, told a meeting of the American Philosophical Society in November, 1960, that life elsewhere in the universe is likely to be the same as life on earth. Because of the appropriate properties of carbon, oxygen, nitrogen and hydrogen, he said, it seems probable that living organisms everywhere must be constructed primarily of these four elements. One month later the Reverend L. C. McHugh, S.J., associate editor of the Catholic magazine *America,* stated in that magazine his belief that intelligent life not only exists beyond earth but is quite a "common" phenomenon in space. Exploring the theological side of the question, he said, "Organic life on earth evolved toward a specialized animal form that in God's design was apt material for the infusion of a spiritual soul, while at the same time the lower forms were ordained to serve as a substratum for rational existence and its needs." Whether or not one agrees with the Reverend McHugh's theology, his theory concerning life and its manifestations elsewhere is sound.

There is also the question whether observations of human-type creatures in the vicinity of discs as early as 1954 were prompted by wishful thinking or were physical realities. Certainly they were not the result of an attempt to tie in the nature of the occupants with accepted fact or theory, for the idea of humanoid denizens in outer space was not generally considered plausible at that time. Nor were these observations the result of subconscious hope, for human nature and tradition generate a tendency toward the belief in the uniqueness of man. The fact that so many science-fiction fans, artists and writers picture other-worlders as horrible-looking, antennaed creatures indicates their own subconscious desire to remain unique. The ego dictates that if these creatures do indeed exist and can traverse space (which make them at least technologically superior to man) they simply cannot resemble us physically. They must be ugly (by our standards) to "compensate" for their superiority in another area.

At this point we should evaluate whether the reporters of humanoid disc occupants were observing real creatures. There is a considerable difference between reports of disc occupants by casual observers and the sensational claims of "contacts" by members of the quasi-religious "saucer" cults. Almost without exception the latter claim that they were "chosen" for contact with the superior alien beings because of some characteristic of their personality or philosophy. The tall, very handsome disc occupants with whom they claim contact speak good English and have come to help us with our problems. This is the tendency of some people to look for a "savior" from without, to allay their pressing fears. The world has been presented over and over again with "saviors" whose teachings and examples offer man a happier life—Buddha, Krishna, Confucius, Jesus and, most recently, Gandhi. But the believers in "elder brothers," etc., are not the only ones looking for help. In his book, *Flying Saucers —a Modern Myth of Things Seen in the Skies,* Dr. C. G. Jung points out the ready acceptance of intelligent beings from outer space by the public in general. This acceptance is based on a hope for a better existence when it seems to humans that they have failed in their personal quest for peace and happiness.

Civilians as well as a good share of the military in other countries are more prone than we are to scrutinize the facts and accept the logical conclusion that UFOs are interplanetary. In 1954 a member of the Royal Australian Air Force told the *Daily Telegraph* that the RAAF was keeping an open mind on the subject and that he believed, from information the RAAF had received, the objects could have an interplanetary source—"people on earth should be able to fly into outer space within forty years, so why shouldn't other people on other planets already have reached this stage?" I have noticed a definite tendency on the part of our military men to dismiss the possibility of interplanetary visitors. This is to be expected from the military of a leading world power. The Air Force is not particularly anxious to accept the idea of superior beings and air machines; that recognition would automatically place it in "second place."

Among those who have closely scrutinized the evidence (and there are more than is generally supposed) the attitude is that the objects are from outer space and that the evidence proving it, or the knowledge itself, is being kept secret "for a good reason." Such knowledge would cause panic it is suggested, and either the Air Force or the government, or both, are keeping the matter secret, discouraging reports which would verify it and generally ridiculing the idea—or through a set of circumstances beyond their grasp the military and /or the government have failed to comprehend the situation. The evidence in this book suggests censorship, but many instances could be a result of lack of coordination, failure to report facts (on the part of the investigators) or a tendency to misinterpret the facts due to subconscious preference.

In January, 1953, a group of scientists was called by the Air Force to review the evidence and make recommendations. This was five months after unidentified objects had buzzed areas off-limit to air vehicles in the Washington, D.C., region. According to Colonel Tacker's book the recommendations were: (1) immediate steps to be taken to strip UFOs of the aura of mystery they had unfortunately acquired; (2) the public be reassured of the total lack of evidence of inimical forces behind the phenomena; and (3) Air Force investigative personnel be trained to recognize and reject false indications quickly and effectively.* To implement these recommendations AFR 200-2 was issued, and has since undergone several revisions. In its present form it states (paragraph 3) that the Air Force has the objective "to explain or identify all UFO sightings"; the philosophy to guide Air Force personnel reporting UFOs (paragraph 3c) is that all UFOs can be explained as conventional phenomena if enough information is available. The implication is quite clear—if Air Force investigators follow the regulation reli-

* A fourth recommendation to the effect that UFOs should be publicly debunked by the Air Force was classified until June, 1966.

giously either insufficient evidence will be gathered for a sighting or incident or it will be explained away.

In 1947 when the UFO mystery first became a matter of public record the Air Force was a new branch of the military. The sightings reported at that time concerned objects apparently at high altitude, and few particulars were supplied; pictures taken were lacking in detail. Although there was sufficient evidence that something unusual was happening and being seen it was by no means conclusive. When detailed observations became common (objects hovering, making low-altitude flights, etc.) the panel's recommendations and the regulation dealing with UFO investigation were made—to hinder the subsequent gathering of valuable data.

UFO "believers" and "nonbelievers" alike have relied on the works of Jung to support their theories. The believers quote a short passage from his book on flying saucers indicating that there may be a case for material, or physically real, UFOs. The "nonbelievers" quote Jung's writings on the myth of UFOs and their psychic reality to bolster the claim that the UFOs are nothing but hallucinations. Neither believers or nonbelievers have made any real attempt to understand Jung's general approach to psychology. If they had they would have concerned themselves with the *whole* of the situation as presented by Jung. A careful study of his book has helped me immeasurably at those rare times when I encountered a UFO incident which had all the earmarks of a psychic rather than a physical experience.

I have watched with growing interest the rocket-propelled attempts of man to penetrate space. With this interest came a growing awareness that rocket power, at least in its present form, is not the answer to our problem of escape and certainly not to prolong flight. In fifteen years of investigating reports of unconventional aircraft I have had the privilege of reading many volumes on space and its problems. One of the most interesting books I have ever read dealing with propulsion theories is *New Principles of Quantum Mechanics*[1] by Dr. Horace C. Dudley. Dudley laments the over-eager acceptance by the scientific world of the Einstein theory as the theory to end all theories. He cites the tendency of science to forget that the Einstein theory is just a theory—unproven. As do Fontes, Rehn, Hritsco and others, Dudley

[1] Exposition Press, New York, 1959.

dares to question orthodoxy. He encourages the young scientific mind to ask the questions which chafe it—this is the way to knowledge and progress. If there had been no sincere doubts about the orthodox theories of science, meteors still would be only the result of imagination, just as UFOs have become things to be denied, ignored—anything but studied.

At the inception of the UFO mystery as a historical fact in 1947 scientists went on record with such explanations as balloons, reflections, spots before the eyes, etc. These same childish explanations are still offered, but unlike 1947 the year 1966 offers any interested individual a host of facts from which to draw his own conclusions. Oddly enough, individuals so eager to discount UFOs as something quite explainable and commonplace have not studied the facts involved. One cannot get a clear picture of the problem by reading the newspapers. But breaking with tradition is not easy. Dudley says: "A wise man once observed that men will love you if you make them think that they think, but will hate you if you make them think." Speaking of his book, he says: "This volume, if it is to accomplish its purpose, must make you think. It must make you question. If you are timid, or proud of the extent of your knowledge, this volume may well be unacceptable." It is obvious that Dudley is a scientist, but it is equally obvious that he is also a philosopher. Dudley is concerned about the tendency among scientists to resist scientific discovery. New ideas and extensions of theory may well be the answer to a propulsion system which would open the door to outer space.

Dr. Dudley joined the ranks of APRO members in 1958. His opinions on UFOs are rational and concise: "I recommend we use a bit of scientific curiosity to see what ever is the physics of the phenomena so many people are describing as UFOs. Ascribing the phenomena as due to psychological aberrations is nonsense. There is a series of physical phenomena that needs explaining; let's get on with it in an open-minded, scientifically oriented manner. Then let the *data* provide the answer."

Since the launching of Sputnik I in October, 1957, the frequency with which UFOs were seen quickened considerably. Although it is possible to get a glimmering of trends as sightings are made, a thorough study of the overall history of UFOs from time to time is most lucrative.

The "hairy little men" may be some type of lower form of life such as our anthropoids, which are pressed into service for the purpose of gathering various samples of flora and fauna, and routine jobs such as gathering mineral samples. They certainly do not react to the presence of humans as do their more human-appearing counterparts, the "little men." This is not a completely unlikely theory—in man's first attempt to put a living thing into orbit around the earth a dog was utilized, and later, chimpanzees. The "dwarves" may even be conscripts from a planet within our own solar system.

The years since 1961 included only spotty reports—significant, but not to be compared with the flaps of 1952 and 1957. The first major sightings involving water sources, and specifically reservoirs, were recorded in 1962. The Sheffield, England, reservoir complex was reconnoitered by a UFO on August 19. On September 15 of the same year the Oradell, New Jersey, reservoir was visited at 7:15 P.M., and an object was observed as it fell into it. The Horsetooth Reservoir near Masonville, Colorado, was the scene of another UFO visitation at 6:15 A.M. on October 26.

Other UFO incidents which seemed to be forerunners of later reconnaissance began to manifest themselves in the early '60s. On a Thursday night in late December twenty-year-old Jerry Hislope of Kentland, Indiana, claimed he had been buzzed by a strange object while driving his car two miles north of Lafayette. The incident, related in the December 28 issue of the *Indiana Journal*, involved a small (eight feet in diameter, three feet thick) glowing white object which dived on the car, sometimes descending as low as ten feet in altitude. It then flew off into the sky at high speed. Other apparent close-up observations of humans followed in the ensuing years as we will see.

One of the most terrifying reports I have ever examined came to my attention in late 1962. The only remaining witnesses were three young boys, Raimundo, twelve years old, Fatimo, six, and Dirceu da Silva, two, whose home is located near Duas Pontes, district of Diamantina, Minas Gerais state, Brazil.

The initial report was made in *Diario De Minas,* (Belo Horizonte), and later was printed in *Correio Da Manha* (Rio de Janeiro). On the night of August 20, the three boys and their father Rivalino Mafra da Silva went to bed as usual. In the middle of the night they awakened and were frightened into a cold sweat by the presence of strange noises like voices and shadowy figures moving about the house in a "gliding" manner. The four prayed and shortly the figures apparently left. No one slept and the four were still badly frightened when morning came. Raimundo arose and started out to the field to get the horse. When he walked outside he saw two large ball-shaped objects floating in mid-air side by side, about six feet off the ground. They were only a few feet from the door and separated from each other by about one yard. One of the objects was black with an antennalike protuberance and a small "tail." The other was black and white with the same configuration. Both objects emitted a humming sound and gave off a fire from the bottom which flickered like the light of a firefly. Raimundo called his father, who came out of the house. Mr. da Silva seemed to become hypnotized by the objects, unable to look away. He warned the boys to stay away and then began walking toward the globes. At a distance of about seven feet from the objects da Silva stopped, whereupon the two balls seemed to merge with one another, raising dust and discharging a yellow smoke which soon enveloped the whole area. Making strange noises, the object approached da Silva. The three horrified boys watched as their father was enveloped in the yellow smoke. Raimundo ran toward his father, into the smoke which had an acrid smell, but found nothing. When the dust and smoke cleared his father and the globes were gone.

Considerable investigation was carried out and duly reported in the newspapers. A careful and extensive investigation into the background of da Silva was made but nothing was found to indicate enemies or any apparent motive for the disappearance. The authorities suspected that perhaps Raimundo may have been concealing something more mundane than the globes and had made up the story to protect himself or someone else. When police investigators searched the area they found nothing except a few drops of human blood about 200 feet from the house. The area around the house was smooth as if swept clean by a broom and there were no tracks except those of the boys. A careful search of the house and area with the help of police dogs was made but nothing was found. In one last desperate effort to get information from the boy, police took him to a room at headquarters where a body was lying on a table covered with a sheet. Dr. Joao Antunes de Oliveira, who had already established Raimundo's sanity to his own satisfaction, told the boy that his father's body had been found, indicating the body on the table, then accused the boy of telling a lie. The da Silva boy began to cry but he stuck to his story, and said that perhaps the globes had brought his father back. When Dr. Oliveira was interviewed by the press, he said, simply, "I don't wish to discuss the facts in the case; they are beyond my competence. But I can tell you that the boy is normal and he is telling what he thinks to be the truth." Lt. Lisboa, the policeman in charge of the case, was equally puzzled and the case was never resolved beyond the fact that da Silva had completely and inexplicably disappeared.

Some additional facts were gathered during the investigation. Jose Avila Garcia, the vicar at the Diamantina cathedral contacted Lt. Lisboa to inform him that his friend Antonio Rocha had been fishing at the Manso river close to Duas Pontes on 4 P.M. on the 19th and had seen two ball-shaped objects hovering over Rivalino's house. Rocha confirmed his observation and said the two globes were flying in a circular pattern low over the da Silva's home. Da Silva was a diamond prospector. Two other miners in the district who were interviewed by Lisboa said that Rivalino had told them of his discovery of two strange-looking small men of about three feet in height who were digging near his house. When he approached them they ran into the bushes and shortly a strange red, glowing hat-shaped object took off from the bushes at high speed. This had purportedly taken place on the 17th, three days prior to da Silva's disappearance.

Exactly one year and one day after the da Silva incident, reporters descended on the home of Senor Antonio de Moreno at Tranca, Argentina, to interview the family concerning the events of the night before. They found some very frightened people. At 9:30 P.M. October 21, 1963, Senor Antonio de Moreno was awakened at his ranch near Tranca by a fifteen-year-old employee who told him there had apparently been an accident at the railroad tracks a half mile away since there was a lot of light and people moving around at that location. De Moreno wakened his wife and they both looked out the window. Over the railroad tracks and just a few feet in the air, an oval-shaped object was hovering and projecting a light to the ground where "people" were walking to and fro in single file. While watching the scene, Senora de Moreno spotted another similar object close to the house. She later described a domed disc-shaped structure of about twenty-five feet in diameter, as well as windows or ports of some kind which were arranged around the circumference. It was hovering just a few feet from the ground.

The senora got a flashlight and shone it toward the disc, whereupon it shot a bright, white tubular beam of light toward the house. When this happened, the senora and her sister rounded up all the children in the ranch house and hid them. Then both of the de Morenos began a systematic check of all the windows and discovered that there were five discs hanging in the air around the house. Three stayed between 210–225 feet away and the other two, including the nearest one which she first saw, stayed only a few feet away. One projected a white tubular light and the other a reddish-violet tubular light. These beams did not diffuse or spread—they were the same size, apparently, at the point of origination as they were at the point where they projected against the house. Shortly after the lights hit the house the inside began to heat up until it was "like an oven" and there was a strong smell of sulphur in the air. Although the heat became so extreme the family didn't think they could stay there, they were afraid to leave because of the strange machines outside. Senora de Moreno spent the time quieting the children. After approximately forty minutes of this discomfort, the witnesses, who had watched the proceedings from a window, saw the object at the tracks elevate itself and move away followed by the discs which surrounded the house. Just before taking off the light on the two closest discs went out and they followed the others off in the direction of some neighboring farms. Where the two closest discs had hovered there remained a misty smokelike deposit for several minutes.

Several hours after the incident a reporter from *Clarim*, a Cordoba newspaper, arrived on the scene. He later reported that when he got to the de Moreno home the strong sulphur smell was still apparent both around and inside the house and the inside of the house was still suffocatingly hot. Corroboration of this incident came from a neighbor, Francisco Tropuano, who reported to *Clarim* that he had seen a formation or squadron of lighted disc-shaped objects moving through the sky at 10:15 P.M., which was about the time the de Morenos said the discs had left their area. Tropuano made his report before he heard of the de Moreno incident.

The da Silva and de Moreno incidents naturally raise some questions: Why the interest in a miner's diggings and why kill him? Why the interest in railroad tracks? Why did a whole family have to be held under siege? In both instances the principals saw something they apparently should not have seen. The de Moreno incident is only one of many in which railroad tracks have seemingly been scrutinized. The discs have buzzed trains. They also have buzzed cars—and stopped them. The locomotive, however, does not operate on the same principle as a car and perhaps the occupants were attempting to find some clue to the motive power in the tracks.

Since 1954, when the UFOs spent several months in low-level examination of South America and Europe, it has been quite apparent that regardless of what UFOs are, they are definitely a global problem. As we will see presently, landings have been taking place on a worldwide scale but have not been given wide publicity. Considering the absolutely bizarre nature of some of the reports, as demonstrated by the foregoing accounts, this is not surprising. Examination of these reports, which come from people who have no motivation for concocting such hair-raising tales, indicates a dire need for even more careful investigation than the existing UFO researchers have been able to manage with limited personnel and funds.

In the de Moreno story, a sort of "ray" or "weapon" which is heat-inducing is described. This correlates closely with the experience of the soldiers at Itaipu Fortress, Brazil, in 1957, which is described in Chapter 10 and which at the time of the de Moreno incident had not been published.

One of the few reports of a disc in trouble came out of Brazil in October, 1963. On the 31st, several fishermen and an eight-year-old girl, Rute de Souza, watched as a 25-foot diameter disc wobbled through a clearing, hit the top of a palm and tumbled, apparently out of control, into the Peropava River. One of the fishermen, Japanese Tetsuo Ioshigawa, estimated the disc's size, and its altitude when it struck the tree, which was about twenty feet. It looked like a "wash basin," he said, and was shiny like polished aluminum. Although the total number of observers was not great, the girl's aunt and uncle, alerted by Rute's shouts, arrived on the scene in time to see mud and water "boiling" up from the river where the object had fallen in.

The Peropava River is twelve feet deep at the point where the disc sank, and has a muddy bottom composed of about fifteen feet of mud and clay. It was theorized at the time that if the disc sank through the water and in turn, the mud—as the boiling up of the water and mud seemed to indicate—it may have proceeded through the riverbed to solid rock underneath. At any rate, subsequent efforts by civil engineers, utilizing mine detectors, to reach the disc, were unsuccessful. Considerable space was devoted to the sighting and especially the ensuing search in various Brazilian papers, including *O Globo,* Rio's largest circulation daily.

The first few months of 1964 were quiet as far as UFO reports were concerned. During this period I had time to study the events of the first years of the 1960s and noted that my prediction of water and electrical power reconnaissance had been accurate and that interest in cars continued. Low-level flights and hovering maneuvers seemed to become more numerous, but despite this indication I was in no way prepared for the occurrences of late April.

At about 11 A.M. on the morning of the 24th the telephone rang and when I answered I found it was a long distance call from Mr. Arlynn Breuer, Editor of the *Alamogordo Daily News.* He informed me that an object had landed near Socorro, New Mexico, on the edge of the White Sands-Holloman Air Force Base Integrated Range. Two small men were seen, he said, and suggested that Mr. Lorenzen and I should proceed there immediately for the incident was only about eighteen hours old, having occurred at 5:50 P.M. the evening before. By 5 P.M. we were heading east out of Tucson and arrived at Socorro at 2 A.M. on the 25th.

Before we left Tucson I had called Terry Clarke of Radio KALG in Alamogordo, only to find that he was aware of the news and had already interviewed one of the principals in the case, Sgt. Chavez of the New Mexico State Police. The word had spread around and the press wires were giving the story unusually prominent play.

At 9 on Sunday morning my husband and I walked into the police station at Socorro. Barely a half hour later we were proceeding to the "landing" site, which was a scant mile and a half from the center of Socorro, in the Police Chief's car, accompanied by Sgt. Chavez and Chief Polo Pineda. Curious spectators were already roaming the area, but fortunately the marks made by the UFO's landing gear had not been damaged. They were curiously arranged and their location (four of them) indicated self-leveling gear. The landing site was in a rocky wash (or ditch) between two small mesas. After looking over the area and taking notes,

we headed back to police headquarters where we interviewed
patrolman Lonnie Zamora. This is his account:

At 5:50 P.M. on the 24th he had been in his cruiser,
headed south on Park St. in hot pursuit of a speeding car. As
he drew abreast of the Church of La Buena Pastor his attention was diverted by a loud roaring sound and out of the
corner of his eye, to his right (southwest), he saw a blue
flame which disappeared down toward the ground and out
of sight. Thinking quickly, he abandoned his chase of the
car (he said he knew who it was and could get him later)
and headed toward the area where the object disappeared,
which was near an abandoned dynamite shack. He was
afraid some teen-agers were "fooling around" the shack.
After he left Park Street he followed a trail which led up
onto a small rocky hill (often called a "mesa" in the southwest). Since there was no real road he had to make three
runs before his car would make the grade, then he drove
across the crest and down the other side. At this point, and
for only a few seconds, the gully or wash to the south of
him was visible; in it he glimpsed a white object which from
a distance of 450 feet appeared to be an overturned car
standing on end with two children or small adults standing
by it. The figures were dressed in white clothing which he
thought looked like mechanics' uniforms. One of the figures
appeared to turn and look toward him as if startled.

Zamora then took his mike from its bracket, called Chavez
and asked for assistance. He thought there was something
odd about the whole situation, and asked him to come
alone. Zamora then drove his car up and across the next
mesa, where he stopped it. He heard two loud metallic bang-
ing noises. He got out of the car, but in doing so, dislodged
his microphone, which he picked up and put back in its
place. Taking three steps toward the gully, he was now in a
position to see the object down the short slope and a little to
his left. Suddenly an ear-splitting roar filled the air and the
object "began to kick up dust." Thoroughly frightened,
Zamora threw himself on the ground. Looking up, he saw
that the object was rising in a slanting trajectory toward the
southwest. He got up, ran and bumped into his car, and in
doing so dislodged his glasses, which fell to the ground. As
the object rose, it displayed a particularly brilliant blue
flame from its middle underside, which was three or four
times as long as it was wide. As suddenly as it had started,
the roar ceased and Zamora stopped in his headlong flight

and looked around. The thing was headed southwest, making a high-pitched whining sound. It was ascending at a very shallow angle, approximately twenty feet off the ground, when it cleared the dynamite shack. Zamora then ran to his car, called headquarters and asked the people there to look into the southwest and see what they could see. Just three minutes later Sgt. Chavez pulled his patrol car to a stop on the mesa and Zamora hurried toward him.

"Do I look strange?" Zamora asked. Chavez replied, "You look like you've seen the devil."

"Well, maybe I have," Zamora said, and related his experience. The two men then walked toward the gully to look at the ground where the object had rested. It was still smoking: several clumps of range grass were burned and a stubby mesquite bush which was located almost dead center of the landing site was burning. There were four 8x12 wedge-shaped depressions, three to four inches deep, arranged in an irregular rectangle. There were also four circular depressions about 4½ inches in diameter and approximately three inches deep not far from one of the large indentations.

Sgt. Chavez immediately put in a call to Captain Holder of Stallion Site range station, who was at home in Socorro, and to an FBI operative who was in Socorro at the time. Holder and the FBI man came out to the site, took measurements, and the FBI man piled rocks around the indentations to preserve them. Then Zamora and Chavez were questioned extensively. During this activity Chavez searched Zamora's car for any equipment which might have been used to start the fire or make the indentations. He found none. I later asked him his motive for doing this and he replied that he was following the regular procedure to establish evidence. He had never put any stock in "flying saucer" stories before. Mr. Lorenzen asked Chavez about Zamora's request that he come to the site alone. Chavez said that Zamora felt he was viewing something unusual and wanted a sympathetic and objective person to verify the object's presence. All questions concerning Zamora's honesty and integrity were met by Chavez with absolute endorsement. He was personally convinced that Zamora experienced exactly what he claimed. The same opinion was held by Zamora's fellow officers and friends, including Chief Pineda. Deputy Sheriff James Luckie had also heard the call for Chavez, had gotten into his car and gone out to the location of the landing, arriving shortly after Chavez. He also testified as to the condition of the smoking ground and the indentations.

During our investigation Zamora was reticent about the markings on the object and said that Captain Holder had instructed him not to talk about them. He also denied that there had been any "little men," but after questioning he admitted that the FBI man had suggested he not talk about them beyond his initial report to the press. He quoted the FBI agent as saying that no one would believe him anyway. However, in the presence of Deputy Luckie, a reporter from the local paper, the *El Defensor Chieftain,* as well as Mr. Lorenzen and myself, he described the little men and noted that the area was dusty, apparently from the landing, so that he did not get a good look at them.

After we finished interviewing Zamora, Mr. Lorenzen called Captain Holder and we were invited out to his home, where we talked about the incident for about two hours. During that time we identified ourselves as representatives of APRO, and Captain Holder proffered his Army ID card which identified him as a Captain in Army Intelligence. He then allowed me to look at his complete report, which was unclassified at the time and which he stated would be forwarded to the "UFO Board." I assumed it would be routed through Army Intelligence channels. This was the first time that we had ever come upon direct evidence of a military UFO investigative organ other than the U.S. Air Force Project Bluebook at Wright-Patterson Air Force Base. It was an interesting bit of information.

I think it is significant that Holder represented Army Intelligence and was stationed at Stallion Site, for the range sites in that vicinity had been visited by UFOs before the Socorro landing and were to be the sites of several more later.

The upshot of the Socorro incident was considerable international publicity and the first in-depth press notice of a UFO incident involving occupants in the United States. At first the exact markings seen on the object were withheld from the press, but Holder told us that he felt that for purposes of future identification in case of other sightings it would be important not to circulate the exact configuration of the markings. He had a good point. The markings which the press were touting were completely wrong. The markings were in red, consisting of a vertical line topped by two slanting lines that gave the impression of an arrow. This was surrounded by a horizontal line on the bottom, a vertical line on each side, and a semicircle over the top of the arrow. It is still not clear whether this mark denotes a double door in the craft or an actual marking of some sort. The small circular impressions were probably the marks from ladder feet, for they were too deep in that rocky soil to have been made by the weight of a person, and certainly not one the size that Zamora described.

Analysis of the whole incident leaves one rather perplexed. It has been suggested that the object was a secret military test craft and that the size of the "men" was misjudged. This solution lacks conviction, for the object was on the edge of one of the largest test ranges in the world and yet came from the direction of the range, landed off range and when it left again, and seemingly with no trouble, it headed away from the range. If it had been a test craft with technical trouble, it would have at least headed back to the range after its untimely landing. Unfortunately, considerable press noise was generated by a statement by Dr. J. Allen Hynek, the Air Force's consulting scientist on the UFO problem, to the effect that he wondered why the Socorro object had not been picked up on radar. The solution to that puzzle is really quite simple. Missions involving radar at Holloman-White Sands had terminated at 5 o'clock. The radars were not in use at the time. Long-range radars from the main base at Holloman or at Kirtland Air Force Base in Albuquerque would not be able to pick up an object flying at such low altitude in that hilly area.

Within the next few weeks other landings and sightings in the southwest tended to bolster the theory that the Socorro object had been a true UFO. Unfortunately it is not possible to document all the sightings for that period, so I will deal only with those which offer the most detail and indicate the presence of unexplainable objects.

At 1 A.M. on the morning of April 26 (a Sunday), only thirty-one hours after the Socorro sighting, Orlando Gallegos of Espanola, New Mexico, who was visiting his father in La Madera, went outside to chase some horses out of the yard. His attention was arrested by a bluish glow about 200 feet from the house. He walked toward the glow and was surprised to see a "butane-tank-shaped" thing which appeared to be "as long as a telephone pole" apparently resting on the ground between a parking and dumping area and the dirt road which led from Petaca to La Madera. Gallegos went into the house and told his family, who laughed at him. He went back outside to check on it, but it was gone. He judged that the object had been about fourteen feet in diameter; it had shot blue flames out of holes in the sides along the bottom and made no noise. The next day Gallegos, bound for home, heard about the Socorro incident and stopped in Espanola to tell police officer Nick Naranjo what he had seen. Eventually several police officers were notified of the incident. Captain Vigil and patrolman Albert Vega and patrolman Kingsbury then went to the Gallegos home, where they found the ground still smoking, twenty hours after the incident had purportedly occurred.

When I interviewed Vigil by telephone, I got the impression that he believed Gallego's story. This is how he described the scene of the landing: The ground was hot and smoking; there were bits of glass which looked as though they had been melted and four 8x12 inch indentations which were wedge-shaped at the bottom. There were at least a dozen circular "tracks" about 3½−4 inches in diameter. An area of 35−40 feet in diameter had been scorched. The scorched area, the wedge-shaped indentations and the circular tracks and their size correlate generally with the Socorro ground markings. The dimensions of the Socorro markings were not available in the press until Sunday so it seems unlikely that Gallegos had this information on hand Sunday morning if he were disposed to attempt a hoax. Other tales of objects similar in appearance, which "buzzed" cars and homes in the general area from Las Cruces north to Albuquerque along the Rio Grande river, seem to support the evidence that strange objects were flying and landing there. One other important point is that none of the markings appeared to have been dug, and it would have required considerable weight to make those deep marks in that hard, rocky ground.

Four days later, on the 30th, several youngsters living near the lake at Canyon Ferry, Montana, claimed that at 10:30 that night they had seen a lighted object which landed and then took off from an area about 125 feet from the rear of the Davis residence. Witnesses were Linda Davis, eleven, and children of the Harold Rust family, who lived nearby. Investigation by the sheriff's office the next day showed four 8x10 rectangular indentations about four to eight inches deep arranged in an irregular rectangle, roughly thirteen feet apart. The area showed signs of scorching and a big cactus near the center of the arrangement of holes was scorched. The ground was still warm.

I noted considerable reticence about the incident on the part of the Sheriff and investigating Air Force officers. I then put in a call to Mr. and Mrs. Harold Rust and learned that the Davis and Rust families live in a federal housing project. Neither family had heard on radio or TV or read in the papers about the dimensions of the Socorro markings. Mrs. Rust was reluctant to talk any more about the incident for fear of jeopardizing their position in the housing project. She promised to write and inform APRO about the pertinent details if her husband felt it was all right. Nothing more was heard from the Davis or Rust families. This seemed to be another instance in which the principals in a UFO case were hesitant to talk of their experiences because of a prior exposure to the "censorship" propaganda. Mrs. Rust had been contacted by many enthusiastic UFO "researchers" who had warned her that she might not be able to "talk."

Socorro, La Madera and Canyon Ferry were the locales of the major sightings of UFOs in the spring of 1964 but on the same day as the Canyon Ferry landing an interesting and sobering incident took place on the north range of the Holloman-White Sands test range. In this instance I'm sure the military felt justified in keeping the information secret, and I must admit that I agree.

The pilot of an RB-57 bomber engaged in a routine bomb test mission in the vicinity of Stallion Site, a few miles west of San Antonio, New Mexico, called Mission Control on the range radio network and informed the controller: "I'm not alone up here." Control came back with: "What do you mean?"

"I've got a UFO," the pilot explained. When the controller asked for a description the pilot said that the object was egg-shaped and white. Another question came from Control:

"Any markings?" The pilot replied, "The same as the one at Socorro. I'm going to make another pass."

Minutes later the big bomber had completed its turn and came in over the area where the UFO was first seen. The pilot excitedly reported: "It's on the ground." At this point communications ceased. Photo crews were alerted and asked to stand by.

The instrumented range at Holloman-White Sands is controlled by the Army. The Navy and the Air Force are resident-guests with certain projects which they test. This incident involving the RB-57 was under control of the Army from the beginning to whatever end there was. Any inquiries from Air Force test personnel concerning the conversation on the range radio network could have been blithely explained away in one of many ways and Air Force or Navy personnel would have been none the wiser.

My first information of the incident was relayed by a very reliable contact at White Sands. I verified it through Breuer at the *Alamogordo Daily News* and Terry Clarke of KALG, both of whom were already aware of the reported "landing" before I was informed. Clarke's information had come from a ham radio operator friend who was monitoring various frequencies while checking out some of his equipment, when he picked up the frequency which the bomber and Mission Control were using. He listened, fascinated, until communications ceased. He then reported to Clarke, who he knew was interested in the UFO subject.

Breuer had learned of the incident from his own news contacts, and when he tried to check it out through Air Force Public Information channels at Holloman he was informed that no such thing had happened. The Air Force at Wright-Patterson knew nothing about the incident for the simple reason that it was handled by the Army. This is supported by the fact that months later a man identifying himself as an employee of the Foreign Technology unit at Holloman contacted me through a friend in Tucson, and when Mr. Lorenzen and I spent an evening with him he tried to extract the identity of our initial informant. He indicated that the Air Force knew nothing about the incident and he may have been telling the truth, for succeeding inquiries indicated that Wright-Patterson was ignorant of the matter also.

In a later exchange of correspondence concerning the matter with Major Quintanilla of Wright-Patterson, Mr. Lorenzen offered to provide the name of our informant providing Quintanilla could guarantee immunity from reprisal for the individual. He said no more about our offer in subsequent correspondence.

Two other range sightings of UFOs were gathered in the course of the investigation of the landing on the north range. On May 15 between 11:30 A.M. and 12:15 P.M., surveillance radar as well as FPS-16 radars at Stallion Site tracked two objects in the vicinity north of the station. The UFOs performed "perfect, precise flight maneuvers" including side-by-side flight, separating, then rejoining each other in formation and up-and-down "pogo" maneuvers. Visual confirmation was made by a trained radar operator who saw the two objects and described them as brown in color and football-shaped. They were flying at very low altitude and disappeared out of sight beyond buildings at the instrumentation site where the radar operator observed them.

Somewhat disturbing is the fact that one or both of the objects were alternately responding with the standard Federal Aviation Agency's recognition signal, sometimes called IFF. To avoid the necessity of having to depend entirely on radar "skin track," (i.e., reflection of the radar beam from the plane's surface), there is in use in most military and commercial aircraft a "transponder" system. It operates generally as follows: An "interrogate" signal is transmitted periodically from the tracking ground station. This signal consists of a series of pulses arranged in a particular time sequence or "code." When the "transponder" (a combination receiver and transmitter) receives the correct code, it responds by transmitting a code of its own which is displayed at the ground station. This is called a "recognition signal." Either of two frequencies are commonly used, with a different code on each frequency. The two football-shaped objects were alternately beaming both of these codes while in flight on the range north of Stallion site.

The summer of 1964 yielded several good sightings but they were considerably different in type and behavior from the incidents of the spring. One chilling incident in June involved a small boy, Charles Davis, of Hobbs, New Mexico. On June 2, Charles, eight, was standing outside the back door of his grandmother's commercial laundry. Mrs. Frank Smith, the grandmother, was just inside the screen door, cutting cake for lunch. Suddenly Mrs. Smith was horrified to see an apparently metallic object, pouring smoke, swoop down out of the sky and hang just above Charles' head. The thing stayed only a few seconds, then with a "whooshing" sound it elevated and disappeared up into the sky. Mrs. Smith then ran out to Charles and put her arms around him. He had begun to swell about the face and neck. There was a sooty deposit on his face and neck and T-shirt. The terrified boy cried, "Grandma, am I going to die?" several times. Mrs. Smith rushed him to the hospital.

According to Mrs. Smith, the object had looked something

like a top and had given off black soot and fire. Charles had stood there, petrified, with his eyes shut tight and his hair literally standing on end, until the object left. When I interviewed Mrs. Smith she corrected earlier press reports claiming that Charles had been "burned bald"—he hadn't. He was badly swollen, however, and his hair singed. One of his ears looked like a "piece of raw meat," she said, his nose was scarcely visible because of the swelling and his eyes were swelled shut. Samples of the boy's skin and hair, along with his T-shirt and Mrs. Smith's apron, against which she had held the boy, were taken by local fire authorities and were sent to the FBI. At the latest report, Mrs. Smith had not been informed of any analysis or conclusions by the FBI. However, I contacted the doctor who attended Charles in the hospital. He did not care to have his name used but did give us this rather puzzling information:

The boy was at the Lee County Hospital for five days. The burns, which were second degree with some embedded soot, were on the face, ears and neck and according to the doctor were "nothing unusual," except for one thing— Charles suffered no pain during his ordeal. Treatment of burns consisted of sulphathiazol ointment applied directly to the affected areas. When Charles began to heal it was necessary to administer a sedative because of the intense itching. Although the doctor was frank and readily answered questions, he would not offer any opinion about the nature of the object or the possible cause of the burns, but he seemed to believe the story told by Mrs. Smith and Charles. This incident seems to be one of those relating to a UFO in trouble. Soot and fire have not been recorded as being typical of the objects.

The remainder of 1964 sightings seemed to follow the pattern of objects observing humans at close range. An example involved Mr. and Mrs. Harry Taylor, their daughter Linda, seventeen, and a friend, Eddie Pfund, twenty-one, who were "chased" along Route 60 near 20-mile Bend in Florida on the night of June 23. The objects when first seen looked like a cluster of lights in the rear view mirror. When observed more carefully, they appeared to be fifteen to twenty disc-shaped amber objects. They seemed to be moving through the air at about sixty to seventy feet from the ground, turning so that their configuration was easily visible. The party estimated the objects' size at about five feet in diameter. When they stopped the car and got out to have a better look, the objects stopped also. As they watched, the glow diminished and nearly disappeared. As soon as they continued their journey the objects showed up again, keeping pace behind the car and appearing considerably brighter than before. When the Taylors turned the car around and headed toward the things, they disappeared again. In an attempt to get away from them, the Taylors pushed their car to 100 miles per hour. Finally, hoping to alert the occupants of a house, they pulled the car into a driveway. The objects then split formation and passed on either side of a clump of nearby trees and disappeared again. When Mr. Taylor mentioned the incident in Vero Beach several days later he found that a Mr. Street and his son, of Keenansville, had seen the objects at about the same time. The whole story was contained in the Fort Pierce, Florida, *News-Tribune* on June 24.

As the year 1964 waned, UFO activity seemed to dwindle to a mere trickle of reports. This was somewhat fortunate for me for at the time I had come into possession of a copy of the original Portuguese text of the secret Brazilian Navy report on the Trindade incident and photos discussed in Chapter 11, and I spent several weeks with the translation. Included with the document, which was forwarded by an ex-Brazilian naval officer who knew of my interest in the case, were copies of confidential letters between Brazilian military officers concerning the Trindade sighting. One of them, from the Chief of the Navy High Command, Fleet Admiral Antonio Maria de Carvalho, to the General Director of Hydrography and Navigation, stated: ". . . the existence of personal reports and of photographic evidence of very great value concerning the circumstances involved permit the admission that there are indications of the existence of unidentified aerial objects." After making this declaration, de Carvalho suggested that the Trindade Island Oceanographic post be kept alerted and subsequent information be relayed to his office. The document also included a polite letter from M. Sunderland, U.S. Navy Captain and U.S. Naval Attaché to the U.S. Embassy at Rio asking for copies of the photos. This is further corroboration of my conclusion that the Air Force Project Bluebook has merely been a public relations organ and that research is being done elsewhere. Sunderland was ultimately sent copies of the photos under cover of a letter, dated February 25, 1958, from Rear Admiral Luiz Felippe Pinto Da Luz of the Brazilian Navy High Command. After considering all information, the document concluded that the object was seen by many witnesses, was photographed and that there was no evidence of a hoax involved. This is quite important in view of Dr. Donald Menzel's conclusion, in his book, *The World of Flying Saucers*, that the Trindade photos were hoaxes. Menzel had no connection with the official Brazilian investigation and it is difficult to determine how he arrived at such a conclusion.

15
1965–The "Big Year"

EARLY 1965 was quiet as far as UFO activity was concerned. However, the "season," as the press so often calls a flurry of UFO activity, seemed to have begun when sixty-five-year-old John Reeves of Weeki-Wachi Springs, Florida, claimed to have not only seen a UFO on the ground, but the occupant as well. His description of the object did not correlate with accumulated material concerning those seen in the past and although the "man" he described was "small"— about five feet tall—and his clothing generally resembled that seen in other incidents, the whole episode lacked authenticity and was generally written off by most researchers as being impossible to accept. Nine days, later, however, a well documented report out of Ft. Myers, Florida, involved a man who was injured by a UFO. The Reeves incident had received considerable publicity, internationally as well as on United States press wires. The incident we will now examine received limited local publicity.

James Flynn, forty-five, is a respected rancher and resident of Fort Myers, Florida. On Wednesday, March 17, he walked into the office of ophthalmologist, Dr. Paul Brown, and asked for an examination. He had just returned from a hunting trip in the Everglades, exhibited swelling around the eyes, and was nearly blind. Brown called Flynn's wife, who

came and took him to the hospital, after which he told
what had happened.

On Friday, the 12th, Flynn took his swamp buggy, camping
gear and four dogs and set out for the Everglades, about
eighteen miles east of the Big Cypress Indian reservation. On Sunday night three of the dogs jumped a deer and
ran off. Flynn whistled and called until about midnight, then
started the buggy and headed in the direction in which he
had last seen them. About an hour later, at 1 A.M. on Monday,
Flynn saw a huge light in the sky above the trees about a
mile away. It moved from east to west and back to its original
position four times. It then settled to the ground and appeared to hover at about four feet altitude. Flynn drove
closer, turned off the buggy's lights, then got out his binoculars and watched the thing. It was a cone-shaped object
about thirty feet in height and about twice as wide as it was
high. Eight feet from the top was a row of windows below
which there were three more rows of windows of the same
size—about two feet square. Around the windows was a
black strip about two inches wide. From the bottom of the
lowest row of windows to the bottom of the ship there was
a distance of about twelve feet. Flynn estimated the size
and dimensions by comparing the object with surrounding
cypress trees which were about twenty-five feet tall. Instead
of coming to a peak like a normal cone, the object was
rounded on top. A typical "disc."

The whole object appeared to be metallic and comprised of
pieces of material about four by four feet and held together
by rivets. The windows gave off a dull yellow light and the
area under the object was lighted by an orangish-red glow.
Flynn watched the object for thirty to forty minutes with the
aid of his glasses. By this time, Flynn was about one-
quarter mile from the object and decided to investigate
further, so he cranked up his buggy and approached it. He
got within a few yards of the edge of the light and stopped,
switching off his lamp again. The dog he had on the buggy
began to try to tear itself out of the cage. The next details
support the contention of many that the UFOs are at best
indifferent to man and at worst, inimical. Flynn walked to
the edge of the lighted area, raised his arm and waved. He
got no response and, after waiting a half a minute or so, he
walked about six feet into the lighted area and raised his arm
to wave again. A short beam of light erupted from just
under the bottom of the lowest tier of windows and struck

Flynn on the forehead, a little to the right of center, above his right eyebrow. He lost consciousness. When Flynn awoke he had no idea how long he had been unconscious. He was lying on the ground behind his buggy and the dog in the cage had nearly torn the cage apart. Flynn realized he was nearly blind, but managed to look around the area. He found a perfectly symmetrical circle of burned ground cover where the object had hovered. Several of the cypress trees on the opposite side of the circle were burned at the tops. Marks in the vicinity of his buggy indicated that he had crawled around during his period of unconsciousness but he had no recollection of doing so. Flynn felt extremely hungry and weak, but managed to drive his buggy back to his camp site two miles away, where he cooked bacon and eggs and ate. He then drove to the home of a Seminole Indian friend, Henry Billy, who offered to go back to Fort Myers with him. Flynn declined, feeling he could make his own way, and set off. When he arrived at Fort Myers, he sought medical aid from Brown and ended up in the hospital, where he remained for five days.

Investigation yielded the startling information that Flynn had been unconscious for twenty-four hours, for he arrived at the home of Henry Billy early Tuesday morning. From the reservation to Fort Myers took nearly twenty-four hours, for the major part of the journey was slow-going through swampy Everglade terrain. Upon examination by doctors, Flynn's face was found to be red and puffy around the eyes. His right eye looked like a bloody marble and was sightless. The sight in the left eye was very blurred. I wrote to Flynn's personal physician and received the following letter in answer:

"I have known Mr. Flynn for twenty-five years and have always considered him a reliable, emotionally stable individual. I also accompanied him to the site of his observation of the flying object. I have made a few pictures of the burned area which is not conclusive of anything but a fresh burn and scorched treetops in a perfect circle are near the area marked by Mr. Flynn as site of the hovering object. There were also fresh scuff marks on two trees twelve or fifteen feet apart in the area underneath the burned circle of trees. The marks were as if a heavy object in a straight line had slid down the trees about two feet and stopped there. There was no mark of any kind on the soft dried marsh underneath. No animal, human or vehicle tracks of any kind. I couldn't account for those scuff marks." Unquote.

Dr. Stipe's medical report reads as follows:

"I asked to see Mr. Flynn about forty-eight hours after he was admitted to Lee Memorial Hospital by an opthalmologist, for an injury to his right eye. The eye condition was hemorrhaging into the anterior chamber of the eye, apparently traumatic.

"Mr. Flynn gave a history of being hit by something like a flash of light while approaching an unidentified flying object hovering just above the ground.

". . . When I first examined Mr. Flynn, he had both eyes covered by bandages and I was not able to observe his eyes or forehead. He was alert and cooperative. The physical examination showed a well-muscled, well-nourished male. The heart and lungs were normal. The abdomen was normal. The only abnormal findings were neurological. No paralysis was noted, but the deep tendon reflexes of biceps, triceps, patellas and achilles were absent. Plantars and abdominal were absent, but cremaseterics were present.

"Mr. Flynn was observed carefully for several weeks. His reflexes gradually returned over a five day to one week period but returned irregularly. The forehead was finally examined and presented a thickened area just above and medial to the right eye; in the center of this area was a depressed, slightly abraded spot about 1 centimeter in diameter. Very small amount of haematoma was noted across the right upper eyelid. There was never any mental confusion or evidence of hallucination.

"About the fourth day in the hospital, Mr. Flynn complained of hearing reduction and numbness in arms and hands. This cleared in about twenty-four hours.

"When last seen about 16 April 1965, approximately four weeks after the injury, Mr. Flynn was again checked. The abdominal reflexes were not present, but all others were normal. The depressed area over the right eye was still present and prominent. He still has a cloudy vision of the right eye. No other abnormal physical or neurological findings were noted." Unquote.

Upon receipt of the foregoing I consulted my personal physician in Tucson for interpretation of the various medical terms. Stipe had said, in a telephone conversation with me, that the lack of those reflexes indicated to him that Flynn had had a real rather than a psychic experience. My doctor told me that this lack of reflexes could have been caused by emotional shock. The injuries to Flynn's face and the lack of deep tendon reflexes cannot be explained by citing the usual causes. His wounds were strange and could not have been feigned. Nor were they self-inflicted wounds, either, for they would have been impossible to achieve.

The Flynn case seemed to be the one which awakened some researchers to the possibility of hostile UFO occupants, although it can be rationalized in any number of ways. However, the events of 1965 and 1966 made it impossible to rationalize any more and the warnings which I had voiced as early as 1958 began to make some impression.

Dr. Fontes, who continued to closely monitor UFO news not only in his native Brazil, but in South America, appeared on television in Rio de Janeiro in June, 1965, and made the prediction that the next UFO activity would begin in July of that year. He reasoned that if the UFOs were permanently based on Mars, as we suspected, the arrival of Mariner on its photographic mission in the vicinity of Mars, would bring a concentration of UFO sightings on earth. He was right. On July 15 press wires carried the details of the sighting of a mysterious glowing object which hovered near Canberra Airport in Australia while the U.S. Mariner space probe was taking pictures of Mars. Press reports said that Canberra officials were "baffled." The object, spotted by air traffic control officers and other expert aircraft observers at 10:50 P.M., hung suspended at about 5,000 feet for forty minutes. When an Air Force plane was sent out to identify it it zoomed out of sight. In the initial account, the wire services said that experts were quoted as "wondering if it was coincidence" that the object was sighted shortly before nearby Tidbinilla tracking station was scheduled to pick up Mariner signals. The station, the report said, had "unusual difficulty" in locking on to Mariner at the time.

The first reports became press sensations. On the first of July a lavender farmer, Maurice Masse, forty-one, of Valensole, France, told friends of an encounter with small "men" in his lavender field near the town of Valensole. Although the story got considerable space in international press releases, little detail was given and it was exploited for its amusement value. Exhaustive investigation, however, yielded the following information:

At five that morning Masse went to his field as usual. He heard a strange noise like "whistling" and upon investigation saw a strange object sitting in the field beyond a terrace about 250 feet distant. The object looked like a large rugby ball, was about the size of a Dauphine car and had a cupola on top. It stood on six extensions or legs. Wondering if it was some new kind of craft, Masse approached the object, whereupon he saw two small beings of generally human appearance who were bending over a lavender plant. Masse walked closer to them, intending to talk to them, but when he was about fifteen–twenty feet away one of the creatures noticed him, pointed a tube of some kind at him and he became paralyzed. Masse stood helpless, unable to speak or move. The two conversed between themselves making strange sounds which he could not recognize as ordinary speech and which did not seem to emanate from their mouths. They looked at Masse in a rather scornful manner but did not demonstrate any hostility as such. After a few minutes the two got into the craft via a sliding door, and the craft, emitting a whistling sound, took off westward at great speed.

Masse's description of the "little men" is somewhat unnerving although he was not frightened by them at the time. They were "about the size of eight-year-old children," he said, and had huge heads about three times the size of a normal adult's head. They were completely bald, had no facial hair and had very white, smooth skin. Only their heads were visible for the rest of their bodies were encased in an overall-like suit of greenish-gray material. Their faces seemed normal except for the mouth which was a lipless hole. Masse's experience is not unique when considered in the context of all the reports in which diminutive bipeds have figured. Although he gives a more definitive description of facial features, his report generally follows the others as far as the small "men" and the type of craft described.

The next incident given wide press exposure involved the sighting by scientific and military personnel of a strange object maneuvering over Antarctic bases. On July 2 and 3, Chilean, Argentinian and English bases on Deception Island reported the presence of an unconventional aerial object over the area. After the initial word about the sighting got out, the press pressured the Argentine Navy for more information and on July 6 a report was issued by the Argentine Navy Secretary. The basic information was as follows:

At 1940 hours (local time, Deception Island), a giant lens-shaped object, solid in appearance, mostly red and green in color and changing at times to yellow, blue, white and orange, moved in a zigzagging trajectory toward the east, occasionally changing course to the west and north with varied speeds and no sound. It disappeared over the horizon at 45 degrees elevation and was judged to be about ten to fifteen kilometers from the base. During the maneuvers the witnesses noted the object's great speed and also the fact that it hovered motionless for fifteen minutes at an estimated 5,000 meters. Among the witnesses was a meteorologist, three Chilean subofficers and thirteen others. The observation lasted twenty minutes and photographs of the object were taken. There was a clear sky, some stratus-cumulus clouds and perfect visibility. The report also stated that in the afternoon of the same day the same or a similar object was observed from the Argentine base on the South Orkney Islands, moving away toward the northwest, at an elevation of 30 degrees above the horizon and a distance estimated at ten to fifteen kilometers.

After persistent efforts APRO was able to obtain the complete text of reports received from Pedro Aguirre Cerda base (Chilean) pertaining to the 4 P.M. sighting of an object on June 18. The same type of object as that observed by English and Argentine personnel was seen, and the maneuvers were generally the same—high speed, swift course changes and hovering. This object, however, disappeared by ascending vertically at high speed.

As soon as the above information was made available, Brazilian and Chilean reporters requested and obtained a direct interview by radio with Commander Mario Janh Barrera, Commanding Officer at the Pedro Aguirre Cerda base. He stated:

"It is nonsense to say that we saw a "flying saucer" like those from science-fiction stories. What we sighted was something real, a solid object which was moving at incredible speeds, performed maneuvers, emitted a greenish light and caused interference in the electromagnetic instruments of the Argentine base situated close to ours. It hovered in mid-air after performing one of its maneuvers, remaining motionless for about twenty minutes and then moving away at high speed. We observed this object through high-power binoculars and theodolites."

The rest of Barrera's statement is graphic and most interesting: "I don't believe it could be an airship of terrestrial manufacture. As an officer of the Chilean Air Force, my knowledge about man-made machines gives me absolute conviction that nothing similar exists on earth in shape, velocity and mobility in space. We have taken ten color photographs which will be developed in Santiago.

"As soon as we sighted the object we tried to contact via radio the Argentine and English bases. But such contact was impossible because there was a very strong interference on the radio—all channels." Unquote.

The interference with radio transmission and reception is not a new factor where UFOs are concerned—it has been noted often through the years. The notable thing about the Antarctic sightings is the fact that a large number of qualified scientific personnel observed an unconventional aerial object which interfered with radio transmission and reception, was observed with optical aids, interfered with electromagnetic instruments including variometers and magnetometers *and was photographed*. To my knowledge, however, the photographs have yet to be released to the public.

After the spate of sightings abroad, unidentified aerial objects began making their appearance in the United States and, as usual, witnesses of sightings prior to the July incidents came forward to report their experiences. At Page, Arizona, on June 3 at 8:45 P.M. Edward Coyle, mine foreman at the Zontelli Western Mining Company, observed an egg-shaped object near Coppermine, twenty miles south of Page. He notified Pat and June Patterson, owners of the Coppermine Trading Post on the Navajo Indian Reservation and the three watched the object for fifteen minutes. They described it as egg-shaped, with a white light on the leading edge and entirely surrounded by a reddish, misty glow.

On the same night, at 10:00 P.M. a Tucson importer (who has requested anonymity, fearing ridicule) observed a "dirigible-shape" object hovering in a canyon just off the Black Canyon Highway near the Verde crossing. Bathed in a "cold blue glow," the object was clearly silhouetted against the hills. Mr. X was driving south out of Flagstaff when he rounded a curve and his headlights picked up the object. It then slowly ascended straight up, headed southwest and disappeared in the direction of Buckeye. The entire sighting lasted about fifteen minutes. The observer said that he had never "believed in these things" but that he had to yield to the evidence before his eyes.

Quite often one or two good reports spur the interest of the press and as a result, ensuing UFO information gets considerable attention. This seems to have been the case in the summer of 1965, although activity around the states of

Oklahoma, Kansas and Texas was sufficient by itself to demand attention.

Wynnewood, Oklahoma, police officer Lewis Sikes was one of the first to report a UFO sighting during the "Western Flap." At 1 A.M. on the morning of July 31 Sikes watched an object which emitted red, white and blue lights as it hovered for forty-five minutes northeast of Wynnewood at 8,000 feet altitude. Sikes reported to the Highway Patrol that the object made no noise, and was picked up on radar scopes at Tinker Air Force Base near Oklahoma City and at Carswell Air Force Base in Texas. The object was tracked as it made its way toward Oklahoma City and within fifteen miles of Tinker where it was lost from the scope's display. Fifteen minutes after the object left the screen it, or a similar object, was picked up again and tracked to a point twenty-nine miles south of Tinker where it disappeared and was not tracked again.

The next day, August 1, brought sightings all over the west. Sikes' sighting was the first observation made by a police officer and tracked on radar at the same time. In the two weeks preceding the Sikes report the objects were seen hither and yon all over the United States, but the police reports seemed to merit more attention. It is difficult to give a true picture of the events of 1965 without narrating sighting after sighting and that is not possible in the limited amount of space in a chapter or two, or even, for that matter, a book. Therefore it is necessary to stress that the following are only a smattering of the large number recorded for the August period. Many sightings of single objects were made, but formations were seen in unusual abundance. We might note here that in some cases there is doubt as to whether an actual formation of objects were seen, or whether the "formation" was actually one object sporting more than one light.

On the 1st, a diamond-shaped formation of white objects was seen by police officers at Chickasha, Shawnee, Cushing and Chandler, Oklahoma. Mrs. Bill Tipton of Chandler claimed she had seen a single object which was red on the bottom and white on the top and which hovered over the town for fifteen minutes before moving into the west at high speed. At about 9 P.M. officers in three different police cars in the Shawnee, Oklahoma, area observed the diamond-shaped formation for about thirty minutes. During their flight into the north the objects, which looked like brilliant stars, changed from red to white to blue-green and at times zig-zagged or moved from side to side. The same type of formation with the same colors was reported by police at Cushing.

Police at Hobbs, New Mexico, near the Texas line, observed a round white object with an orange tail which moved into the west. Shortly thereafter a police dispatcher at Carlsbad, sixty-nine miles west of Hobbs, reported a similar object, and police at Artesia, thirty-six miles northwest of Carlsbad, received four reports of a bright white spherical object with a red tail which passed overhead northeast of the town.

The biggest spectacular of the night, however, took place at Wichita, Kansas, when the Weather Bureau radar there tracked several objects at altitudes of from 6,000 to 9,000 feet. This information was given to the press by the Sedgwick County Sheriff's office at Wichita. "Red objects that exploded in a shower of sparks" and others that "fluttered like leaves in the sky" were some of the descriptions by multitudes of observers who could hardly believe their eyes. One was a police dispatcher at the Sheriff's office who said, "I was a disbeliever but I saw something up there tonight and so did other observers at the Weather Bureau and McConnell Air Force Base." McConnell personnel were reticent about observers and the observed, though, and the usual "no comment" preceded official referrals to AF Headquarters in Washington, D. C.

On the night of the 2nd, Ed O'Brien, PIO officer at Tinker AFB, let fly with the famous "explanation" that some of the reports could have been of the observations of a delta meteor shower which occurs from July 26 through August 6. He admitted that between fifty and seventy-five calls had come in during a 1½ hour period starting at 8:15 P.M. on Monday night, August 2.

Still on the first of August pressrooms hummed to the tune of reports of vari-colored objects at Broken Bow and Grand Island, Nebraska, Sioux City, Iowa, Medicine Lodge, Kansas, Mountain Home, Arkansas, and various points in Colorado.

At the Colorado State Penitentiary at Canon City, two tower guards observed a glowing white object which remained stationary for about thirty minutes in the northeast. One guard, Don Stites, said the object was first spotted at 2:15 A.M. on the morning of the second and appeared to be about halfway between Colorado Springs and Pueblo. During the observation it would dim, then brighten, and finally just disappeared.

Another early morning sighting of the 2nd got more play than most in news accounts, and, piecing together the events occurring over a period of time, we get some interesting information. At 3:40 A.M., the Wichita Weather Bureau tracked an unknown object on its radar to a point south and west of Wellington, Kansas. First showing up at 22,000, south of Wichita, it gradually descended to 4,000 feet, when it disappeared from the screen. At 3:40 A.M., police officers Dave Lowe and Eddie Roberts were patrolling Caldwell, Kansas, when they heard a police radio report about two objects moving in a southerly direction toward Wellington, South Haven and Caldwell. The two officers headed their police car toward the airport on the east edge of town. They spotted two glowing objects, but not clearly enough to identify them; so they sipped coffee and talked about the situation. Shortly another radio report told of a UFO being tracked north of Caldwell and the pair looked around but saw nothing at first. Then Lowe spotted something which he described as a "halo of light like a city has at night" behind a rise in the ground about fifty yards away. Lowe jumped on the car's running board to get a better look and saw the object—a red, white, bluish-green irridescent object "as bright as a hundred searchlights." He said it didn't resemble a "flying saucer" at all, but looked more like a 100-yard-long egg. After the two regained their composure they got into their cruiser and raced after the object in an attempt to get a closer look. As they pulled onto U.S. Highway 81 and headed east, the object ducked behind a hedgerow and they lost sight of it. They later conjectured that the object may have turned out its lights, thereby preventing them from seeing it again. Total time of close-up viewing of the object at Caldwell was about three minutes. Meanwhile, variously described objects were being observed at Wellington and South Haven. And just a couple of hours earlier, in northern Texas, photographic history was being made. Just after midnight on the morning of the 2nd, TV news photographer Robert Campbell was lying in his bed at home at Bells, Texas, listening to a police broadcast. He listened with mounting interest to an account of an object being tracked by radar, apparently at Tinker Air Force Base, and which was heading south. The end of the conversation that he was monitoring was that of the Texas State Police. The information which ultimately propelled him into motion was that a blue-white light was south of Durant. He grabbed his 4x5 Speed Graphic and went into Bells, where he encountered Chief of Police Pete McCollum. The two drove around until they were one mile east of Bells on Highway 82, where they spotted the object hanging motionless at 45 degrees elevation in the northeast. Campbell immediately set up his tripod and took four time exposures of two minutes each at three-minute intervals. The photographs, on black and white film, show a misty, glowing object with traces of what appears to be vapor on its surface. After watching for 2½ hours the two men left and went home to bed. The remarkable aspect of this particular incident is that, having been alerted by the same radio broadcast, several other individuals were also watching the object. Campbell and McCollum were one mile east of Bells, Oklahoma. Highway patrolman Bill Quires was watching from Durant, thirty miles north of Bells, and Department of Public Safety dispatcher Jim Faglia was watching from a point seven miles south of Sherman, which is twelve miles west of Bells. All descriptions put the object between the town of Bells, Durant and Sherman, thus precluding the possibility that the object could have been a planet or star.

After August 2 sightings seemed to drop off sharply and it was generally assumed that the flap was in its dying throes. Toward the middle of August, however, APRO began receiving airmail packets of clippings, translations and personally gathered reports from South American members. The UFOs had not deserted the earth's skies—they had merely moved south.

This account would not be complete without the story of truckdriver Don Tennopir of Beatrice, Kansas, who was driving north of Highway 15 about twenty-five miles south of Abilene, Kansas, on August 4, en route to Lincoln, Nebraska. Suddenly all the lights on his truck went out. They came back on, then went off, then came back on again. At about this time a strange object came down over the truck with a sizzling or "wind-blowing" sound, Tennopir told reporters. It seemed to almost touch the cab of the truck. The strange thing then swooped down over the road in front of the truck and hovered about 100 feet in front of the startled Tennopir. "I tell you, I was standing on those brakes. It looked like it was going to fall right in the middle of the road but it didn't. I got my rig stopped and about that time this thing raised up a bit and slowly took off to the west and then headed south." Tennopir described the object as round, about fourteen to fifteen feet in diameter and "sort of orange-colored." It appeared to be shooting off reddish rays, he said, and seemed to be about two feet thick with a "hump" in the middle which "stuck up four feet or so." He also noted a dark spot on the "hump." The classic disc with cupola.

Scarcely a state in the United States went unvisited by the discs during those hectic days of early August, and APRO gathered reports from virtually every country in the non-Communist world. Some of those in South America were outstanding because they involved incidents in which hundreds and sometimes thousands of observers watched objects cavort in the sky for minutes and sometimes hours. Major cities such as Buenos Aires, Argentina, Caracas, Venezuela, Lima, Peru, were treated to such spectacles. Some of the more sensational included a cigar-shaped reddish object which hovered over the Rio Plata, a 28-mile-wide river which separates Argentina and Uruguay, on July 17. It was observed by many people. A plate-shaped object giving off red, yellow and green lights, hovered over Diamante, Argentina, on July 25. On the 27th hundreds in Barroca, Calfate and Gameleira, Brazil, watched a glowing plate-shaped object crossing the sky in Bel Horizonte state. It flew slowly at first, then rapidly, in a zigzag course, leaving a yellow-blue and orange trail behind it.

Also on the 27th, Prospero Alva, an employee at the Chosica Electric Company in Lima, Peru, heard a strange noise like the "buzzing of bees," looked outside and saw an object ten to fifteen feet in diameter, saucer-shaped and with "holes" through which light emanated. The object had a "turret" on top which rotated constantly and from which came forth an elongated object which Alva interpreted as some sort of a "scanning device." The object was on or near the ground within forty feet of the startled observer. Shortly the "armlike" protuberance withdrew into the turret, the object moved slowly off the ground, then disappeared into the sky at high speed. Coincidentally, all of Lima suffered an unexplained power outage on June 8, 1966, during which two million people were without electrical power for from thirty minutes to three hours. There are more of these "coincidences"; after spotty sightings of low-flying and hovering objects in Nebraska, Colorado, and Wyoming in April and May, 1966, spotty blackouts affected these areas.

A class of fledgling radio operators and their instructors at Grano De Oro Airport, near Maracaibo, Venezuela, observed visually and tracked on radar three luminous discs at 7:30 A.M. on July 28. The objects were only observed for about ten seconds on radar, but visually they appeared as elongated objects with a "bulge" in the center—the disc with cupola.

These are only a few of many sightings in South America. After the end of July activity switched to the United States for just a few days and then proceeded south again where landings and appearances of occupants were recorded.

A glowing oval-shaped object maneuvered over the water reservoir near the Hills of Carrizol about 20 miles from Caracas, Venezuela, on August 17. Seen by several workers at a house nearby, the object hovered momentarily over the water after wobbling precariously in the air. The men who observed it said it left the vicinity, flew toward the house and landed briefly on the grass. This activity was also observed by people driving along the nearby highway. One witness said his car engine acted up while the object was in sight. When the object neared the ground it extended several stiltlike protuberances to the ground. The workers said they expected something or someone to come out of the thing but the "legs" were drawn up into the object again, it glowed intensely and left.

Euclides Bencomo, Jesus Zapata and Juan Ramos were hunting in the Bum-Bum forests of Barinas, Venezuela, on August 18 when they saw a strange glow behind some bushes. When they approached the source, they saw a huge egg-shaped object hovering some six feet off the ground. It was giving off multicolored lights which emanated from large round windows and it made a whistling sound. The three dropped their guns and ran, later coming back with a posse. The guns were there but no evidence of the object's earlier presence was found.

A rather spectacular incident took place shortly after midnight on September 15 on a highway near Pretoria, Africa. Two police officers, Koos de Klerk and Jochn Lockem, were on a routine mission at a farmhouse and on their way back to headquarters saw what appeared to be a "sea of flames" on the highway ahead. Some ten seconds later they saw a top-shaped object which ascended at high speed and took off into the northwest. No noise was heard, but jets of flame spurted from the underside of the object through two openings. A circular area of the asphalt highway covering, about six feet in diameter, was found to be burning and grass on both sides of the road was also scorched. The highway continued to burn at that spot for some time after the object departed. The two officers said they had passed that spot not five minutes before and everything had been normal.

About one month before the above-mentioned incident in Africa, Dr. Silva Guillen reported to APRO member Joe Rolas of Caracas, Venezuela, that he and his family had seen a strange disc-shaped object at about 8 P.M. in the middle of August while driving in Eastern Venezuela in the vicinity of Cumanacoa. His niece had just called attention to a "flaming meteor" which had passed the car on her side, and when Guillen looked, he saw what appeared to be a "brush fire." Then he noticed that the flames actually came from a round-shaped metallic object and were projected downward toward the ground. The object was hovering about ten to twenty feet above the ground. Guillen stopped the car to look, whereupon the object began to approach him. At the urging of his wife and niece he got back in and resumed driving. The disc followed the car for a short distance, then sped out of sight. Dr. Guillen is an engineer and president of the Sugar Refining Corporation at Cumanacoa. The object involved in the Guillen incident seems to resemble at least generally the object sighted by the police in Africa, and the flames projected downward in both cases is another correlation. The Guillen sighting was not published until APRO included it in the January-February 1966 *APRO Bulletin,* so there was no chance of collaboration between the police in Africa and Guillen in Venezuela.

If, as some seen to think, the sighting of UFOs is nothing more than a symptom of psychological aberrations, then the human race has been infected by a highly contagious kind of progressive mental disease.

The next outstanding sighting in South America took place on November 1 over Huanaco, Peru, at 5 P.M. A globe-shaped UFO with an encircling ring which made the object resemble the planet Saturn (like the IGY photos) came out of the south, appeared to be rotating at high speed and hovered within 400 meters from the observers, who included the editor of the local newspaper. The object gave off multicolored light and displayed an antenna on the top which revolved continuously. When observers attempted to approach the object the light became blinding and the UFO moved off into the north and out of sight.

Several incidents took place on October 26 which were sensational in nature. At about 8:30 P.M. Dr. Oswaldo Cardoso, in a taxi on his way to a house call in Mogi-Guaçu, Brazil, observed a bright round object which came up from behind the car, caught up with it, then swerved to the left and disappeared at incredible speed. The other witnesses were the taxi driver and another passenger. In the same general location, in the early hours of the 26th, a farm woman walking along the road near the Champion Cellulose Works, saw a green, round, luminous object which appeared to be landing near an oil refinery in the neighborhood.

Around the middle of November a strange object showed considerable interest in the field adjoining the farm of Dario Anhaua Filho, a landowner and chemist who lives near Mogi-Guaçu, Brazil. Several sightings were made of a landing or nearly landed object and then on the 11th, after Mr. Filho had gone into town on business with the mayor, Mrs. Filho saw a strange light. The time was 9 P.M. Because of preceding sightings, the woman was afraid but nevertheless, followed by her grandson, she walked to the farm gate where she could see the object sitting on the ground in a nearby field. Two small humanoid figures were standing beside it. One began to walk to and fro along the furrows in the field, picking up twigs, branches and leaves, which he carried in his arms. The other figure stood by the fence and seemingly watched the mare on the other side. During this time, a truckload of shouting and singing people went by, whereupon the object moved away. As it moved one of the "dwarves" entered it quickly up a "green-colored tube," which suddenly had appeared on one side of it. When the truck had gone by, the object came back, and the same procedure of picking up plants, etc., took place again. Another car passed—the object switched off its light and moved away. During the second departure Mrs. Filho noticed that two similar objects were hovering in the sky. After the object reappeared and landed again, one of the dwarves turned on a green light which issued from an object about the size of a drinking glass, and an explosion was heard. Thereafter the object and the dwarves left.

The third occurrence on the 13th was the most revealing of all, and the bank manager who had been invited out to watch the curious proceedings, Filho, his wife and grandson all observed the strange goings-on. The object came in after dark and landed about 400 feet from the observers and focussed a bright beam of light upward. At the same time, the local sheriff and a police clerk, who had been traveling by car to Catagua, which is Senator Auro Moura Andrade's farm, came close to the farm, stopped and witnessed the object hovering over the farm prior to its landing. So excited did the bank manager become at the sight that he dropped his camera, which he had brought along to take photographs, and couldn't find it in the dark.

The beings appearing in this incident were small, about the size of a seven-year-old child seen from about a distance of 70 feet. One was wearing overalls, the other chocolate-colored pants and a gray collarless shirt. The third being had a squarish, flat head and was wearing what appeared to be a surgeon's apron. All three, as well as the ship in which they arrived, glowed brightly and were viewed by Father Longino Vartbinden, parish priest at Mogi-Guaçu, and scores of police, from a nearby farm. The latter had been summoned as soon as the object showed up.

On the same night, in the same general area, a couple driving their Volkswagen from Mogi-Mirim to Nova Lousan in the middle of the night, saw a huge light blocking the road; so they turned back. They then encountered a truck and warned the driver. While they were talking to him another car sped by them in the direction of the light, but soon came speeding back. The three vehicles then made their way along the highway in a bunch, driving slowly toward the source of light. As they approached it, it soared up above the approaching cars and lighted up the whole area. Dozens of other witnesses saw the object when the three vehicles arrived at a gas station and alerted the people there.

Also on the night of October 30 a night watchman working at the Ipe Ceramics factory noticed a light in the yard, went to examine it and saw a huge luminous disc floating slowly by the large chimney towers. When it reached the high-voltage wires it returned and seemed to head straight toward him. He ran into the factory and locked himself in.

The foregoing cases were investigated by Professor Flavio Pereira and Doctors Leo Godoi Otero and Renato Bacelar of São Paulo, Brazil, and turned over to APRO's representative, Dr. Olavo T. Fontes of Rio de Janeiro.

One of the best-documented incidents during the fall activity in the United States took place near Angleton, Texas, at 11 P.M. on September 3. Chief Deputy B. E. McCoy and Deputy Sheriff Bob Goode of Angleton, Texas, south of

Houston, were patrolling the West Columbia area of Brazoria County on the highway between West Columbia and Damon. McCoy spotted a brilliant purple light at horizon level beyond vast pasture land and was unable to identify the source. The officers were heading south, with Goode driving. McCoy was on the driver's right, and the object was in the west. Next, McCoy noted a somewhat smaller, less powerful blue light which seemingly emerged from the purple light and moved some distance to its right. He later realized this effect probably resulted from the object making a 90 degree turn so that it "faced" them, and the blue light, which had been parallel with and behind the purple one, now became visible. Until this time, Goode had maintained that the lights were in an oil field but McCoy had disagreed. The lights then rose simultaneously slightly above horizon level and Goode swung the car around for a better view since they were now directly opposite it. Based on their knowledge of the area, both men estimated that the object at this point was five to seven miles away. Suddenly the light came toward the police cruiser and within three to four seconds was within 150 feet of the highway at an elevation of about 100 feet and parallel with the car. The men later estimated that the object was at least 200 feet long and between 40 and 50 feet high. The purple light appeared to grow much brighter when it moved toward the men's position. Goode's window was down and his elbow was extending beyond the window ledge and he reported that he definitely felt heat when the object was at its closest point. Frightened, the men left the area as fast as the patrol car would take them—110 miles per hour. As they left, McCoy continued to observe the thing and was surprised to see it literally "snap back" to its original position. Suddenly it shot straight up in the air, the purple light becoming tremendously brilliant, and disappeared completely at about 20 degrees elevation in the west. An interesting point is that the purple light had illuminated the object itself, the pasture over which it was hovering, the highway and the exterior and interior of the patrol car.

On the same night that Officers Goode and McCoy fled the strange object in Texas, strange things were happening a half continent away in northeast United States. Literally hundreds of people observed strange disc-shaped objects sporting flickering red lights in the vicinity of Exeter, New Hampshire. Mr. John Fuller of the *Saturday Review* completely covered these incidents in his book *Incident at Exeter,* so we will deal with them only briefly at this time, because of their importance to our overall presentation.

On that night at about 2 A.M. Exeter police officer Eugene Bertrand was called to headquarters to get eighteen-year-old Norman Muscarello, who had reported a huge red-blinking UFO on Route 150 about two miles from town. Bertrand proceeded to the police station, where he heard young Muscarello retell his story about having hitchhiked home from Amesbury, Massachusetts, about twelve miles away, and walking most of the distance because of light traffic. He saw the UFO as he was approaching a farm and he watched the object as it moved over the Clyde Russell home and appeared to hover just a few feet above the roof. The thing was noiseless and he estimated that its diameter was eighty to ninety feet. The boy took refuge in a ditch near the road and watched as the object disappeared over some trees. He flagged a ride to Exeter where he told his story to police. Officers took note of his state of high agitation and obvious fright and called Bertrand.

Bertrand and the Muscarello boy went back to the scene of the initial sighting, got out of the cruiser and went into the field where Bertrand shone his flashlight about, seeing nothing. Then horses in a nearby corral began to kick and neigh and neighborhood dogs began to bark. The two stood almost petrified as the "thing" rose from behind some trees with a yawing motion and headed straight toward them. At this point they took cover in the cruiser. Bertrand started to draw his gun but thought better of it. Another police officer, who heard Bertrand's subsequent call on the radio about the object, arrived in time to see it disappear from view. Therefore, there was a total of three witnesses to this one sighting; all of the witnesses checked out as reliable, competent people.

The most interesting of the Eastern sightings which came to light and which seemed to have a bearing on future happenings, however, took place on October 21, when young Joseph Jalbert of Exeter noticed a reddish cigar-shaped object high in the sky at dusk. As the amazed young man watched, a small, reddish-orange disc detached itself from or came out of the larger object and slowly descended to the ground. It appeared to draw nearer to the boy's location, then skimmed along the power lines which line the road near the Jalbert house. The most unusual aspect of this case is what happened next. The object stopped, approximately 200 feet from Jalbert's position and just a few feet from the wires. Then, a silvery, pipelike extension descended from the object and appeared to touch the wire for a few seconds, then receded into the disc, whereupon the disc returned to the cigar which immediately flew out of sight. Considering the large number of observations of objects in the Exeter area, which are painstakingly and accurately documented by Mr. Fuller, it seems likely that the operation just described may have taken place many times. The majority of the sightings in the New Hampshire area, including hovering and landed objects, *almost invariably took place over the high tension power lines in that area!*

Extending this conjecture, we may have the explanation for the flap of 1965 in the west. In the East, which is heavily populated and which is also quite densely forested (at least in comparison to the west), the routes of the power lines are easily discerned—they cut a swath across the landscape. In the west, however, such maneuvers could be carried out either in the daytime or at night and hardly be noticed because of the vast unpopulated areas as well as the deserts and mountains. That the same sort of reconnaissance of high voltage electrical transmission lines may have been carried out during the UFO activity in the northwest in 1965 is suggested by the sighting of two disc-shaped objects which hung over high tension lines between Renton and Kent, Washington, on January 31. William E. Bolson of Maple Valley reported that he and his fellow musicians had observed the phenomenon at 6:15 that night.

Among the many sightings in the latter half of 1965, from August through December and into January, 1966, there occurred several incidents involving water storage areas. It can logically be assumed that besides the many incidents which were reported and recorded, a comparable number were not reported, and still more objects were not observed in these areas because of the hour of the day, the location of the water sources and other circumstances.

An object was observed passing within 100 feet of the Lewisville Dam at Denton City, Texas, on the night of August 2, and many residents called to report that an object appeared to have landed at Eagle Mountain Lake in the same area. Sheriff's deputies at Johnson City and Coralville, Iowa, and Iowa City police observed a brilliant object flying a circular pattern over the huge Coralville Water Reservoir north of Iowa City on the night of August 4. The last "big" case of objects over reservoirs in the United States took place on the nights of January 11 and 12, 1966, near Wanaque, New Jersey when hundreds of citizens and local police watched an object alternately hovering and maneuvering over the Wanaque reservoir. This particular reservoir is only one of many in that part of the state.

In an attempt to learn something more about the UFO concentration in 1965 than the mere fact that there had been a flap, APRO members carefully logged all sightings gathered, then, discarding the "flyovers" (i.e., horizon-to-horizon flights of high-flying objects) we found some curious patterns:

1. Seemingly deliberate exhibition by the discs over populated areas (Buenos Aires, Lima, Mexico City, Oklahoma City, Dallas, etc.).

2. Preoccupation with power stations and high tension lines.

3. Apparent interest in freshwater sources.

4. Preoccupation with police cars.

It was suggested by several members that the interest in water might be due to a need for hydrogen for fuel if the discs utilized nuclear engines. This doesn't seem to be a good explanation, however, for there are ample water supplies in mountain lakes, springs and, of course, in the oceans.

There has been considerable support for the theory that the discs were drawing electrical power from the power lines in the Jalbert case. This doesn't hold up either, for the discs have been flying about earth's atmosphere for hundreds of years (before the advent of electricity) and the presence of UFOs in the proximity of high power transmission lines only became manifest during the two years preceding the 1965 flap. Also, the Jalbert incident is the only one on record (to date) which involved a disc extending a device to the vicinity of the power lines. This was obviously an innovation.

The concentration on police cars may have been inadvertently caused by Lonnie Zamora's accidental chase of a UFO in 1964. Just one year after that incident, when the objects were maneuvering about cities and towns during the activity of July and August, 1965, officers in police cars began to take up the pastime of chasing the things whenever they had the opportunity. If the object involved in the Angleton, Texas, incident of September 3, 1965, was intelligently controlled, there seems to be little doubt that the occupants were aware of the police car.

On the morning of April 17, 1966, hundreds of residents in the vicinity of Ravenna, Ohio, and others east toward Pittsburgh, Pennsylvania, including many police officers, witnessed the passage of a strange object which sped eastward following main highways. Behind (and at times below) it, in hot pursuit, sped the county patrol car of Deputy Dale Spaur. Some of the details of this "chase" were carried in AP and UPI wire stories and most large American dailies, and Attorney Carl Funk of Zanesville, Ohio, was asked to investigate on behalf of APRO. In brief, these are his findings:

The first reports placed the object east of Ravenna, traveling along U.S. Highway 224 north of Canton. At 5 A.M. Deputy Wayne Huston was cruising about East Palestine, Ohio, when he heard a message on his car radio stating that a woman had reported from east of Akron that she had sighted a bright UFO which was apparently headed eastward. Portage county Deputy Dale Spaur received the message and along with another county deputy he took off in search of the object and picked it up "near Brady's Park going into Rochester" on State Route 224. The vehicle followed the UFO at speeds of between 80 and 100 miles per hour, later leaving Route 224 and taking State Route 14 toward Pittsburgh. During this time the deputies were using their car radio and were heard from the first by officer Huston of the East Palestine local police. As the chase passed East Palestine on Route 14 at about 5:35 A.M. at the highway junction just north of town, Huston joined the chase and all three, the UFO, the Portage deputies' car and the East Palestine cruiser proceeded eastward toward Pittsburgh at 80-100 miles per hour. Attempts were made to alert Pennsylvania officers, but with no success, due to differing radio systems and frequencies. However, on reaching Conway, Pennsylvania, contact was made with the local officers and the matter was turned over to them.

The police described the object with such phrases as, "so bright they could have driven without their lights"; "there were no windows, no irregular surface features, no exhaust or contrails"; it looked like "an ice cream cone, big end up," etc. There was no sound heard by any of the police except for a whirring noise similar to that made by a rapidly turning motor. The average height at which it flew was about 800 feet but once or twice it dipped to 200 feet. The deputies said there was no oscillation or erratic flight and the only variation was when it ascended, which it did, very rapidly. They assumed that it was intelligently controlled and it seemed to be capable of much greater speed than 100 miles per hour, but was holding back. They felt their radio communications were being monitored and their changes in procedure anticipated. Mantua Village's police chief, Gerald Buchert, obtained a photo of the object but it showed only as a blob. Spaur said it appeared to be about thirty-five to forty feet in diameter. Deputy Robert Wilson said that at one time during the chase, he heard Spaur say that an object "something like an antenna" protruded from the bottom of the object as it hovered over the cruiser in which he and his companion were riding. Buchert said the object appeared round until it was some distance away, then it appeared like two saucers, lip-to-lip, the top half bright and the bottom half dark. At one point, when the deputies reached a highway interchange bridge, they had to slow down and the object appeared to slow and hover, waiting for them. After the Ohio police abandoned their chase and turned it over to Pennsylvania authorities, information dwindled and no more was said publicly.

If the thing chased by Spaur and the others was intelligently controlled, just what did the occupants learn? They learned that cars with sirens and red lights on top are some kind of official vehicles for which all other similar land-based vehicles stop, or at least to which they yield. They learned that the top speed of such vehicles is about 100 miles per hour. They also learned that even these official vehicles are slowed by highway junctions, traffic interchanges, etc. And if they are capable of monitoring radio broadcasts as Spaur seemed to think they were doing at the time, they learned that communications between certain areas are limited for some reason and that this results in a lack of co-ordination.

The United States has not been the only area in which police cars interested the discs. On June 6, 1966, two constables pursued a bright object which maneuvered at low altitude over Grafton, Australia, for two hours. Hundreds of local residents watched the object cavort about the skies during the "chase." It would not seem illogical, then, to expect similar incidents in the future. The Grafton incident was given big play in Australian newspapers because UFO activity in that country had aroused public interest. On

April 2, 1966 a well-known Melbourne businessman (who refuses to be identified but is known to APRO's Representative there, Attorney Peter Norris), snapped a photo of a bell-shaped object which was suspended on edge over Balwyn, a Melbourne suburb. (See *Plate 7*.) Using a polaroid camera, he got a clear color photograph of the polished metallic object, which was reflecting the pink roof of a building below. All the Melbourne papers included the story because of the qualifications of the observers.

After the sensational sightings in northeast United States during the fall of 1965, and the Exeter sightings in particular, the blackout of November 9, 1965, came as no surprise to APRO members and the office was immediately notified by members in the East. One of our contacts, a wire service newsman, forwarded literally hundreds of thousands of words which came over the wires during the early hours of the blackout and which were invaluable in assessing the whole situation and evaluating the evidence. During the ensuing days clippings and first-hand information from sighters of strange objects over New York City and elsewhere in the northeast indicated that the UFOs were on the scene during those hours of darkness. But why? Some enthusiastic researchers intuitively linked the UFOs with the blackout, assuming that they were at various points and had some direct relationship with the blackout at several points. However, in view of the scant existing evidence to indicate "foul play" that night, APRO staff people theorized that the objects seen and reported were merely observing the chaos and probably learning a lot.

There was little or no panic in the Northeast area during the blackout because radio stations switched to emergency power almost immediately and went back on the air, keeping the citizenry advised about any progress being made to end the outage, and keeping them posted concerning what authorities were saying and doing about the situation. Not so in Buenos Aires, Argentina, on December 26, however, when for lack of emergency reserve power, half the population was kept in total darkness for seven hours. Panic reigned since there was no contact between the people and the voices of authority. Added to the inconvenience of the blackout, electrically driven pumps failed after an hour and there was no water.

But—back to the States and November 9. Shortly after news reached us, we were surprised by a call from Richard

Gerdes, electronics engineer and owner of Optical Electronics Incorporated. He said he felt that the blackout was so extensive that there had to be something radically wrong. It seems he was right. During the first few hours, press stories continually referred to "trouble up north" and "the vicinity of Clay." Two days later we received word that some very unusual sights were observed by people north of Syracuse at about the time the blackout started. This was what we were looking for. Although we later received accounts of strange objects hovering over New York City and other points, we were looking for some incident which coincided with the inception of the outage.

On the press wire, the phenomena observed by Weldon Ross and Robert Walsh were described in such a way that they may have been accepted by some as UFOs. Their descriptions, however, indicated something other than a solid, material machine.

Ross, of Carrier Corporation in Syracuse, is a part-time instructor-pilot and on the evening in question he was in the air with a student pilot and preparing to land at Hancock Field when the lights went out. He was north of Syracuse, headed east when he saw a "huge fireball" in the vicinity of the New York Power Authority's 345,000 volt lines that run from Niagara Falls to the Mohawk Power Corporation Station in Clay. The time: 5:15. The lights went out in that area at 5:15. In New York City, at 5:15, the lights dipped. The Consolidated Edison facility in New York was monitoring a flow of 300,000 kilowatts from the upstate facilities at the time. Checking his instruments, Edwin J. Nellis, in charge of the plant, found that all of his facilities were functioning normally but that the instruments showed an immense *flow to the north*. Nellis then received three calls: from Flushing, Orange County and Rockland County, notifying him of "trouble to the north." He began to put through a call to the Syracuse control station. They reported "trouble to the North." New York blacked out at 5:27.

Syracuse had been blacked out for several minutes when Robert Walsh, Syracuse's Deputy Aviation Commissioner, was on the field at Hancock putting out emergency lights. He saw a ball of fire which "came into being," grew to huge size, then shrank to nothing. It resembled a huge cloud of burning gas, he said. This was the same description as that given by Weldon Ross. Walsh estimated that he observed this phenomenon at about 5:25 or thereabouts. It appeared to be a few miles south of Hancock Field in the vicinity of the power lines from Niagara Falls. This "fireball" approximately coincides with the loss of power in New York City.

The third in this series of observations took place about ten or fifteen minutes after Walsh's first sighting of the strange vaporlike cloud, and in a slightly different location. Although the third ball of fire did not exactly coincide with a particular power loss, the first two definitely did. Northern New York and Canada lost their power at 5:15 when Ross saw the first ball of fire, and New York cities and points east blacked out about ten minutes later.

After this information had reached the office, my mind leapt back to the Jalbert incident and I pulled out the file. I had an idea what the connection might be, but I called Mr. Gerdes to coordinate with him. He agreed with me—that instead of "drawing power from the lines," as some thought, the red disc seen by Jalbert was probably measuring the parameters of that leg of the northeast power grid. The exact amount of power being shunted along the high tension lines *at dusk,* when the peak flow was reached, would be necessary information if a blackout was considered.

I then asked Gerdes to give me a short but concise description of his theory of how such a power outage could be brought about. He said that two or more coherent energy beams (e.g. infrared *laser*) could be aimed to intersect at some point along a high tension group of power lines. If the critical energy level was exceeded, a mass of plasma would be produced enveloping the wire group and causing a short circuit. To all intents and purposes this would appear to anyone monitoring the circuit as a massive short circuit or "flow of power into a ground." Now let's look at a statement by a Con Ed spokesman about the blackout, which was carried by both wire services on the 10th: "Like a giant water main break, the interconnecting electrical power networks lost vast amounts of electricity through a main into a ground, causing last night's massive northeast blackout." Although Federal Power Authorities in the United States eventually pinned the blame for the northeast blackout on the failure of a breadloaf-sized relay at the Sir Adam Beck Plant at Queenston, Ontario, they had to admit that they still could not account for the *initial cause of the immense short circuit.*

On December 3 over one million people from Juarez, Mexico, to Socorro, New Mexico, and Alamogordo as well as Holloman AFB, White Sands Proving Ground, Fort Bliss and Biggs AFB (the latter two in Texas) were plunged into darkness. First reports said a defect at a gas plant in Juarez was the cause, then later it was blamed on a defect in two units of a power plant at Newman, New Mexico. A few weeks after the southwest blackout, Robert Achzehner, a Motorola Company field representative was in El Paso and was asked to comment on the 1965 UFO flap on a radio program. After the program a telephone caller who insisted that his name not be used said that he was at his home in northeast El Paso and looking toward Newman when the blackout began. His attention was drawn to that direction because of the presence of a glowing object over the power plant. Whether or not it had any connection with the blackout cannot be stated with absolute certainty, but it is certainly too much of a coincidence that unusual objects or phenomena were present during both of these blackouts. The area covered by the power outage in the southwest on December 3 had been visited by UFOs during the summer 1964 flap. The area covered by the November 9 blackout had experienced UFO visitations in 1964 and 1965.

Prior to the November 9 blackout in the northeast, many residents of Syracuse had reported objects in that particular area which might indicate a preblackout reconnaissance.

It almost seemed the season for blackouts during November and December, for the eastern section of the Netherlands experienced a power outage due to a "defect in a power plant at Zwolle." An unexplained blackout hit Conroe and Johnson City, Texas, on December 7. This was the third big blackout in the U.S.A. within thirty days. The electric power dropped for five minutes before the complete failure, which lasted for thirty minutes.

In Naples, Italy, on January 8, 1966, a blackout took place which also affected all of Southern Italy except for the Calabria area in the toe. Naples was blacked out for an hour and other cities as long as two hours. Officials of Italy's nationalized Electrical Power Authority attributed the blackout to "an overload of four high tension lines feeding current southward from generating stations in central Italy." On the same date a "globe of fire appeared in the sky and hovered over Capri" for several minutes and disappeared when two NATO jets approached it. Witnesses who saw the object stated that household animals showed great nervousness during the object's presence.

The advent of the blackouts, specifically those in north-east and southwest United States and Buenos Aires, implies that experimentation with our dependence on electricity was being carried out. In an editorial in the May-June issue of the APRO Bulletin, members were asked to forward information about UFOs in connection with water, electrical power transmission wires and installations, radio and TV transmitters, telephone installations and microwave relay towers, water reservoirs, water tanks and pumping stations. Shortly thereafter, we received sketchy information about landed and hovering UFOs in the vicinity of the main antennas of the major wire services, Bell Telephone transoceanic relays and several parabolic microwave transmitters on Long Island.

On April 26 portions of Colorado, Wyoming, Nebraska and Utah experienced unexplained blackouts which began at 3:46 P.M. and lasted for varying periods. Harry Caperton, supervisor for power in the Reclamation Bureau's Region 7, said that alternating current in transmission lines throughout the West as far as Arizona and Oregon began showing violent fluctuations shortly before the Rocky Mountain area outages. Reclamation Bureau officials in Loveland, Colorado, said power systems throughout the area are interconnected in such a way that it might be days before officials could determine what happened.

An earlier blackout, at Laramie, Wyoming, on March 12 also included the sighting by many residents of a "brilliant blue flash" north of the city which was seen at the same time the lights failed at 10:17 P.M. A similar phenomenon was observed at 8 P.M. on the night of November 26, 1965, in East St. Paul, Minnesota, when unusual aerial objects were seen as momentary electrical power outages occurred. Several residents, including Nick De Vara and Mark Wilcox, saw a light which resembled a welding light passing overhead. As it did so, the lights in a nearby service station went out, only to return after it was gone. Just a few blocks north of Maryland and Supornick Lane, where De Vara and Wilcox saw the blue light, the Don Roush residence experienced a power outage and shortly afterward the Roush son came in saying he had seen a brilliant blue light in the sky at the same time the lights went out. A motorist in the area reported the same type of light coinciding with the failure of his car radio and lights. Two drivers on Warner Road south of the Roush residence reported that at 9 P.M. they saw a blue light which appeared to be on the ground south of them.

They claimed the light appeared and disappeared three times and was red at first, then turned to blue almost immediately. Later they noticed that power seemed to be out in that area.

Police and the Northern States Power Company received complaints from residents in the general area of Totem Town along Highway 61 to the effect that their lights were out; some residents also reported seeing strange orange and blue lights in the sky. The company was unable to determine what caused the outage and a weather bureau spokesman ruled out lightning. Although authorities later tried to blame snow-laden and wind-whipped power lines for the shortage, most in the area could not accept this as an explanation for the effects on car radios and lights.

The four factors—water, electrical power and police vehicles, as well as communications facilities—indicate something more than a chance concentration of "natural" phenomena. These four factors are very closely related to everyday life and, indeed, to survival on this earth. In addition to irresponsibly badgering authorities, some UFO fans seemed to intuitively link the UFOs with power outages; however, they did not attempt to link, by means of a workable theory, the phenomena present during the outages. It seems logical that if, as some claim, the UFOs are indeed interplanetary craft and intelligently controlled, there would be some purpose behind these various types of reconnaissance. Through the years I have observed the growth of a pattern of behavior on the part of the UFOs which is somewhat disconcerting to even the most objective investigator. I have used this pattern to formulate a theory which was suggested entirely by the pattern and which involves only the most authenticated reports.

In 1877 two unusual satellites were discovered circling Mars. When one considers the hundreds of years of apparent earth visitations by the UFOs, it is not difficult to theorize that those strange satellites may have been the culmination of several centuries of exploration by an advanced civilization.

Any interstellar craft would, of necessity, have to be very large. Today man is launching successively larger and heavier objects into space with rocket power. We can be almost certain that heavier and larger objects will be launched as time progresses. If a civilization which is advanced, say, five hundred years or more beyond our present technological ability were to explore space and find a planet bearing

similar life they might want to attempt contact. Their first
move would be to locate a colony within comfortable telescopic viewing distance and establish a base. If the planet
under surveillance had a natural satellite of its own, it would
be another ideal way station. Astronomical journals and
popular lay magazines have from time to time commented
about strange and unexplainable lights and light phenomena on the moon. We now have the beginning of a reasonable theory.

Two huge interstellar ships may have come in from outside the solar system in 1877, unloaded men and materiel
to the surface of Mars and left the empty shells of the ships
in orbit. These may be the two "new," strange, unexplained
"moons" of Mars, Deimos and Phobos. From a vantage point
on Mars, a small base could have been established on earth's
moon. This could account for the unexplained light phenomena observed for many years on the surface of the moon.
With these bases established, it would have been no large
problem to observe the birth of the atomic age when the
1945 explosions of the A-Bomb on the New Mexico desert
and, later, twice over Japan took place. At the time Mars
and the earth were in excellent relationship to one another
for adequate telescopic observations. A flotilla of reconnaissance ships could have been launched to size up the situation.
Within two or three years, the following could have been
deduced: The planet which had been a "backward" abode
had become highly industrialized and a huge world war had
taken place. Nuclear weapons had been used—not once but
twice—by the inhabitants against members of their own race.

Just as earth nations carry on their espionage operations in
countries considered to be peaceful, as well as those that
constitute a threat, the interlopers from space might have
deemed it desirable to reconnoiter earth's terrestrial defenses.
Thus there followed the activities of the discs. In 1950 they
surveyed atomic installations in the United States; in 1952
they visited defense installations of the United States, now
known to be the most wealthy and powerful nation in the
world; and in 1954, they reconnoitered Europe and South
America—South America, probably because it was felt to be
next in importance as far as potential goes, and Europe next
in power. When 1957 and the first earth-launched satellite
came along, the visitors might have become genuinely concerned. Two and two make four. Nuclear fission and satellites

add up to nuclear-powered space travel, and space travel by warring earthlings might not be particularly desirable.

In any military rconnaissance, infinite pains are taken to learn as much as possible about those under scrutiny. Of prime importance is civil authority and its extent, transportation—whether by air, sea or land—natural resources, industrial and power resources, and communications. So far, we know that reports of hovering and/or maneuvering UFOs have concentrated on military installations, land-based vehicles (trains, cars, trucks) as well as planes and ships. That takes care of the transportation angle. Within the area of transportation a special interest has been shown in police cars (civil authority). Industrial capability in a world dependent on electrical power is nonexistent without power and water, and both of these resources have proven to be of interest to the UFOs.

Some of my colleagues have questioned this theory because of the preponderance of evidence indicating the UFOs' interest in South America. It seems to me that two considerations are important here: the abundance of minerals—Brazil in particular has been the site of hundreds of good observations—and the abundance of land. Especially in Brazil the citizens tend to herd together in cities, leaving vast expanses of virgin territory virtually untouched, and inadvertently providing the opportunity for UFO bases to exist undetected. The availability of land which is inaccessible to ordinary means of transportation should not be overlooked either. The maneuverability and speed of the UFOs would render any mountain fastness completely accessible.

In view of the progressive nature of the UFO reconnaissance, if that is what it has been, we might keep a watchful eye on anything which has any remote connection with communications. I do not think that our visitors have followed a plan which might easily be detected. That would be foolhardy. Taking into consideration the patterns and evidence involved, it would seem that "they" have followed a general plan with occasional modifications, always careful not to "overplay their hand." Surveillance of the electrical power in one area, for instance, would not be followed immediately by a blackout.

It may be that "they" found their plan to be defective when, during the northeast blackout, power was restored to military bases within minutes and, despite the blackout of television and radio facilities on the east coast, information seemed to be flowing to the west coast and other points. This knowledge would have been easy to come by had high-flying ships been monitoring TV and radio broadcasts across the United States. It would have been natural, then, for them to deduce that some other type of communications was being utilized. Perhaps "they" did deduce just that and we ought to keep better tabs on our telephone nerve centers and in particular the microwave relays which carry the greater portion of our long distance telephone calls.

I am deeply concerned about the present trend of converting underground television coaxial cable systems to above-the-ground, easily available microwave relay facilities. I am also deeply concerned about the growing electrical "grids" in the United States whereby so many power companies and areas are so interdependent that a new and exotic weapon could black out large areas within seconds. In case of emergency, the United States would be quite incapable of any kind of coordination—whether it be concerned with military movements or otherwise—without television, radio and long distance telephone. If one can picture such a situation, one can conceive of the urgency of the problem at hand. We are currently faced with a problem which yields only "circumstantial evidence" of the observational type and which does not appeal to the scientist, who should be attacking it. On the other hand we are dealing with emotional individuals who apply only very rudimentary approaches (I am speaking now of the majority of UFO enthusiasts)—accusing "authorities" of betrayal and completely ignoring the real problem—the UFOs. They seem to want an endorsement of their personal convictions concerning the interplanetary nature of the UFOs. They expect quite a bit, however, for it is a matter of fact that there is only fragmentary physical evidence, a weighty amount of circumstantial evidence and *no absolute proof of the real nature of the objects.*

Besides the cold back of hauteur offered by the majority of scientists, and the repetitious emotional tirades of the "believers," we are also faced with the nationalistic nature of existing civilian UFO research. Prior to 1960 most American UFO researchers largely ignored the reports and investigations of "foreigners." It is still assumed by some that a confession or admission concerning the interplanetary nature of the UFOs by the U.S. Air Force will automatically make their existence and identity a declaration of dogma for the whole world. One need only look at the state of American prestige the world over to realize that an American pronouncement is not necessarily the "last word" anywhere. Our anti-Air Force colleagues may very well have contributed to this state of affairs in the last seventeen-odd years.

A kind of psychic revolution, in terms of acceptance of the phenomena heretofore considered too bizarre for consideration, is in process at the present time. The new, critical attitude of the press may even be part of it. This is lamentable, at times, for it would seem that now is the time for some sort of cooperation between the public, researchers, the military and the press. If the Air Force, like the press, only echoes the popular sentiment of the majority of the people relative to the UFOs, then they may have been ignorant and who can blame them? Perhaps disgust with the crackpots and hoaxers and their constant attackers has tended to color the judgment of those charged with the UFO problem. And perhaps irresponsible writers who twist and color the facts have contributed to the overall confusion also. Had it not been for the fact that I have seen several unexplainable airborne objects myself (and this truly makes me unique among researchers), I might seriously doubt the veracity and credibility of all purported witnesses because of many instances, which I know of from firsthand sources, that have involved misinterpretations of ordinary objects.

The subject of water reconnaissance is an intriguing one. It does not seem reasonable that an alien race would be interested in such a large number of water storage facilities as they have indicated. What, then, are they after? If we consider the blackouts in conjunction with the water reconnaissance, a very sobering possibility comes to mind. Suffice it to say that an invading force could black out strategic military bases, communications centers and government seats and, employing sleeping drugs of some kind, probably simultaneously released in strategic reservoirs and water tanks, bring a nation or a world to its knees within a few hours.

Just as there is no proof of the interplanetary nature of UFOs, there is no proof that the occupants are hostile, either. But on the other hand, despite their origin, strange occupants of strange airborne ships have demonstrated no indication that they want contact. In some instances, already described, they have indicated a rather indifferent attitude toward individual man. Apparently the occupants observed to date have wanted nothing to do with man and, being superior in every way, have gone about their own business—whatever their business is.

Are we, then, merely the subject of an Interstellar Geophysical Year study?

Are we a threat to other races on other planets, and will we be policed?

The possibilities are intriguing, to say the least.

The earth is apparently being observed by intelligent beings from outer space, but information reaching the general public promotes an opposite impression.

A hoax has been perpetrated.

We, the people, are the victims of that hoax.

And we, the people, in our eagerness to worship the orthodox and embrace mediocrity, have also served to perpetuate that hoax.

It would be impossible, in the course of years of close affiliation with the subject of UFOs not to have formed some definite opinions of my own concerning their origin. Much has been recorded and written about the elusive objects, and since the monumental works of the late astronomer M.K. Jessup many UFO researchers have gained a clearer picture of what the real answer may be. Jessup, an instructor in astronomy and mathematics at the University of Michigan and Drake University, compiled an impressive amount of UFO data in his book *The Case for the UFO*.[1]

In the chapter "The Incredible Decade," dealing with the period 1877–87, Jessup did a remarkably thorough search of astronomical journals for significant data. In addition to a large number of comets of unusual characteristics, reported by Jessup, three astronomical events which accompanied a veritable flurry of strange airborne objects within the earth's atmosphere suggested a fantastic theory to me. (1) One incident was the sudden appearance of a tiny companion crater to Hyginus on the moon. After no little disagreement among lunar astronomers who did not believe in changes on the moon, this tiny erratic was dubbed Hyginus N. (2) In 1878 a huge disturbance was noted in the atmosphere of Jupiter, the big-brother planet of our solar system. The storm, later

[1] Citadel Press, New York, 1955.

to be known as the Great Red Spot, was pecan-shaped, between six and seven thousand miles wide, thirty thousand miles long, and it raced about the planet's atmosphere at a surface speed of approximately two hundred miles an hour, pushing aside all other surface features. (3) The most fascinating of these incidents was the sudden appearance of the two tiny moons of our sister planet Mars in 1877, which I discussed previously. Here are some curious facts about these satellites:

The great astronomers Herschel and Lasselle discovered the moons of Uranus through their powerful telescopes, but they never spotted the moons of Mars which, with the benefit of their instruments, should have been much less difficult to find than Uranus's satellites. The credit for the discovery of Deimos and Phobos, during the 1877 conjunction, goes to Asaph Hall. His find was verified by astronomers throughout the world, and they since have been successfully observed through smaller telescopes with much less power than the reflectors of Herschel and Lasselle. Why? Perhaps because they were not there before 1877! This is far more plausible than the assumption that they were entirely missed by the telescopes which had been used in a search for Martian moons in prior conjunctions. In fact, by 1862 it had been generally accepted by the astronomical world that Mars had no satellites. I am surprised that astronomy did not ring with the words "strange things are happening" during that incredible decade.

The proximity of Deimos and Phobos to the surface of Mars, their small size and great speed, as well as their high degree of reflectivity, point to a strangeness which indicates artificiality. If these tiny moons are of the same degree of reflectivity as their parent planet, they are probably about five and ten miles in diameter, respectively. If they are metallic, they could be considerably smaller and yet highly reflective, so as to suggest larger sizes than they actually are. We can hardly deny the unusual brightness of these tiny bodies.

The Russian astronomer I.S. Shklovsky has pointed out that Phobos exhibits a strange acceleration during its orbit around Mars, which can be explained only if the satellite is a hollow sphere—an impossibility for a natural astronomical body. Shklovsky's theory that Deimos and Phobos are artifi-

cial satellites generally has been scoffed at, but nevertheless
is a sound one, another instance in which prejudice re-
places reason and logic; we cannot discard the facts.

Shklovsky and other Russian scientists further specu-
late that these artificial space platforms are evidence that
Mars supports intelligent life—that, in fact, Mars became
capable of space exploration and travel late in the last century. This certainly would explain the sighting of craft in the
skies of earth during that incredible decade. However, other
data must be discarded in order to accept *in toto* Shklovsky's theory of Martians with a technology only a few hundred years ahead of that of earth.

Shklovsky's theory would also appeal to a scientist with
feelings of inferiority (an outstanding characteristic of the
Russians) in the face of facts, such as those concerning the
nature of Deimos and Phobos. Who can argue that it is not
preferable to accept the existence of a species of space
travelers only a century ahead of earthmen in scientific
achievement rather than a species hundreds and possibly
thousands of years ahead of us?

If we consider the order of events by which space travel by
man came about, and compare it with the facts available
about UFOs, we must conclude that the intelligence in-
habiting Mars has, in fact, been capable of space travel for a
considerable period of time prior to the discovery of the
Martian satellites. Earthman first orbited tiny objects and,
as his technology advanced, larger ones were launched.
Eventually we hope to build a permanent space station at a
convenient distance from earth which will facilitate the fuel-
ing and launching of space ships bound for the moon and
then the planets. However, if we can easily launch huge
space ships, such as those seen throughout the years prior to
the existence of the Martian satellites, why build small space
stations comparatively close to our planet? The moons of
Mars appeared in 1877, but astronomical records of unidentified aircraft predating those satellites by hundreds of years
indicate that some intelligence has been capable of space
flight for quite some time. Did these beings build the satellites
(admittedly a gigantic engineering feat) to facilitate space
travel? Hardly—they exhibited a great deal of talent in that
direction before. *Something* was very busy in the solar
system in 1877. The exact nature of those strange happenings is not precisely clear.

If, however, we postulate that several giant interstellar

space ships arrived in this system in 1877, climaxing several hundred years of interstellar exploration by an advanced race, we at least have the beginnings of a workable theory which will explain in large part the strange happenings since 1877. Two such ships could establish powered orbits around the planet which had been explored and selected for colonization (in this case, Mars) during previous surveys. This would also account for sightings of discs and cigar-shaped objects dating back five hundred or more years prior to 1877. After men and material were unloaded on the surface of Mars, the shells of the giant space arks may have been stabilized and left to orbit as a memorial to this gargantuan feat. Then, of course, depending on the needs of the visitors or colonists, they would set about adjusting to the surroundings or changing the surroundings to fit their needs. This would include a careful examination of the other planets in the solar system, possibly with an eye to the conscription of lower intelligences for labor purposes, etc. Bases could be established on the moons of the various planets to keep a close eye on the inhabitants and developments on the main planet.

At this juncture we must remember some strange new facts about Mars which have come to light in our century. In 1952 Tsuneo Saheki, the famed Japanese astronomer and Mars expert, observed a strange "explosion" on Mars, consisting of a brilliant flash of several-minutes duration followed by a luminous cloud. Saheki could offer no satisfactory explanation for the spectacle. Those he suggested but found inadequate, considering the characteristics of the phenomena, were: reflection from water (but there is no water on Mars); reflection from an ice field (but ice does not form on the equator where the explosion was observed); impact of a meteor (which would have lasted only momentarily); an atomic explosion (but earthmen did not possess the capability to rocket an atomic warhead through millions of miles of space to Mars). One other possibility remained—a nuclear device had been detonated by the inhabitants of Mars. This, of course, was ruled out because it was not felt at the time that Mars could sustain intelligent life.

Times have changed, however. I quote from *Space Handbook: Astronautics and Its Applications*—a staff report of the Select Committee on Astronautics and Space Exploration to the Eighty-fifth Congress: "Although human life could not survive (on Mars) without extensive local environmental modifications, the possibility of a self-sustaining colony is not ruled out." I can remember quite vividly when it was heresy to suggest any kind of life could exist on the red planet. In fact, I was called a heretic, as well as a radical.

In April 1954 the *Australian Post* carried an article on space travel and quoted the famed Dr. Girard de Vaucouleurs: "We cannot doubt that there is something remarkable on Mars." Indeed there is. Let's examine some of these:

On earth spring starts at the equator. On Mars it starts at the poles, moving toward the equator. In spring those strange Martian surface configurations, which have been dubbed "canals," are the areas which become green first. This could indicate the presence of an intricate pumping system which utilizes polar moisture. In 1952 a new green spot, the size of Texas, appeared. It becomes darker each year. It seems that some race with daring genius has undertaken a stupendous technological project. Our picture is almost complete.

Any individual curious enough to read this book is of course concerned with the intentions of our hypothetical race of interstellar pioneers. If he is a little fearful that is only normal, for the implications are fairly clear. But at the risk of seeming to soothe the reader I must explore the possibility that the examination and surveillance of the earth is only precautionary. There is a good deal of evidence to support this possibility.

America, the most advanced nation on earth, had not yet launched its industrial revolution at the time of the discovery of Deimos and Phobos. To advanced space travelers we would have seemed rather primitive. Therefore, only a cursory inspection was carried out periodically, possibly from a number of ships stationed on our moon—observational outposts. With powerful telescopes it would have been fairly easy to observe the burning cities of World War II, and by the time news of this holocaust had been relayed to headquarters on Mars, more attention would be concentrated on Planet III. The supposedly harmless race on earth would bear closer scrutiny, and the two atomic blasts of 1945 were easily detected. Knowledge of the discovery of nuclear fission by earth dwellers would be a growing concern for the colonists of Mars. Comparatively small in number, they would become preoccupied with our future scientific developments and military potential, and would begin methodical geographic mapping and military reconnaissance to determine the aggressive and defensive strength of the planet. They would be extremely interested in developments indicating our progress in space travel, for this could endanger their position in the solar system. A timetable of closer reconnaissance would be set up; thus we come to the pattern of visitations which have become obvious since 1947.

Every atomic installation, military base and rocket launching station in the Western world has been visited by unconventional aerial objects during the past 19 years. Information from behind the Iron Curtain indicates that Communist satellite nations have experienced similar visitations. Whenever a new military base is established or reactivated it is the subject of UFO visits. Mysterious, unidentified satellites have been observed circling the earth. Every time a major rocket launching is executed UFOs are there. Both prop-driven and jet planes have been paced by UFOs; some have mysteriously disappeared or crashed—specimens? Automobiles have been paced and even stopped by some mysterious method. People have been closely watched, approached—and there are thousands of mysterious disappearances of individuals in the United States alone each year—specimens?

The Current Trends

THE spring of 1966 brought hundreds of detailed sightings of UFOs, not only in the United States but also abroad. Two of the best cases came out of Australia and one had an ominous overtone:

On April 5, Mr. R. Sullivan, a steel contractor of Maryborough, was driving home from Wycheproof along a tree-lined road when the beams of his car headlights were suddenly "bent" sharply to the right. They lit up the fence by the road "as though being dragged by a giant magnet," he said. He applied his brakes and barely escaped crashing into the ditch at the side of the road. He was then looking into a paddock in the center of which he saw a 25-foot column of light which was shaped like an ice cream cone. It appeared to be about three feet wide at the bottom and ten feet wide at the top. The bottom appeared to be resting on the ground and was a brilliant white in color but the rest of it looked like a rainbow, exhibiting all the colors of the spectrum. Before Sullivan could move, the object rose silently from the ground at tremendous speed and zoomed away without a sound. On the next day he tested the headlights and found them functioning normally. A small dust depression in the plowed paddock was examined. The "saucer"-shaped depression was about three feet in diameter and two to five inches deep and about fifty yards from the road, where he had seen the spectral object the night before. Two days after Sullivan's experience, Gary Taylor, nineteen, of Carnegie, died when his car unaccountably left the road and crashed into a tree about ten feet off the highway—in the same spot from which Sullivan observed the object and had experienced trouble with his headlights.

Strange depressions of swamp reeds in various parts of Australia were discovered in January, 1966. At 9 A.M. on the 19th George Pedley heard a hissing sound and observed a vaporlike saucer-shaped object taking off from a swamp near his farm at Tully in North Queensland. Upon examination of the area he found a circular area in which reeds were flattened in a clockwise direction. The flattened reeds were dried, whereas the surrounding reeds were green and healthy. The object observed was blue-gray, about twenty-five feet across and about nine feet thick and appeared to be spinning at a high rate of speed as it rose vertically to about sixty feet altitude. Then it made a shallow dive and took off in a southwesterly direction at high speed.

On the following Thursday other "nests," as the press immediately dubbed them, were found in the same general area and later in a swamp at Sydney near the Bankstown Airport. The latter depression was twenty feet in diameter and consisted of tall reeds flattened into the mud as if by some tremendous force. All were in a perfectly clockwise position and a pungent smell hung over the area.

Swamps were the hangout of weird brilliantly lighted objects in March, also, when two well known cases were publicized in the United States. At 7:30 on March 20, Frank Mannor and his son Ronald waded into a swamp near their home outside Dexter, Michigan, to view an object hovering there. They first became aware of it when a "ball of fire" came out of the west, then dropped below a clump of trees about a half mile behind their home. The two got within 500 yards of the object, described it as a somewhat saucer-shaped object with a "blue light in front and in the back a light that kept changing from red to white like it was rotating." They said it was almost flat on the bottom and kind of "high and peaked" on top, and was wrapped in a light like a halo. The object was in the area for some time, either turning out its lights so that it couldn't be seen, or zipping out of sight when observers, including police, got too close. Later, artist's conceptions drawn to the specifications of the observers, closely resembled a photograph of an unidentified object taken in 1957. But the Mannor sighting was only a preview of what was to come.

On the night of the 21st 87 coeds, a dormitory house mother and the civil defense director for Hillsdale County, Michigan, watched a strange object from dormitory windows which maneuvered and hovered over the Hillsdale College arboretum for three hours. They testified that the object would sink down out of sight when the beacon at the nearby airport swung in its direction. The object's general description resembles that given by the Mannor family, and Civil Defense Director Van Horn said the lights on the object appeared to be either fixed and a part of a rotating object or lights rotating around the object. The whole thing was surrounded by a silvery glow.

There were many more sightings in the "Michigan flap," as it was called, which preceded the two mentioned above but were not publicized. APRO members in that area forwarded many accounts of mysterious lights in the sky or hovering near the ground, but out of the whole lot the Mannor sighting with accompanying sightings and testimony of police officers who had gone to the scene seemed to be the most authentic and detailed.

Feelings and expectations ran high, people were driving the back roads and generally keeping their eyes on the sky in hopes of seeing the elusive objects. This highly emotional situation may have led to the "marsh gas" explanation which presently emanated from Wright-Patterson. The explanation does not fit the facts and to anyone who has seen marsh gas, as I have, it is wholly ridiculous.

I have also heard it said that a swamp is not a likely place where an interplanetary visitor would land his ship. I think we should know a good deal more about these interplanetary visitors before we make such a judgment. I do know that a swamp is one good place to take cover if one has a ship capable of hovering for hours and wants to avoid curious people on foot or in cars.

Activity was not confined to the Michigan–Ohio area or even the Midwest as the press wire reports seemed to indicate. Just three days after the Mannor sighting several people including postman Louis Di Paolo and Mrs. Eulah Mae Hoch, Assistant Editor of the Trinidad, Colorado, *Chronicle-News,* observed two disc-shaped objects maneuvering near Trinidad on the 23rd. The time was 5 P.M. and the discs, with their metallic surfaces, flat bottoms and dome-shaped tops were clearly seen in broad daylight between the observers and the mountains in the south. The objects were estimated to be within one-half mile of the observers and most likely huge in size. Mrs. Hoch compared their apparent size to a six-inch object held at arm's length. No surface details were discernible.

UFOs showed up in South America in March, this time concentrating on Brazil. Most of the staff of the Lourenco

Jorge Hospital at Barra da Tijuca observed a bright ovoid object which maneuvered in the area from 2 until 4 A.M. on the 6th. The object alternately hovered, dashed about, dimmed out, increased its brightness and generally exhibited all the characteristics of a UFO. It is important to note that attempts were made to notify the Air Force and the National Observatory but for some unknown reason the telephones were out of order in the area.

On the 12th ten employees of the National Motors Plant north of Rio de Janeiro, observed an ovoid bright object which hung in the sky near the plant at an estimated 1500–1800 feet altitude. Its apparent size was several times that of the full moon. The observers notified the Director of the plant, Army Colonel Jorge Alberto Silveira Martins, who was so impressed and alarmed by what he saw that he notified the Army at Rio, which sent a detachment of troops to the plant armed with anti-aircraft guns. The Air Force was notified and Martins was informed that there were no aircraft in the area. Thirty minutes after it was originally seen the object decreased in brightness and silently disappeared. A few moments later it appeared again, apparently about one-half mile away. It repeated the disappearing act once more and was gone just before the Army detachment arrived. As a precaution, the Army detachment stayed at the plant and on the next night when the object returned the military personnel observed it. One soldier, in near hysteria, tried to fire his gun at the object and had to be physically restrained— the order had been to fire only if attacked. The object's brilliance was the same as it had been the night before; occasionally it shot out bursts of light which made viewing it an uncomfortable experience. In this instance, almost all the observers felt they had observed an alien object from outer space. Besides the fact that the National Motors Plant is an important industrial complex, the high tension wires feeding electrical power to Rio de Janeiro pass about seven miles to the north of it.

Other sightings were made in the suburban areas around Rio in March including that of another object at the Lourenco Jorge Hospital on the 16th and then of a formation of colored objects at Cordovil, north of Rio, on the 17th.

On the 24th, shortly after 2 A.M., policeman Edwar Robson Brun intercepted a man who was running wildly through the streets of Jacarépaguá. The man, a businessman named Jonas Franco, was in a cold sweat. His eyes were protruding and he could not talk. After he was taken to the Carlos Chagas hospital and given an injection, Franco managed to write that he had seen a brilliant, metallic and soundless object which had scared him half out of his wits. With the full story, gathered later, it was revealed that Franco had heard a knocking at his door and when he opened it, had seen a disc-shaped object hovering not fifteen feet from his house. He said it was so brilliant he could hardly see and he was so frightened that he didn't think of going back in the house, but started his wild flight through the streets until apprehended by the policeman. Friends testify that Franco is a normal person (or was), responsible and not given to telling tall tales. The problem now is that he is still unable to talk and his nervous state gets worse each day.

The Jacarépaguá district is located south of Rio near Barra da Tijuca where the disc was seen on several occasions in the early part of March.

Back in the States, there had been several sightings which did not receive the press coverage given the Michigan cases but were nevertheless quite revealing:

On April 8 two twelve-year-old youngsters, walking to school at 8:05 A.M., were delayed for nearly two hours by an object, eight feet in diameter, which dove at them and finally forced them to seek shelter under a bridge abutment. The boys, Mike Dorsey and Gary Hunt, were walking along Redcoat Road on the edge of Norwalk, Connecticut, when they spotted the object in the sky. It made a sound like the humming of bees, was dull metallic in color, saucer-shaped and had an antenna topped by a red light on its upper surface. Recounting their story later to the press and to school authorities, they said, "When we hid behind trees it floated above the trees to spot us. When we hid behind rocks it still spotted us." When they finally crawled under the bridge the object came down to within an estimated seven feet of the ground, apparently trying to locate them. It stayed there for about five minutes, then took off. They heard a sound like a splash after it left, the boys said, and assumed that it had dropped into a nearby water tank or the nearby lake. Both boys were interviewed in the principal's office at school by a man who said he represented a government agency but said he could not identify his agency nor give his name.

On April 25 an anonymous (by request) police officer at Syracuse, New York, observed a circular car-sized object hovering near the Thornden Park water tower. He had seen another object earlier which had come out of the south. This first object appeared as a cloudlike affair (recall the object of the Australian saucer nest). The second also came from the south, dropped at a 45 degree angle and was bluish-green in color and trailing white sparks. It was comparable to an auto in size, circular in shape and had a domed top in which lights were observed. The thing stopped and hovered about three feet above the road leading to the water tower and after five to ten seconds it rose and vanished back into the south.

A round, gray object with a flat base and a hump on top was observed by science teacher Andrew Greenwood and students while it hovered and maneuvered near the Westall School in Clayton, Australia, on April 6. The object was first spotted when it rose into the air from behind pine trees near the school. Greenwood watched it, along with some of the students, for about twenty minutes, looked away for a few seconds and when he looked back it was gone.

One of the most publicized sightings of spring, 1966, involved the sighting of a "bright flying object" by Governor Haydon Burns of Florida on April 28. Four newsmen, the Governor and seven other individuals were on board Burns' Convair and flying south of Ocala, Florida at 8:52 P.M. when Burns spotted the object and ordered his pilot to intercept after obtaining approval from the Miami control tower. The observers all said the object looked like two inverted saucers, lip to lip, with a yellowish light emanating from the area where they joined. When the plane gave chase the object's light turned down and went out completely and the craft disappeared in the night. Although the Burns incident gave some impetus to the subject of UFOs its only outstanding feature was that a prominent public figure had observed one of the illusive things.

The year 1966 has been, by and large, only an extension of the happenings of 1965. We predicted more blackouts—they took place, and frankly I am more than a little concerned. There have been too many "blackouts" in the Wyoming-Nebraska-Colorado area. The latest, at Idaho Springs on July 20, is not too far removed from the vast underground headquarters of the North American Air Defense Command. Perhaps not so coincidental is the fact that telephone service was also interrupted.

We predicted more police car chases and the most recent took place on June 24 when patrolman William L. Stevens, Jr., chased a "white or dirty-gray" dirigible-shaped object estimated to be 1001–25 feet long, from the State Fairgrounds in Richmond, Virginia into Hanover County. The object, said Stevens, was ringed by green and yellow lights and a whitish haze seemed to be coming from it when he first saw it. He filed a written report with the police department stating that the incident took place at 3:30 A.M. Part of the verbatim report is most revealing: "At no time did this object make any sound. It just seemed to be gliding along. The object seemed to be playing tag with my police unit. . . ."

On that same night hundreds of residents of Rochester, New York, watched a silver pipelike object which spun across the skies at about 8:30 P.M. Sheriff's Deputy Joseph Bobortella said he watched the cylinder spin over Aquinas Stadium at Mt. Read Boulevard and Ridgeway Avenue for fifteen minutes. A police officer, Paul Sterling, had viewed it earlier through high-powered binoculars. He said the object appeared to be only 150 feet in the air as it hovered above pickets at the strikebound E. I. DuPont de Nemours and Co. plant on Driving Park Avenue. It appeared to be fifteen feet long and about two feet in diameter, he told the press. Mrs. Linda Gerks of Rochester said she and friends saw it over Taylor Instrument Co. on Ames Street and that it was burning blue and white lights and looked like two saucers fastened together.

Two Gemini flights in the spring of 1966 reported strange objects in space which were never satisfactorily explained and which seemed to be only an extension of other unusual phenomena during space experiments. Unidentified objects were accompanying the Agena target ship and its spent Atlas during the flight of Gemini 9. By the time the astronauts reached the area the objects had disappeared. Later, the closest object was about a thousand miles from the orbiting Gemini.

Everyone laughed a little nervously when David Brinkley cracked wise about "swamp gas" after Collins and Young reported unidentified objects in their vicinity while over Hawaii.

At CBS, on May 10, the great spectacular on UFOs was beamed out to anxiously waiting millions. Some people got what they wanted—reassurance. Others got mad. I almost got hysterical. It was a rather silly repetition of what had been going on for years. Dr. Donald Menzel, the great protagonist of light inversions and antagonist of UFOs made his usual statement about "natural phenomena." Keyhoe made his usual statement about "intelligent, qualified people" seeing things, and the public was ready for the truth and had a right to know. Carl Sagan, eminent astronomer, who writes occasionally for popular magazines concerning his theory that earth has been visited by spacemen in the past (his "evidence" is mostly myth and legend), reiterated his conviction that there is no evidence to indicate visitations now, or even the existence of UFOs. He did not say whether or not he had examined the evidence and it is doubtful that he had.

Joseph Nyman, an APRO member in Boston, Massachusetts, wrote to Dr. J. Allen Hynek, of the Smithsonian Institution and Major Quintanilla of Project Bluebook, asking about the Smithsonian official's implication (on the CBS UFO dissertation) "that every inch of sky over the United States was covered by satellite tracking cameras, and that every object recorded on film of these cameras was known or explained." On the program, Nyman recalled, the Air Force admitted to more than 600 unknowns, of which presumably at least one had taken place at night (for instance in Exeter, New Hampshire, September 3, 1965). The answers, copies of which he forwarded to me, were enlightening. In his letter he pointed out that "what seems obvious from their replies is the apparent lack of communication among the three parties that would indicate an 'organized silence group' being in control of the dissemination of 'official' UFO information."

"I can only conclude," Nyman continued, "that the program and the letters reflect the strong personal biases of people who cannot get themselves in the psychological position of examining the evidence objectively because they may not be able to face the enormous significance of the real situation."

I agree. Now let's look at those answers:

From Dr. Nynek: "The entire sky is not covered by satellite tracking stations and they go into action only when a satellite is passing. The satellite tracking cameras do pick up unknown objects which are, however, presumably airplanes and weather balloons. An occurrence near Exeter, especially one near the ground, would certainly not have been picked up by satellite tracking cameras." Unquote. I concur.

In part, from Smithsonian: "Unfortunately, the implication was probably unintentional and the result of overzealous editing by the television." There is more than just that one sentence, but that is adequate for our purpose. The buck was passed to "television."

From Major Quintanilla: "Your statement is true that over

600 unknowns remain in our files. The statement regarding the Smithsonian Satellite Tracking Cameras is also true." There is much, much more to Quintanilla's letter, but not sufficient space here to quote it in its entirety. He did endorse the statement that the Smithsonian Cameras covered "every square inch of the sky," whereas Hynek and the Smithsonian denied the validity of that statement.

This series of letters illustrates what I have tried to get across for so many years concerning the lack of coordination between official agencies, including the military, which precludes the possibility of organized censorship. There is considerable emotional bias where this subject of UFOs is concerned. I would be completely dishonest if I did not admit that I have some trouble with it. Fortunately, though, my prejudices have not, to my knowledge, prevented me from steadily gathering facts about the subject even though the facts are often bizarre and possibly a little frightening. The time has come for the formation of an International Commission which will deal with information concerning the UFOs on a global scale. Ranking high on the list of qualified scientists should be psychologists, for they will be direly needed.

APRO has gathered impressive evidence that some UFOs sometimes affect the function of cars and planes; that some UFOs give off a substance called "angel's hair" (a thin, fibrous stuff resembling spider's web); that huge chunks of ice falling from the sky cannot be explained in conventional terms and seem to occur during UFO influxes; that occasionally slag, a by-product of metal production, falls from the sky; that a woman suffered apparent radiation effects including ruptured surface blood vessels, a whitening *and scaling* of her normally oily skin, disruption of her normal menstrual cycle accompanied by severe hemorrhage and pain—all after having observed a glowing UFO at close range for twenty minutes. In the light of the foregoing we cannot with conscience ignore the UFO mystery.

There can be little doubt that the treatment of the UFO subject in the first years of its acknowledged existence has had much bearing on its present treatment by authorities and the public alike. This is tragic, for sufficient evidence is mounting to indicate that very real unconventional airships directed by real, intelligent beings are operating within the earth's atmosphere, at times landing and often exhibiting more than passing interest in people and things.

Thousands of UFO buffs have written hundreds of thousands of letters to our lawmakers demanding a release of the facts about UFO. But perhaps there are no facts to release —no facts upon which the Voices of Authority can agree, that is.

Perhaps to us the idea that we are being fooled is preferable to the idea that no one has the answers. Perhaps our demands are based on naive assumptions. To get a proper answer we must ask a proper question.

In March 1961 APRO forwarded a briefing, prepared by my husband, Leslie J. Lorenzen, to President Kennedy and various members of Congress. Presenting evidence which we felt was important, the brief concluded:

> It may seem, upon superficial consideration, that the UFO problem is merely one for military intelligence— one that would succumb readily to a "scientific study." It is not. It is (1) above all a violently emotional problem; (2) a red-hot political problem; and (3) only incidentally a scientific problem.

Basically, the scientific problem is the easiest of the three. Science invariably gives an exact answer to a properly phrased question. But the other two aspects are not characterized by the same clear-cut simplicity and, moreover, are powerful enough to encourage the scientific world to avoid the problem.

The violent emotional responses stem from the fact that the idea of vehicles from another planet or star system attacks one of the basic tenets of our world picture. It is not easy for the scientific man, who believes sincerely that his life is entirely rational, to accept or appreciate that he is human and that his reactions are emotional.

He manages to overlook a very basic tenet—that observational data should never be discounted on the basis of authority and/or theory. In our present ideological structure the scientist and militarist are cast respectively in the "father-image" roles of "sage adviser" and "warrior-protector." To expect either to endorse the *fact* of extraterrestrial visitation is in effect to expect him to attack his own potency, prestige and security—the very validity of his own existence.

The layman, however, interprets the matter differently. He is faced with the fact that official opinions often contradict the available evidence. He concludes that a "conspiracy of official silence exists" concerning the "true facts." "Father lies" is preferable to "Father just doesn't know." He consoles himself with the thought that this is "all for his own good."

We are in urgent need of the acquisition and objective analysis of basic data. The United States is at present putting all its eggs in one basket and has thus fallen victim to a program which inadvertently stifles vital information at its source and plays ostrich in the face of potential danger.

There are no definite indications of hostility on the part of our visitors; but equally important there is no indication of friendliness either. Possibly we are only the subject of a routine survey—an Interstellar Geophysical Year, so to speak. To fail to educate the public concerning the facts at hand, however, is to court danger of a particularly insidious nature. The existence of a species of superior beings in the universe could cause the civilization of earth to topple. Even on earth societies have disintegrated when confronted by a superior society.

The UFO problem embodies an urgency which defies expression. Certainly procrastination is no solution. To leave matters as they are would seem to indicate that we are anxious to re-learn the bitter lessons of history: Billy Mitchell—Maginot—Pearl Harbor—and so on.

Other SIGNET and SIGNET SCIENCE Books
on Space Exploration

THE RELUCTANT SPACE-FARERS
                        by Frank B. Gibney and George J. Feldman

The political and economic consequences of America's space effort assessed by two experts who headed the House Select Committee on Astronautics and Outer Space.
(#P2887—60¢)

THE MOON   by V. A. Firsoff

Based on the facts and theories that have been gathered from telescopic observation and the expeditions of Rangers 7 and 9, the author presents a vivid picture of what the first man on the moon can expect to encounter. Lavishly illustrated with drawings, maps, and photographs.
(#P2985—60¢)

SATELLITES, ROCKETS AND OUTER SPACE
                                             by Willy Ley

An expert's report on the science of rocket development and its tremendous expansion in the 20th century, traced through the flights of Titov and Glenn and the launching of the Telstar satellite.   (#P2218—60¢)

RANGER TO THE MOON   by Willy Ley

This account of lunar science includes the facts behind the Ranger, the first U.S. rocket to reach the moon. With photographs of the moon taken from the Ranger, and line drawings by the author.   (#P2668—60¢)

MARINER IV TO MARS   by Willy Ley

A record of the historic flight which revolutionized science's conception of Mars, including an hour-by-hour log of the final phase of the mission, and an evaluation of the twenty-two photographs taken by Mariner IV.
(#P2932—60¢)

THE NATURE OF THE UNIVERSE   by Fred Hoyle

A noted astronomer explains the latest facts and theories about the universe with clarity and liveliness. Illustrated.
(#P2331—60¢)

To Our Readers: If your dealer does not have the Signet and Mentor books you want, you may order them by mail enclosing the list price plus 10c a copy to cover mailing. If you would like our free catalog, please request it by postcard. The New American Library of Canada, Ltd., 295 King Street East, Toronto 2, Canada.

THE BEST READING AT REASONABLE PRICES

signet paperbacks

SIGNET BOOKS *Leading bestsellers, ranging from fine novels, plays, and short stories to the best entertainment in the fields of mysteries, westerns, popular biography and autobiography, as well as timely non-fiction and humor. Among Signet's outstanding authors are winners of the Nobel and Pulitzer Prizes, the National Book Award, the Anisfield-Wolf award, and many other honors.*

SIGNET SCIENCE LIBRARY *Basic introductions to the various fields of science—astronomy, physics, biology , anthropology, mathematics, and others—for the general reader who wants to keep up with today's scientific miracles. Among the authors are Willy Ley, Irving Adler, Isaac Asimov, and Rachel Carson.*

SIGNET REFERENCE *A dazzling array of dictionaries, thesauri, self-taught languages, and other practical handbooks for the home library.*

SIGNET CLASSICS *The most praised new imprint in paperbound publishing, presenting masterworks by writers of the calibre of Mark Twain, Sinclair Lewis, Dickens, Hardy, Hawthorne, Thoreau, Conrad, Tolstoy, Chekhov, Voltaire, George Orwell, and many, many others, beautifully printed and bound, with handsome covers. Each volume includes commentary by a noted scholar or critic, and a selected bibliography.*